I0817208

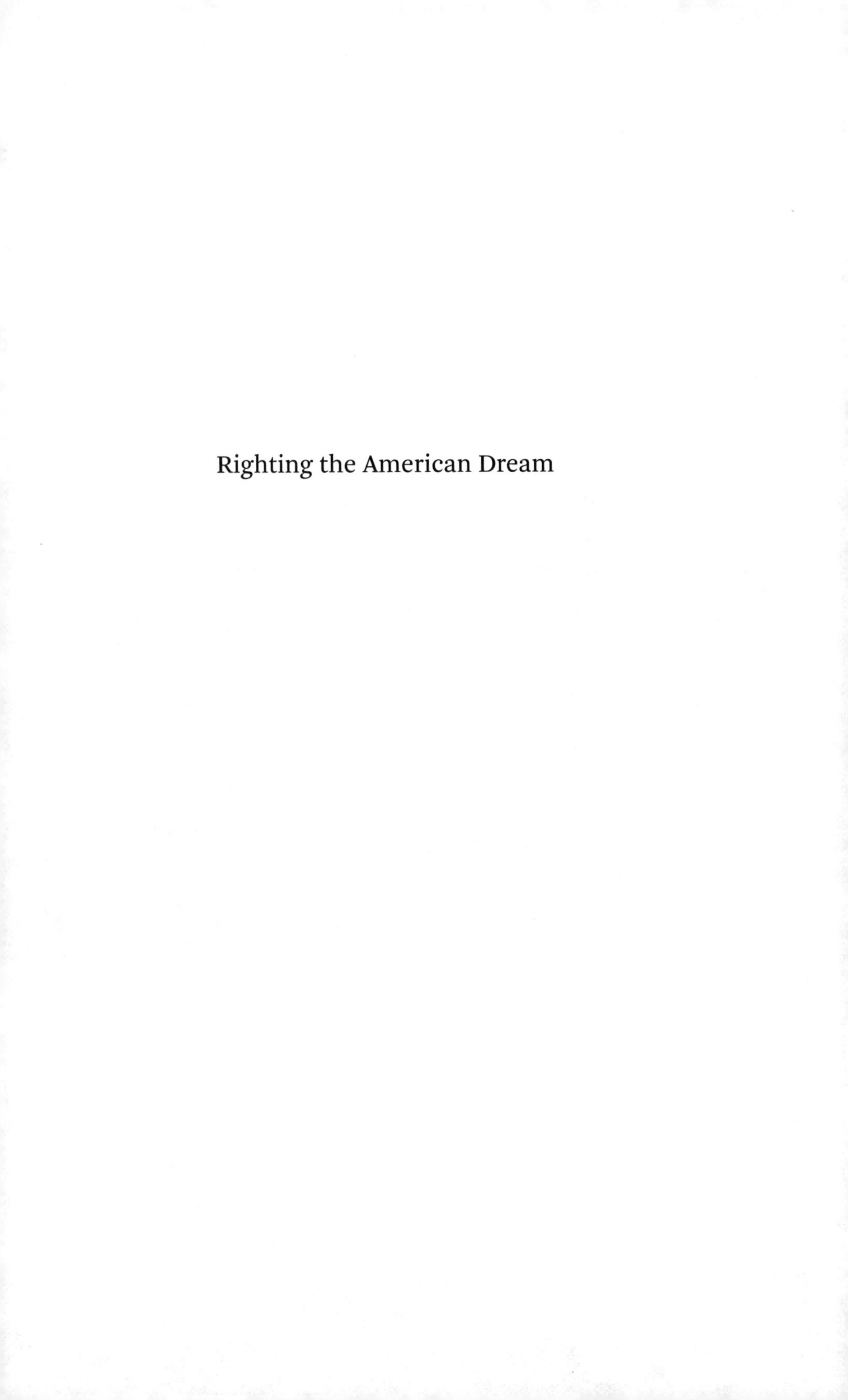

Righting the American Dream

Righting the American Dream

HOW THE MEDIA MAINSTREAMED REAGAN'S EVANGELICAL VISION

Diane Winston

THE UNIVERSITY OF CHICAGO PRESS
CHICAGO AND LONDON

The University of Chicago Press, Chicago 60637
The University of Chicago Press, Ltd., London

Published 2023
Printed in the United States of America

32 31 30 29 28 27 26 25 24 2 3 4 5

ISBN-13: 978-0-226-82452-9 (cloth)
ISBN-13: 978-0-226-82454-3 (e-book)
DOI: https://doi.org/10.7208/chicago/9780226824543.001.0001

Library of Congress Control Number: 2022044588

♾ This paper meets the requirements of ANSI/NISO Z39.48-1992 (Permanence of Paper).

For family, friends, and students who listened,
advised, and inspired.

And for those whose memories are a blessing:

SHARON GILLERMAN

LYNNE LANDSBERG

GINGER MAYERSON

JOHN ADAMS

ROGER WEISBERG

BILL WINSTON

DAN WINSTON

Contents

Introduction

> Our country is a special place, because we Americans have always been sustained, through good times and bad, by a noble vision—a vision not only of what the world around us is today but what we as a free people can make it be tomorrow.
>
> PRESIDENT RONALD REAGAN, State of the Union Address, January 25, 1983

In January 1983, President Ronald Reagan faced an unhappy electorate. By midmonth, his job approval rating would fall to 35 percent—an all-time low.[1] His proposals to cut income taxes and social spending while tightening the money supply and increasing the military budget did not produce the positive results he had predicted. In 1982, the unemployment rate hovered at 10.4 percent and the real gross national product had fallen almost 2.5 percent, the largest drop-off of the postwar era.[2] Housing starts were at their lowest since 1946,[3] while mortgage rates rose to over 16 percent.[4] In fact, the economy was so bad and Reagan's image so tarnished that the president's advisors were desperate for their boss to provide a compelling case for his continued leadership. Even conservative Christians, his strongest supporters, were disgruntled by a lack of concrete change: abortion remained legal while school prayer was against the law.

But if Reagan was worried, he didn't let the public know. Rather than admit anything was wrong, he blamed the news media for erroneous reporting.

"I came in to point out to you accurately where the disarray lies," the president said at a news conference in the White House press room. "It's in those stories that seem to be going around, because they are not based in fact."[5]

Many of those stories were based on leaks from administration insiders, whom the president criticized too. But from a distance of decades, the important question is not who leaked the stories or how true they were. Rather, it's how, in less than a year, a foundering leader turned into America's white knight. By exploring the political, religious, and media history of the 1980s through news narratives that helped propagate and, in turn, shape the Reagan Revolution, this book provides an answer. It focuses on the pivotal year of 1983, when the economy rallied, America's global standing rose, and Reagan convinced many conservatives and evangelicals that he was still their man.

Reagan's ability to set and dominate news media narratives was crucial to his success.[6] And whether discussing international relations, military decisions, or economic policy, he often included a religious or moral dimension in his comments. Critics dismissed his claims of divine justification for secular actions, but their complaints had little impact on the president or his policies. Nor did they stop the recasting of the nation's culture and ideology. Americans' understanding of themselves and their world was changing. The religious worldview that accompanied this shift encompassed more than a set of sacred beliefs. It also enfolded economic tenets, social values, and political practices that would shape the United States and its citizens. Reagan knew or intuited this transformation, which mirrored his own ideas about God and country, and made it central to his political platform.

I call that cluster of religious, economic, and political beliefs an *American religious imaginary*. A commonsense understanding of metaphysical truths, ethical norms, and civic virtues, a religious imaginary draws on traditional religious and/or cultural notions of the common good to provide mission, identity, and purpose for citizens as individuals and as national stakeholders. A national religious imaginary can encompass a belief in the supernatural; but most important, it offers a shared orientation to everyday life, especially political and economic convictions reflecting a higher purpose. Religious imaginaries shape individual identity and social relations, including what people expect of themselves and their world; how they expect others will behave and how they interpret their own daily interactions; and most significantly, what they know to be true, real, and good.[7] In other words, a religious imaginary instills a collective sense of what's normal—that is, the correct way (whether for religious or for ethical reasons) to live one's life as both a private individual and a public person. It also provides a way for people to think about national destiny and their role in its fulfillment.

We can better understand the dynamics of the Reagan-era shift in the religious imaginary by exploring the religious, political, and media worlds of the 1980s. The so-called Reagan Revolution was as much a religious phenomenon as a political and economic one, and the mainstream media, despite its liberal reputation, played a significant role in its spread. The news media accomplished this through its daily narratives, stories about current events that embedded the ideology of elite news sources, most important the president, and media moguls, such as the publishers and owners of news outlets. By the 1980s, a majority of Americans received their news from television. Nonetheless, newspapers remained central to the media ecology, so in the pages that follow I focus on their coverage.

Owing to their size and daily publication schedule, newspapers contained more information and in-depth coverage than did radio, television, or weekly newsmagazines. Strong regional dailies with a tradition of solid reporting—such as the *Louisville Courier*, the *Baltimore Sun*, and the *Atlanta Journal-Constitution*—along with big-city broadsheets held pride of place in the journalistic world. The *New York Times*, the *Washington Post*, the *Los Angeles Times*, and the *Wall Street Journal* attracted the best and the brightest reporters and editors. As these newspapers were powered by healthy profit margins brought about by a monopoly on print advertising, their publishers could finance the smartest features, the sharpest analyses, the savviest columnists, and the most enterprising reporting. Moreover, the de facto recognition of a media pecking order allowed leading newspapers to play a central role in setting and shaping coverage. *60 Minutes* was a top-ranked television newsmagazine that broke significant stories, and National Public Radio (NPR) attracted an affluent and educated audience by delving into selected subjects. (NPR is an outlier in the elite media sphere, since it is publicly financed; poor business practices led to a brush with bankruptcy in 1983.) But these and other broadcast outlets tended to follow the lead of major newspapers in deciding what stories to cover and which angles to emphasize. The nation's political leaders, policy makers, cultural elites, and even other journalists looked to newspapers, specifically the *Times*, the *Post*, and the *Journal*, to find out what was important and why it was worth knowing.

During Reagan's tenure, the news media helped normalize a neoliberal worldview—a market-oriented outlook advocating individual freedom and unfettered capitalism—rooted in a sense of America's divine identity, mission, and purpose.[8] For decades, this same imaginary had circulated in conservative Christian media, where it was grounded in evangelical terms.[9] Its hallmarks were a clear sense of good and evil, a fervent belief in American exceptionalism, and a deeply individualistic notion of virtue. In practical terms, this meant support for a strong but limited democratic government that protected free markets and religious liberty.

Ronald Reagan viewed free markets and limited government as the products of sound religion and good politics. The flip side of his commitment to America's God-given democracy was his abhorrence of communism. When he became president, his agenda encompassed religious, political, and economic transformations, which, I argue, helped change the mainstream understanding of American identity and purpose. In speeches and interviews, Reagan spread this worldview through salient narratives about current events reported in the news media. The Soviet Union was not a geopolitical rival but an evil empire. International crises were not diplomatic problems but confrontations with godless communism. Single mothers on welfare were not victims of an unfair system but frauds and freeloaders who refused to work. To make his point, Reagan often used evangelical terms that his religious base valued but outsiders failed to hear. In fact, his religious imaginary appealed to Americans of other religions or even no religious affiliation, because it aligned with their ideas about America's greatness, and it renewed their faith in both the nation and their own future.

Reagan's words—mainstreamed by the media and enacted through government policies, social practices, and commonsensical assumptions—transformed his version of the religious imaginary into the nation's lived religion. Lived religion does not refer to institutional practices such as attending worship services or Bible school. Rather, it describes the ways people express meaning in daily life, from personal rituals to political and economic choices. In these everyday actions, as much as in any worship service or belief system, people nurture and reinforce their sense of meaning, identity, and purpose.[10] There are many national religious imaginaries—for example, sociologist Robert Bellah's civil religion, Martin Luther King Jr.'s beloved community, and early twentieth-century American Jews' golden land. Each has a different set of truths and virtues that inform its lived religion, its adherents' way of being in the world. But they all participate in a foundational American religious imaginary that affirms the possibilities of a free people in a democratic nation that God has blessed.

Since the mid-twentieth century, this foundational religious imaginary has taken inspiration from John Winthrop's 1630 treatise *A Model of Christian Charity*.[11] Many Americans believed that Winthrop delivered this monograph to his fellow Puritans before alighting in the New World.[12] More likely, his words on divine love and communal responsibility had limited circulation among readers in England and the Massachusetts Bay Colony; then, slipping into obscurity, his vision lay dormant for almost three centuries. When scholars in the 1950s and '60s rediscovered his manuscript, they read it into American history.[13] *A Model of Christian Charity* was deemed a social contract rooted in God's love for America, a visionary

FIGURE 1. The Reagans on Inauguration Day, January 20, 1981. Courtesy Ronald Reagan Presidential Library and Museum.

statement from the Puritans, whom some envisioned as the nation's founding fathers.[14] This vision of society, this Protestant imaginary, came to include the notion of American exceptionalism, which may have reflected the nation's new prosperity and emerging status as a global power after World War II. And although there are multiple religious imaginaries that inspire Americans, this one—based on seventeenth-century Protestant providentialism—has dominated for several decades and is shared by many citizens, whether Christian, Jewish, agnostic, atheist, Muslim, Hindu, or Buddhist. That is why I call it an American religious imaginary.

What is most familiar to Americans today is Winthrop's invocation of the biblical call to be as "a city upon a hill." He wrote, "The eyes of all people are upon us. So if we shall deal falsely with our God in this work that we have undertaken and so cause him to withdraw his present help from us, we shall be made a story and a byword through the world."[15] Winthrop meant that the world was watching for signs of failure and the withdrawal of God's favor from this new endeavor. But in 1969, Ronald Reagan began describing the United States as "a shining city on a hill," and the meaning of the phrase changed from a warning to a benediction and a belief that America has a divinely sanctioned calling.[16]

Reagan's reinterpretation appealed to a nation reeling from the social and cultural upheavals of the 1960s followed by the political and economic cataclysms of the 1970s. Americans, accustomed to stability and prosperity, were unnerved by inflation, unemployment, challenges to "family values," and international showdowns, such as the 1979 Iranian hostage crisis. Citizens distrusted their government, and they questioned how much they owed other nations or even the domestic poor when their own livelihoods were threatened. What Reagan's predecessor Jimmy Carter termed a national "crisis of confidence"[17] was the culmination of a decade long disintegration of common understandings that had inclined Americans to trust their leaders, bankroll big government, and believe in a beneficent universe. In 1980, when voters were asked to choose between Carter's call for sober self-reflection on national limits and Reagan's summons "Let's make America great again," their preference was clear.

REAGAN'S CONSERVATISM AND THE ROLE OF THE MEDIA

At the heart of the American religious imaginary that Ronald Reagan helped promote is the conviction that God chose America, resulting in Americans receiving God's greatest blessings: freedom and democracy. American exceptionalism, the shorthand for this conviction, encompasses and justifies an entire worldview. In Reagan's judgment, which reflected a conservative Christian perspective, it warranted unequivocal and unilateral military action—such as the 1983 invasion of Grenada—since whatever America does is good because America does it to spread freedom and democracy. Domestically, American exceptionalism meant that each American, created in God's image, is an individual bastion of freedom. Freedom is more than an existential notion; it is a lived religion with three key elements: the political freedom of democracy, the "soul" freedom of religious liberty, and the economic freedom secured through free markets and limited government. This entwining of religious and political freedom was written into the First Amendment, but a full-throated religious rationale for the sanctity of free markets and a small federal government is a more recent invention.

Beginning in the 1920s, coalitions of clergy and businessmen promoted the idea, which Bruce Barton embodied in his 1925 best seller, *The Man Nobody Knows*. Barton's book depicted Jesus as a strong outdoorsman and a successful businessman. Critics mocked Barton's creation, but the depiction of a powerful and prosperous Jesus rang true for many Christians.[18] A successful advertising executive, Barton parlayed his publishing success into a political career. Citing Jesus as his central proof text, he declared, "I must be about my father's business." His linkage of religion, free markets, and limited government informed a countercultural current among conservative Protestants and fundamentalists for decades after his death.

Their efforts, bankrolled by many of America's richest men, used print and radio, sermons and church bulletins to convert the masses to their cause.

Reagan's narratives, subtler than many of these earlier efforts, had outsize effects in the media environment of the time. Unlike the twenty-first-century media universe, which can target niche audiences, the late twentieth-century news industry was dominated by a small number of corporations seeking mass saturation. It was the era of CBS News and *Time* magazine, not Fox or Breitbart. Since owners needed large audiences to attract advertisers, editors sought the widest common denominator rather than the fiery extremes. As a result, news was more standardized and less polarized than it would become in the digital era.

Reagan's words, directly quoted, had maximum impact as they echoed via radio, television, newspapers, and newsmagazines. Striving for objectivity, reporters did their best not to editorialize. Expressing a personal opinion was not only unprofessional, it also was bad business, since it could alienate consumers holding alternate views. Thus, despite assumptions about mainstream media's liberal bias, most news outlets were conservative insofar as they presented narratives that were recognizable and acceptable to a broad audience. Reporting on a familiar world from a normative perspective was better business than challenging the status quo.

Options for Americans who wanted something different were few, small, and siloed. Evangelicals watched *The 700 Club*, progressives subscribed to the *Nation*, and Latinos listened to Spanish-language programs. Funded by public support and special interest groups, these news and information outlets reflected political extremes, religious commitments, or a common language and culture. But even Americans divided along ethnic, racial, religious, and political lines likely watched network television news, read a newspaper, or subscribed to a weekly newsmagazine.

The mainstream media had a lock on its audience. News outlets disseminated the Reagan administration's talking points to radio, television, and print audiences, and subsequent public discussion propelled those same messages back up to the highest levels of government and media. This feedback loop, which shaped public opinion and influenced public policy, started with a top-down flow of information.[19] Reagan was not the first modern president to make use of the news media's power. Franklin D. Roosevelt's "fireside chats" series of evening radio addresses gave him direct access to the nation. John F. Kennedy befriended reporters who supported, then reported, his agenda. Richard M. Nixon, seeking control of the information flow, established the first White House communications office. But Reagan and his team outdid them all. Their plan was "not simply tame the press but to transform it into an unwitting mouthpiece of the government."[20]

The mainstream news media, bound to cover the words and activities of the commander-in-chief, reported on Reagan as objectively as possible. It also quoted surrogates, aware that his inner circle reflected the president's positions. When editorialists disagreed with Reagan and his men, they still restated the president's positions, normalizing them through repetition. This kind of news and editorial reiteration has the effect of setting cultural and political agendas, as the sheer accumulation of talking points and key ideas shapes what news consumers see, hear, and consider. As one political scientist put it, the news media "may not be successful much of the time in telling people what to think, but it is stunningly successful in telling its readers what to think about."[21] The circulation of Reagan's narratives not only mainstreamed his opinions but also provided news consumers with a frame for internalizing those opinions and making them their own.[22] And it was this dynamic that accounts for the changes in America's religious imaginary. Media narratives, more than simply circulating Reagan's positions, provided a framework for understanding the nation's mission and purpose. This framework helped legitimate an American religious imaginary that set norms for a virtuous social compact expressed through specific political and economic policies. In this way, moral propositions led to political practices, and the religious imaginary inspired a lived religion for citizens.

Reagan's religious imaginary reflected the conservative worldview that had circulated for decades among opponents of communism, the "welfare state," and perceived threats to the family. Barry Goldwater's 1964 presidential campaign highlighted some of these concerns, but his stridency alienated voters. Goldwater received only 39 percent of the popular vote, among the weakest election showings ever. Reagan, who had supported the Arizona senator, saw the defeat as a referendum on the man, not the message. That's why his 1966 campaign for the governorship of California projected a different style of conservatism. Reagan eschewed the brittle, censorious edge that, fairly or not, had characterized Goldwater. He also let voters know that his Christian faith shaped his political views. His born-again bona fides were common knowledge in California, as were his friendships with the state's evangelical elite. A law-and-order candidate, Reagan also appealed to voters vexed by the Watts riots, antiwar protests, and student radicals at the University of California, Berkeley, a state-subsidized public university. His support for fiscal conservatism and limited government impressed those who considered incumbent Democratic governor Edmund

"Pat" Brown a free-spending liberal. Maybe most important, his genial and folksy manner reassured voters across the political divide.

Reagan's rise preceded the emergence of the religious Right. But in the years between the 1966 gubernatorial election and his 1980 presidential run, hardline religious conservatives became a national political force. Their influence was based on grassroots organizing and electoral victories coordinated by local ministers, directed by parachurch organizations, and inspired by televangelists such as Pat Robertson, Jerry Falwell, and Jimmy Swaggart. Televangelism's reach was nationwide, and whether through broadcast worship services or *The 700 Club*, a daily televised newsmagazine, millions of Americans, especially those who did not read the *New York Times* or tune into NPR, absorbed the religious imaginary that Reagan would subsequently dispense through the secular press. This confluence of mainstream news narratives with evangelical media messages aligned two very different audiences. Their opinions diverged, but their discourse converged, influencing the parameters of public debate. For example, in 1983, when AIDS became a major story, Jerry Falwell's proximity to President Reagan made him a top source for reporters covering the response to the epidemic. Falwell's opinion, already familiar to his television audience, now entered the mainstream as the press circulated and normalized his view that AIDS was a divine punishment for individual and collective sins.

The appeal of Reagan's vision and its dissemination in both mainstream and religious news outlets help explain its success. Over time and through many reiterations, these narratives became the commonsense worldview, affirming conservative political, economic, and social values in contrast to those that predominated in postwar America. This change in perspective enabled Bill Clinton, a Democratic president, to oversee the repeal of the Glass-Steagall Act, which separated commercial and investment banking; to roll back welfare benefits, including the Aid to Families with Dependent Children program; and to greenlight the US bombing of Serbia without the sanction of the United Nations. However, tensions over the specifically evangelical aspects of the religious imaginary helped spark "culture wars"[23] over abortion, gay rights, and prayer in public schools. These social issues, which were much more polarizing than competing views on the defense of democracy and the limitations on government, sparked fierce debates over the definitions of a good society and a responsible citizenry.

Despite maxims about newspapers being good only for lining birdcages and wrapping fish, the news is neither ephemeral nor transparent. Rather, it is a collection of constructed stories whose significance lies not only in the act of their telling but also in how they are told: who is interviewed, what is emphasized, where the stories are placed (top of the broadcast or the very end; front page or deep in the second section), and how they are composed (language, framing, and organization). News is part of a cultural web that assimilates new information and turns it into conventionally accepted perceptions of reality. The news likewise sets permissible parameters of debate around acceptable topics of discussion.[24] This becomes the basis for a public agenda that shapes and reflects public opinion, creating and sustaining consensus on everyday reality through news narratives and their repetition.

News establishes what is significant. It influences not only what its consumers know but also how they think about what they know. In the United States, the first order of news is what powerful people say and do. Therefore, the president and those who speak for him have a primary role, not just in setting the national agenda and influencing public opinion, but also in establishing a normative understanding of American politics specifically and American mission and identity more broadly. Yet comprehending the relationships among the president, public opinion, and the news media requires more than studying the presidency, reviewing polls, and scrutinizing the news. It entails a deeper cultural investigation.[25]

MAPPING THE ARGUMENT

Righting the American Dream begins with an examination of the long-entangled relationship between American religion and the news media, especially their competing claims to be cultural arbiters and civic leaders. The chapter also looks at the newspaper industry in the post–World War II era, culminating with the far-reaching changes of the 1980s. Chapter 2 takes a step back, exploring the cultural context for the Reagan era and the reasons why so many Americans were open to his ideas. Social, cultural, political, and economic dislocations, many of which came to a head in 1973, undermined citizens' sense of mission, identity, and purpose. These upheavals coincided with a decline in the national mood and in Americans' trust in government, buoyed only briefly by Jimmy Carter's 1976 election to the presidency.[26] The country was ready for a Great Communicator, as Reagan was called, who could articulate a clear and compelling national vision of destiny and greatness.

The era's religious landscape is described in chapter 3, which examines the overlap between modern evangelicalism—the Protestant movement that asserts that a personal relationship with Jesus is fundamental for salvation—and the Reagan-era religious imaginary. It describes how and why different strains of the post-1960s evangelical world resonated with

Reagan's policies, and it discusses alternate examples of baby boomer spirituality that were compatible with the new religious imaginary. Evangelicals, influenced more by religious media than secular outlets, provided grassroots support for Reagan's vision. This is key, because although the secular news media mainstreamed Reagan's agenda and his imaginary, the success of his worldview required buy-in from Americans attuned to alternate news sources. The new religious imaginary was as much a grassroots phenomenon among evangelicals as a top-down endeavor of the Reagan administration's management of secular, mainstream news.

The fourth chapter demonstrates this latter point, showing how the president and his surrogates used current events to articulate the theological stakes facing the nation. Both Reagan's formulation of the nuclear freeze as a cosmic showdown between the United States and the Soviet Union and his supporters' assertion that AIDS was a moral issue introduced the notion of religiously based evil into secular sociopolitical debate. Media coverage repeated this language and framing, amplifying religious and moral themes through sourcing, story organization, and writing style. Subsequent repetition—news stories followed by features, analyses, profiles, and op-eds—further disseminated the president's ideas and arguments. While not the primary focus for reporting on either AIDS or the nuclear freeze, the religious/moral framework became a significant part of news coverage and public discussion. Although the framing of these two stories used evangelical Protestant language, Reagan's and his proxies' clear expression of right and wrong attracted members of other faiths as well as secularists disenchanted with the 1960s' assertions of moral relativism.

Reagan's "new patriotism" and his mastery of the liberal media are highlighted in chapter 5, which recounts the context for and coverage of the US mission in Grenada. President Reagan, warning Americans of a communist coup in the tiny Caribbean nation, provided a justification for the October 1983 invasion. For the first time in more than 125 years, the press was banned from covering a military intervention, and government news sources depicted the incursion as a victory for patriotism. (Press coverage of the Vietnam War had convinced some military and government leaders that American journalists were hostile to national interests.) The successful outcome of the mission, pumped up by White House spin in the absence of independent reports, resulted in two important wins for the president: Grenada boosted his personal popularity and helped coalesce his new patriotism. However, these political triumphs came at the expense of the mainstream press's freedom of movement. Reagan wanted news outlets to spread his message, and in this instance, that meant controlling their coverage. The administration sidelined reporters, stymied independent information gathering, and derailed critical stories of a trigger-happy president and an ill-advised escapade. Such a heavy-handed approach would not be possible outside the special circumstances of a military intervention, but Grenada demonstrated how journalists could be checked and manipulated.

Just as chapters 4 and 5 detailed the Reagan administration's war against an external evil, so chapter 6 chronicles its fight against an evil within: the welfare state and the miscreants who benefited from it. As governor of California, Reagan removed millions of the working poor from welfare rolls. Early in his presidential tenure, he oversaw legislation that cut taxes and reduced federal entitlements. Officially presented as a way to end the recession, the initiatives also coincided with Reagan's moral and religious vision of ending the welfare state, limiting government involvement, and empowering individuals to take responsibility for themselves and their families. The chapter looks at reporting on welfare, tax cuts, and hunger to examine the political, economic, and moral nexus of Reagan's religious imaginary. It argues that the coverage and normalization of the new imaginary contributed to changing notions about citizenship, responsibility, and fairness as well as race and gender.

Reagan's determination to restructure the US economic system and restore its global stature meant redefining cultural credos that had organized American life in the postwar era. In 1981, his draconian budget proposals upended thirty years of liberal New Deal ideology, and by 1983 those changes were recasting America's sociopolitical underpinnings as well as its economic prospects. Yet the sweeping innovations known as the Reagan Revolution were not willed into being solely by the actions of the fortieth president. They also reflected the aspirations that millions of Americans had harbored for decades and turned them into a national reality.

The epilogue for *Righting the American Dream* assesses how the ideological changes advanced by the Reagan-era religious imaginary have fared over the past four decades. One significant change has been measuring politics in terms of good and evil. That notion has inspired true believers to strong words, harsh stands, and devastating actions ranging from zealous antigay protests to the murder of pro-choice physicians. It also paved the way for Islamophobia and xenophobia, and for leaders who take strong stands against what some citizens see as societal sins. Lauding personal freedom and self-reliance, the Reagan imaginary also enabled successive administrations to cut back social welfare programs, lower taxes, and support deregulation. For example, many of President Donald Trump's policies and executive orders would have been unimaginable without Reagan's language of personal responsibility, small government, and American exceptionalism.

Despite a growing gap between rich and poor, the conviction that God helps those who help themselves has not only sanctified the prosperity gospel, a form of Christianity that promotes health and wealth, but also justified billionaires whose corporations pay taxes at lower rates than those available to small-business owners or even citizens. Lastly, the belief in American exceptionalism has sanctioned a dangerous tautology: God has blessed America, so anything America does is blessed by God. In conjunction with the acceptance of a cosmic moral order and the affirmation of personal freedom, American exceptionalism can vindicate anything, from safeguarding gun owners' unfettered Second Amendment rights, to accepting "collateral damage" in international warfare, to spurning public safety guidelines during a global pandemic. *Righting the American Dream* argues that the news media played a crucial role in mainstreaming the religious imaginary that made all this possible.

PART ONE

Context: Media, Politics, and Religion

CHAPTER ONE

Faith in the Media

> Of the forces shaping the destiny of our civilization, none is more crucial to our future than the responsible reporting and truthful analysis of the events of our era.
>
> PRESIDENT RONALD REAGAN, October 6, 1983

In the five years between the release of *All the President's Men*, the 1976 film about two *Washington Post* newsmen who uncovered the Watergate scandal, and *Absence of Malice*, the 1981 movie about a reckless reporter whose work leads to a suicide, America's image of journalists—or at least Hollywood's take on it—had plummeted. Gone were the golden boys whose crusading reportage saved democracy. In their place were callow, compromised women. In *Absence of Malice*, Megan Carter, an ambitious Miami reporter, dupes some sources but is deceived by others. She prints unverified information, sleeps with the subject of her investigation, and sacrifices professionalism for a scoop. But her actions are absent of malice, and as portrayed by Sally Field, Carter is less a villain than a witless wannabe.

Two of her silver-screen sisters, whose stories were released that same year, fared no better. Tony Sokolow, a television journalist played by Sigourney Weaver in *Eyewitness*, is oblivious to her fiancé's role in a murder she is investigating. Perhaps that's because she's emotionally involved with a source. Critics praised Diane Keaton, who portrayed Louise Bryant in *Reds*, for evoking the "alienating and exasperating"[1] aspects of the early twentieth-century feminist and journalist. Bryant leaves her marriage and shakes off bourgeois respectability for a liaison with writer John Reed, and the two travel to Russia to cover the 1917 revolution. For all three women, sleeping with sources, betraying commitments, and doing anything to get ahead were all in a day's work. Although sex was central to these female characters, it remained in the background for the celluloid depictions of Woodward and Bernstein. Their only compromising act, portrayed as an in-joke, is to call their source Deep Throat—a reference to Linda Lovelace, a 1970s porn film star famous for her pharyngeal achievements.

Why in five short years did Hollywood's representation of journalists swing from zealous male defenders of democracy to personally and professionally challenged females? The shift was more than a coincidental plot device. During the Reagan years, female journalists such as Diane Sawyer, Barbara Walters, Jane Pauley, and Jessica Savitch enjoyed high-profile careers that rivaled those of their male colleagues. Nevertheless, distrust of the press and disquiet about female empowerment reflected a growing conservative perspective. The same anxieties that made many Americans doubt the accuracy and objectivity of the news media inclined them to fear and resent the growing number of sexually active and economically independent women. Hollywood's portrayal of journalists as flawed females reflected and reinforced suspicions that working women were duplicitous and that reporting was a sullied profession.

Yet even as critiques of the liberal media increased, changes in the news industry were transforming both the business and the content of the nation's newspapers. The openness to countercultural trends and anti-establishment investigations that defined coverage in the 1970s was an early casualty of industry consolidation and the conservative turn of the Reagan administration. To understand the news media's role in mainstreaming the Reagan Revolution, including its dissemination of his religious imaginary, this chapter surveys the long-standing relationship between religion and the news. It also explains why the economics of the 1980s news business worked in favor of President Reagan's conservative message.[2]

Throughout the 1970s, when Gallup first asked Americans about their opinion of the news media, the public's trust level hovered between 68 and 72 percent.[3] Thereafter, public trust began an almost steady decline, and in 2021 that number was down to 36 percent.[4] Several factors, including political shifts that helped drive distrust, explain the drop in public confidence. But so do economic and social factors. Competition from cable news and alternative print media, often with differing points of view, eroded confidence in mainstream media. But more significant was the increasing cultural polarization that, starting in the 1970s, shattered a four-decade consensus supportive of New Deal liberalism. As politics became more combative, politicians attacked the news media for coverage that conflicted with their point of view. Conservative Republicans were particularly hostile, beginning with supporters of Barry Goldwater's 1964 presidential campaign and continuing through the Nixon White House.

The news media's coverage of the Vietnam War intensified criticism. In 1969, Vice President Spiro Agnew launched a series of attacks on the press. Critical of what he perceived as the liberal East Coast media's hold on information, he asked Americans to let the television networks know they agreed with him. Within days, the three major networks "received nearly 90,000 letters, telegrams, and phone calls, most of which supported the vice president." (Although Agnew repeatedly attacked the press, his oft-cited description of "nattering nabobs of negativism," penned by Nixon speechwriter and future *New York Times* columnist William Safire, actually referred to politicians.)[5]

Fourteen years later, critic Lewis Lapham noted that complaints were common "about the distortions of the news, about the 'rude,' 'accusatory,' 'cynical,' 'meddlesome,' 'arrogant,' and 'self-righteous' behavior of the press."[6] Other observers faulted journalists who they said were unprincipled or out of touch with mainstream Americans. Janet Cooke, a *Washington Post* reporter whose 1981 Pulitzer Prize–winning story about an eight-year-old heroin addict turned out to be a hoax, was the poster girl for their critiques.[7] *The Media Elite*, based on a 1980 survey of reporters' attitudes, would not appear until 1986, but its authors' preliminary research papers argued that journalists in the nation's premier news outlets were more liberal and secular than the general population.[8] The implication was that their reporting could not be trusted. The claim would be nuanced and refuted over the years, but it gained traction, because it substantiated conventional wisdom.

THE PENNY PRESS AND BEYOND

When Ronald Reagan became president in 1980, he inherited an evolving relationship among the news, the government, and Protestant Christianity that stretched back to the seventeenth century. Puritan colonists treated news as a religious hermeneutic. It was a way to decipher God's intention for their mission,[9] which they believed could be known through the working of nature and the outcome of events. A stillbirth signaled God's displeasure. A bountiful harvest meant God was pleased. Reporting was the documentation of objective revelation based on personal observation. This approach echoed down the centuries, differentiating the content and perspective of American journalism from its European counterparts. As a result, American news tended to be written from an omniscient, or objective, perspective rather than a subjective one, and news narratives conformed to biblical themes, such as sin and repentance, sacrifice and redemption, good versus evil.

In the colonial era, American religion and American news were bound in a mutually constitutive relationship that turned militantly competitive by the late nineteenth century. Yet their union played a crucial role in American nation building, because news stories created and sustained a narrative of peoplehood, which included a divine mission and a godly covenant. As Georg Hegel and later Benedict Anderson observed, reading the morning newspaper became the modern analogue to morning prayers, a ritual that structured an unruly world and oriented the self within it. The Puritan notion of God's saints in a New Jerusalem was just one of several religious visions for the New World. Anglicans in the South, Roman Catholics in the West, and Jews in the Mid-Atlantic told their own stories of a chosen people with a divine calling to a promised land. Unsurprisingly, accounts of religious leaders' trials and triumphs were among the first news to travel through the colonies, and they knit readers together with threads of shared concern.

By the 1730s, a thriving newspaper culture had spread throughout the colonies, with weekly news sheets offering a mix of essays, fiction, and current events. Religion was pervasive in the mix: church activities were regularly noted, and hymns, sermons, prayers, and Bible verses were featured. Political stories had a religious dimension, and reports on laws and governmental decrees noted religious motivations. Religion was a fact of life covered by the press, and it also was the primary means for interpreting events, whether a rise in taxes or a series of freakish storms.

By the 1770s, the focus on religion had decreased, and economics and politics predominated. The colonists' growing commercial sector demanded more financial news, and many citizens, chafing under Britain's oppressive taxes, wanted political news too. Newspapers still printed church updates and reported on events, including acts of rebellion, which could be interpreted as part of God's plan. But the earlier identification of news as religion and religion as news had lost currency among a growing and less devout population.

After the Revolutionary War, newspapers played a key role in shaping the new nation. Many were organs of political parties; others specialized in commercial news for the growing mercantile class. Catering to subscribers who paid a hefty advance, editors valued partisanship and debate, offering a narrow focus on a particular topic. The formula worked: By 1825, the United States had eight hundred–plus newspapers, more than any other country.[10] However, new technology transformed content, delivery, and audiences. Innovations in printing and papermaking reduced production costs, and enterprising publishers bet that workingmen would spend a penny for a daily newspaper that informed and entertained. Better yet, advertisers would pay a premium to reach that audience; thus, the penny press was born.

The penny press shifted news gathering, professional standards, and industry economics. The change from subscription-based weeklies to reader-purchased dailies incentivized publishers to seek mass audiences for their advertisers rather than a limited base of partisan subscribers. One of the first major penny press stories was a scandalous tale of money, mayhem, and religion. The Prophet Matthias was a self-proclaimed religious leader who bilked his followers, slept with female acolytes, and allegedly killed a troublesome donor.[11] In 1833 Matthias, who before his spiritual rebirth had been a carpenter named Robert Matthews, founded a religious commune with several of New York's leading evangelical merchants, their wives, and Isabella Baumfree, a former slave who later changed her name to Sojourner Truth. A year later, Matthias's kingdom was in ruins, and he was on trial for fraud, assault, and murder. The proceedings received national coverage, because they fit the business model of the new penny press. Sensational stories that commingled scandal, crime, and hypocrisy were a recipe for commercial success. Matthias's story had all three cast in a narrative replete with sex, money, and false prophecy.

In the same way that colonial news sheets revealed the unfolding of a divine plan, the penny press spotlighted human agency and concomitant vice, especially through tales of crime and punishment. These narratives, presented in titillating detail, appealed to voyeuristic news consumers as well as affirmed the nation's commitment to justice. Divine providence remained in the mix, but its authority over the quotidian realm had receded. In fact, God's role or lack thereof in the penny press was the professed cause of the Moral War of 1840.[12] The fight centered on James Gordon Bennett and his flamboyant *New York Herald*. Bennett, a self-made Scottish immigrant, was a revolutionizing force in the news industry. He pioneered financial coverage, international reporting, and society stories, providing readers with as much news as possible as quickly as possible.

Bennett also is credited with spearheading modern religion coverage. His *New York Herald* printed sermons, hymns, and scriptures as part of the daily mix, but he also provided news reports on religious meetings, activities, and leaders. A Roman Catholic by birth, Bennett was curious about religion and supportive of religious liberty, but he happily exposed any piety that smacked of hypocrisy or malfeasance. He covered religion like any other beat and considered clerical peccadilloes, congregational scandals, and denominational crimes fair game. In fact, the *Herald*'s front page included coverage of Prophet Matthias's murder trial.

Nineteenth-century newspaper editors frequently battled one another for financial gain, but the fight against the *Herald* was different. Critics accused Bennett of packing his pages with sex, crime, and sensation. They also condemned him for satirizing religion and criticizing church leaders. Opponents even organized a boycott to shut down the newspaper. Some clergy may have been less concerned with Bennett's critical reporting than with the *Herald*'s policy of covering ecclesial meetings that they wanted to keep private. Many also disliked stories about the growing entanglement of religion, business, and politics.[13]

In the short run, the Moral War hurt the *Herald*'s finances, but it did not ruin the newspaper. Bennett continued to report on religion, but changes in staffing and news gathering affected the style and substance of coverage. Before the Moral War, Bennett wrote the bulk of the stories: most were about New York and mirrored his own interests. Afterward, he hired correspondents around the country to broaden the scope of articles. By the mid-1840s, the *Herald*'s coverage of religion featured reports on New England's evangelical abolitionists, New York's frontier revivalists, and midwesterners' run-ins with members of the Church of Jesus Christ of Latter-day Saints.

Bennett and his fellow publishers broke news rather than circulating reports from other journals. They made news a marketable commodity and "invented a genre which acknowledged, and so enhanced, the importance of everyday life."[14] Throughout the nineteenth century, the number of American newspapers soared: in 1850, there were three thousand; in 1880, seven thousand. The penny press ushered in an era of reader-friendly content that made newspapers a daily habit for citizens of the new republic. They now turned to the paper not only for tantalizing stories but also for timely information.

Yet one businessman sensed a market for a more serious alternative. In 1851, when Henry Jarvis launched the *New York Times*, he hoped to introduce a level of sobriety to his city's pell-mell press. A decade later, during the Civil War, publishers nationwide followed suit, inaugurating a new era of responsible coverage. Religion, which the pennies usually covered as a foil for scandal and sensationalism, was treated respectfully, woven into battlefield stories as solace and inspiration for families back home. But when the war ended, the flow of positive religion news ebbed. During the 1870s, an economic downturn battered newspapers along with the rest of society. To boost sales, editors peddled shock and titillation, including religion stories that appealed to both skeptics and believers. The Salvation Army's antics—brass bands, women preachers, and services held in saloons—were good copy, as was the Reverend Henry Ward Beecher's trial for committing adultery with his best friend's wife.[15]

Clergy, seeing their day-to-day work as increasingly peripheral to reporters and editors, criticized the press's lack of social responsibility and

FIGURE 2. Image from the adultery trial of the Reverend Henry Ward Beecher.

moral leadership. They castigated the purple prose of sensationalism and condemned advertisements for frivolous products, such as medicinal tonics.[16] They insisted that newspapers had a moral obligation to improve society, which in their view meant inculcating a Christian worldview. That meant publishers should stop printing unseemly details about scandals, divorces, suicides, and executions as well as ban advertisements for illicit activities and disreputable products.

The power to influence public opinion was migrating from pulpit to press. Between 1870 and 1930, changes in the news business, including the growing importance of advertising and the need to reach a diverse readership, further mitigated against a moralizing Christian perspective and sectarian religious coverage. Journalists profiled men and women whom they perceived as oddball religious outsiders: Father Divine and his Peace Mission, W. D. Fard's reinvented Islam, and fake fakirs who compromised their female followers. Overall, however, the number of religion stories plummeted. Between 1905 and 1909, the *Reader's Guide to Periodical Literature*, a sampling of journals and magazines, listed 21.4 stories per year on religion. In 1931, the total came to 10.7. Moreover, stories positively inclined to "traditional Christianity," which had constituted 78 percent of coverage in 1905, fell by more than half to 33 percent in 1931.[17]

Shifts in the coverage of religion reflected changes in the news industry and in society. During the closing decades of the nineteenth century, secularization made significant inroads in both higher education and the professions. Educated Americans linked science to progress and lumped religion with ignorance and superstition. Religious elites, such as Presbyterian and Episcopal clerics whose opinions had graced editorial pages, were not exempt from the new classification. Their essays were out of favor, and their public opining ended. The 1925 Scopes Trial was the coup de grace. Many reporters depicted religion as outmoded buffoonery, and opinion writers disparaged Tennessee laws that forbade the teaching of evolution. Editorialists, noting that fundamentalism was symptomatic of an "ill-balanced mind,"[18] feared that its adherents made America look foolish to the rest of the world. The change in the media's approach following the Scopes trial was palpable: a 1933 survey found that newspapers had shifted from sanctioning biblical authority to privileging science and facts.[19]

Many journalism professionals now believed that their vocation had superseded religion as society's authoritative truth teller and interpreter of events. Whereas preachers wove supernatural tales about a mist-swathed past, journalists reported true stories about today's world. According to much of the American press, Bible-believing Christians may have won the 1925 Monkey Trial, but they'd lost control of the narrative.

THE COMPETING GOALS OF JOURNALISM, 1900 TO THE 1950S

Social and cultural shifts similar to those facilitating journalism's rejection of religion also affected journalists' professional identity, the content of their work, and their industry's finances. Technological advances encouraged industry expansion at the same time that secularization prompted greater professionalization. Growth and gravitas had brought a new level of seriousness and self-importance to both the business and the mission of journalism. As a result, two trajectories developed in tandem, with conflicting missions: one to maximize profits and the other to serve the public.

On the business side, advertising, which subsidized the news, was increasingly important; revenue from circulation alone could not cover the rising costs of labor, technology, newsprint, and delivery. Concurrently, reporters were held to higher professional standards. According to pundits, democracy depended on fair and impartial news gathering, thus imbuing journalists with a special responsibility for the public welfare. The press was responsible for shaping not just public opinion but also public perceptions of culture, politics, and society. As priests and prophets of the secular age, reporters provided the authoritative guidance and vital information needed to negotiate an increasingly complex world. Readers torn between the old, familiar ways and societal shifts in education, urbanization, and mobility wanted guidance, but the Bible was no longer relevant to many Americans. Newspapers, offering insight on the real world, were.

Objectivity was the editorial goal. Walter Lippmann, one of the most influential press critics of the twentieth century, argued that the complexity of the modern world required journalists to stick to the facts. Lippmann posited the scientific method—a model for remaining open, unbiased, and rational—as journalism's lodestar. Implicit in this call for objectivity was the recognition of its impossibility, a way of reckoning with the spiritual crisis and loss of faith following the First World War, the Russian Revolution, the rise of fascism, the Great Depression, and the emergence of Nazism. In this context, objectivity can be seen as journalism's attempt to invoke the omniscient authority that once exemplified religion, even though the attempt would always fail.

But a chasm loomed between lofty ideals and the lived experience of workaday reporters. During the first decades of the twentieth century, few journalists were college educated. Most were working-class white men toiling in a profession that paid the bills but little more. Even during the Great Depression, journalists still had jobs and publishers still made money. Small, independently owned newspapers faced the most difficulties, since advertisers had reduced budgets, especially for local markets. Some newspapers went out of business, and others were sold to newspaper chains. By the end of the 1930s, many American cities had only one newspaper, but overall circulation held steady, even growing slightly between 1929 and 1939.[20]

During this same period, newsreels, newsmagazines, and radio began competing with newspapers for audiences and advertisers. Newsreels debuted in 1911. Shown at cinemas before the feature-length movie was presented, these short films were a hit. In 1923, Henry Luce and Briton Hadden launched a weekly print magazine, which curated and streamlined the news. *Time* used bright, colorful prose for roundups, opinions, and in-depth features. Its success encouraged competitors, and Luce later extended the brand with *Life*, a weekly newsmagazine of photo essays. But the greatest challenge to newspapers was radio, the wireless box that came into its own as a commercial medium after World War I.

In 1925, there were fourteen hundred radio stations in the United States; by 1930, there were fourteen million radios.[21] Music was the mainstay of early broadcasts, but religious services soon filled the airwaves as well. Newspaper publishers quickly realized that radio would be a formidable competitor. Determined to retain their monopoly on news, they tried to prevent the Associated Press and United Press International, news agencies that used wire services to transmit stories domestically and internationally, from providing information to radio stations. The conflict was resolved when radio stations agreed to limit news coverage, and newspapers promised to publish radio schedules. However, the settlement did not stop radio programs from providing news commentary in lieu of breaking news. It also did not prevent the nation's commander in chief from utilizing the new medium of radio to communicate with the American people.

In 1932, when Franklin D. Roosevelt was elected president, radios were in 90 percent of American households, making them the perfect medium for his popular "fireside chats." In thirty broadcasts over eleven years, Roosevelt directly addressed the electorate—"my friends," he called them—to explain complex domestic and international issues in plain English. If his unprecedented four-term tenure was partly a testament to his explanatory skills and rapport with regular folks, his relationship with the news media was more complex.

Deft at getting on the good side of White House reporters, Roosevelt charmed many with his wit, bonhomie, and cultivated candor. But his rapport with their bosses was tenuous. Businessmen that they were, publishers distrusted Roosevelt and disliked his New Deal. Many of their newspapers had skipped lightly over the origins of the Depression, foregoing in-depth coverage of the devastating impact of Wall Street's troubles. Instead of commentary, analysis, or investigative reporting on the stock market's failure and its effect on individuals and institutions, many publishers focused on feel-good reporting that either distracted or reassured readers. Looking back on the decade in 1937, George Seldes, a liberal gadfly and independent journalist, noted, "It is held by many people that the failure of our newspapers to inform us honestly and accurately about the economic situation from 1927 to 1929, and the wish-fulfillment policy from 1929 on, constituted [the press's] greatest failure in modern times."[22] Echoing Seldes, other critics described the press as antiunion, probusiness, and in thrall to the government line.

Just as the press skewed toward favorable coverage of banks and business in the 1920s, so, too, it was reluctant to "politicize economic issues" in the 1930s. According to one study, front-page coverage of the economy did not increase after the stock market crashed in 1929 or during the next two years. It rose only after Roosevelt was elected in 1932 and peaked in 1936.[23] Yet the press's reluctance to take on the causes and context of the Great Depression did not initially hamper reporting on the New Deal. Journalists liked the thirty-second president and reported positively on his plans. Publishers, wanting to appear supportive of the new administration, initially did not object.

But press barons began deriding Roosevelt before his first term ended. Colonel Robert McCormick of the *Chicago Tribune* decided that the New Deal would lead to communism, and others, including William Randolph Hearst, agreed. Nor were businessmen the only critics: Walter Lippmann, the respected press critic and columnist mentioned above, opposed the president's plans, fearful that they would centralize power in the federal government. News pieces tended to put the president and his programs in a positive light, but editorial pages told a different story. In 1932, 41 percent of American dailies and 45 percent of weeklies endorsed Roosevelt's candidacy, while his popular support was 57 percent. When he ran for a third term in 1940, only 25 percent of dailies and 33 percent of weeklies backed him.[24] Notwithstanding this lack of editorial enthusiasm, Roosevelt won 54.7 percent of the vote and thirty-eight of the forty-eight states.[25] Publishers had no more luck than other businessmen in turning popular opinion against the president and his new economic order.

When the war ended and the United States emerged as a global power, commentators inside and outside the news industry challenged journalists to produce a better product. Many chided the press's tendency to trivialize, sensationalize, and distort the news to fit a conservative, probusiness point of view. More than ever, critics said, Americans needed sound information about crucial issues at home and abroad. In 1942 Henry Luce, the founder of *Time* magazine, asked Robert Hutchins, the president of the University of Chicago, to examine the ramifications of a free press, including its responsibilities and challenges. Hutchins agreed, and he and Luce selected sixteen men to serve on a blue-ribbon panel. The Hutchins Commission had its shortcomings; in particular, its members were all upper-class white male academics or elite professionals. But they also were true believers in the ability of a free press to ensure democracy.

With funding from Luce and a three-year mandate, the commission set out to explore how the press was doing and what factors—such as government censorship, audience demand, and managerial reticence—hampered its mission. Between 1944 and 1946, members met seventeen times, conducted fifty-eight interviews, read dozens of documents, and

FIGURE 3. The Hutchins Commission. Holborn Gray Special Collections Research Center, University of Chicago Library.

made nine revisions of their final report. Among their concerns were the declining numbers of newspapers and the subsequent decrease in competition; the spread of tabloid journalism; the influence of owners and advertisers on coverage; the lack of reporting on racial minorities; and the widespread reliance on official sources.

Although several commission members believed that the most effective way to improve the press was to regulate it, the group eschewed that recommendation, wary that it would antagonize publishers and quash any hope for change. Declaring the importance of a free press for a democratic society, its report concluded that the press's "faults and errors have ceased to be private vagaries and have become public dangers."[26] It warned that journalism was more apt to entertain, stereotype, and sensationalize than to provide trustworthy information. Concluding with a series of recommendations to the government, the press, and the public, the commission sought greater accountability, increased competition, and financial incentives for start-ups as means to strengthen the news media and enhance its role as a safeguard of democracy. But the commission's recommendations, the thrust of which threatened business as usual, fell flat. The press ridiculed the report and academics dismissed it. Some critics faulted the commission for not including working journalists among its members. Others rejected its critique as insufficient or out of touch. Still others, predominantly publishers, called it a left-wing attempt to rein in a free press. The charge was spurious, since the group comprised mainstream elites.

The commission's report missed a major change in the media that was already under way. A new technology, pioneered in the 1920s, was about to take off. RCA, the earliest manufacturer of television sets, had expected the new medium to break through in 1939, when the company debuted it at the New York World's Fair. But the war slowed television's spread, and it was another ten years before the talking picture box assumed pride of place in America's living rooms. Television's success was tied to the need to grow the peacetime economy; manufacturers produced six thousand sets in 1946 and three million in 1949. A decade later, televisions would be in 87 percent of American households.[27]

Television news developed slowly. As a first step, news broadcasters' short reports were supplemented with newsreels. By the mid-1950s, anchormen brought personality to network news, but their shows were only fifteen minutes long. However, other types of news programs debuted. Weekend roundups assembled commentators to discuss current events, and morning shows entertained housewives with news and soft features. The new medium's popularity hurt other news outlets. But even though their advertising revenue shrank, newspaper publishers, still earning double-digit profits, did not worry. They told themselves that Americans still needed their newspapers' larger news hole and deeper coverage to supplement television and radio.

But the numbers suggested otherwise. Although the US population grew after the war, newspaper readership was constant and household penetration shrank. In 1945, 1.29 papers were sold per household; twenty years later, that number dropped to 1.05.[28] By 1980, it fell to 0.77.[29] Four hundred newspapers closed or merged in the two decades after the war.[30] Since much of the shakeout occurred in cities with more than one paper, Congress held hearings in 1962 to ensure that publishers were not forming monopolies. Given the role of a free press in a democratic polity, elected leaders worried about decreasing numbers of independent news outlets, and the US Justice Department blocked several acquisitions that appeared to violate antitrust laws. It was a both-and era for many publishers. Costs were going up while circulation stalled, yet profits remained high, especially since newspapers could raise advertising rates in the increasing number of American cities where there was no competition.

POLITICS AND THE PRESS: THE 1950S TO THE 1980S

The emergence of the Soviet Union as a world power in the 1950s ratcheted up anticommunist sentiments that had been present since the Russian Revolution of 1917. America's fear and loathing of the Red Menace was matched by the Soviet Union's hostility to capitalism and its apprehensiveness about US aggression. The resulting Cold War between the two world powers lasted for decades. Its early years were fierce: the United States demonstrated nuclear superiority, adopted the Truman Doctrine to contain communism, and launched NATO to align with European countries against the USSR. The Soviet Union developed its own A-bomb, instituted an Iron Curtain in Eastern Europe, and supported the communist takeover of China. In 1950, proxies for the two sides came to blows in the Korean War.

During World War II, American newspapers had willingly acquiesced to government censors, convinced that an Allied victory was more important than an unfettered press. But in the postwar period, when the government asserted national security reasons for withholding information, journalists pushed back. They didn't want to endanger the fight against communism, but since it was peacetime, they felt justified to expose other secrets. Accordingly, when the junior Republican senator from Wisconsin announced that Reds had infiltrated the government, the military, and Hollywood, reporters jumped on the story.

Senator Joseph McCarthy excelled at using the news media for his own ends. For almost four years, he held the nation rapt with claims that communist agents had penetrated America's most esteemed institutions. Initially, McCarthy was a journalist's dream. Not only was he at the center of the biggest story of the day, but he also provided a steady stream of scoops and colorful commentary. Timing announcements for maximum impact and exploiting the conventions of objectivity, he ensured that his accusations received excellent coverage and, even at their most outrageous, were treated seriously. Opponents characterized his relationship with the press as cynical opportunism at the public's expense. "If Joe McCarthy is a political monster," wrote two critics in 1952, "then the press has been his Dr. Frankenstein."[31]

As McCarthy's power grew, some journalists reconsidered their role in his crusade. Their initial coverage of the Wisconsin senator had been a foregone conclusion, given the news industry's penchant for conflict and controversy. Most reporters sought to be objective, but the ideal of impartiality had reified since Lippmann's day. By the 1950s, the line between journalistic objectivity and stenography was nearly erased: reporters gathered comments from opposing sides and let readers decide what to make of them. Moreover, many journalists were now inclined to give politicians and government officials the benefit of the doubt, a vestige from the war years when safeguarding national interests trumped the press's role as public watchdog. Thus, support for McCarthy initially seemed patriotic, and his crusade worthy of coverage.[32]

By 1954, however, some reporters were questioning McCarthy's charges. Coverage increasingly utilized interpretative reporting to explain and contextualize events. Stories, no longer limited to accounts of McCarthy's latest accusation, now included the history, pattern, and reliability of his prior allegations. Instead of accepting his claims at face value, reporters began examining both his motives and his intentions. Members of the press were not left-wing, but they were no longer willing to play a passive role in a government-sanctioned witch hunt. In response, McCarthy returned the favor, questioning journalists' motives and loyalty, claiming they were communists too.[33]

Not long after the McCarthy era, Wall Street discovered that newspapers were extraordinarily profitable. Until the 1960s, many family-owned papers operated under the radar; as private companies, their books were closed. But some properties that were started in the late nineteenth century faced financial difficulties by the mid-1960s. The three-generation grace period for taxes on family-owned businesses was ending. To avoid a hefty tax bill, owners could either take the company public and trade shares on the stock market or sell to another company.

When newspaper companies took the former route, Wall Street compelled financial disclosures revealing that many family-run newspapers—assumed to be noblesse-oblige ventures operating for the public good—had pretax profit margins as high as 40 percent.[34] Enticed by this new honeypot, banks and other institutional investors swept up 44 percent of the publicly owned newspaper stock by the early 1980s.[35] The turnabout was staggering: in 1945, 80 percent of daily newspapers were owned by families; by 1989, only 20 percent remained in family hands.[36]

The demise of the family paper benefited newspaper chains. Between 1945 and 1964, these groups doubled the number of dailies that they controlled.[37] Chains promised editorial autonomy to local papers, but critics wondered whether corporate owners, more concerned with costs than community, would invest in properties or strip out profits. In some instances, family owners that disliked chains were overruled when shareholding relatives opted to cash out. In other cases, families faced with exorbitant income and inheritance taxes had no choice but to sell. Tax laws favored chains that could keep investing. If companies used earnings to buy related businesses (including other newspapers), their tax bill was significantly reduced. As a result, chains began buying up news properties, eventually taking over one another.

President John F. Kennedy had direct knowledge of the newspaper business because of his father's friendship with William Randolph Hearst, owner of Hearst Newspapers. In 1945, young Kennedy had been discharged from the military and was considering career options. His father called Hearst, and JFK was hired as a foreign correspondent. His journalism career lasted less than a year, but it left Kennedy appreciative of journalism's role in a democracy, even after he won the White House in 1960. During a 1962 interview with a television reporter, Kennedy said, "There isn't any doubt that we could not do the job at all in a free society without a very,

very active press."[38] He was clear that he did not always like what the press reported or its "abrasive quality," but that did not stop him from courting the reporters who covered him. And after his election, a new generation of journalists fell under the sway of the most charismatic leader since FDR.[39] Kennedy was both charming and manipulative. He reached out to reporters as part of a larger strategy to manage the news, an ongoing concern of the modern executive branch. In addition to stemming news leaks and withholding information, his team also misled the press, most spectacularly during the Bay of Pigs debacle.

In April 1961, the US government helped exiled Cubans launch a coup against dictator Fidel Castro. But the small invading force that landed at the Bay of Pigs was rebuffed by Cuban troops. News about the planned attack was leaked in magazines and small newspapers in the months beforehand, but larger news outlets had reported only bits and pieces—an oversight, some said, due to presidential pressure on publishers. When confronted about details in print, Kennedy's men claimed ignorance or dissembled. They covered up their involvement and tried to stop reporters from pursuing the story. With the very public failure of the invasion displayed across the front pages of American newspapers, the administration blamed the news media for the fiasco. Kennedy said the press had written too little about the plan and that more publicity might have prevented the fiasco. But he also criticized reporters for endangering national interests and asked publishers to exercise voluntary censorship.

As with the McCarthy episode, the press was forced to recognize that its interests did not coincide with the government's. If there had been any question about that reality, the 1962 Cuban Missile Crisis underscored the point. After the aborted Bay of Pigs invasion, the Russians sought to install nuclear arms in Cuba. Kennedy countered, saying that positioning Russian weapons so near the United States would be tantamount to a declaration of war. Negotiations between the two sides lasted several weeks. The administration released few details to the press and sought to control what reporters saw, where they went, and with whom they spoke. The world edged toward a nuclear showdown, but journalists were unable to report events.

Thirteen months later, on Friday, November 22, Kennedy was assassinated. Immediately after the shooting, all three networks switched from their regularly scheduled programming to the spectacle that unfolded over the weekend. More than 90 percent of American households had a television,[40] which turned the tragedy into a collective ritual of mourning. For many, Kennedy's death would be the most memorable news event in the postwar era, and it secured television's role as the nation's hub, mirror, and glue. Unsurprisingly, 1963 also was the first year that a majority of Americans said that television, not newspapers, was their primary news source.[41] Broadcast images of the fateful motorcade, Jacqueline Kennedy's bloodstained pink suit, the shooting of Lee Harvey Oswald, the riderless horse, and the black-swathed widow with her two small children engaged viewers with an intimacy and immediacy impossible for radio or newspapers. The president who had sought to control the news media during his lifetime proved its potency with his death.

Kennedy had wanted to manage coverage not only of the Bay of Pigs debacle but also of US involvement in Vietnam's civil war. Concerned about the spread of communism in Southeast Asia, he sent sixteen thousand military advisors to Saigon, the southern capital of the war-torn nation. Kennedy defended the government's right to dissemble and withhold information in service to an important cause—in this case the "domino theory" of a communist takeover in Southeast Asia—and President Johnson continued the practice. His administration sought to keep Americans ignorant of the war's size, scope, and progress. The result was a *credibility gap*, a term signifying the distance between government information and on-the-ground reality. Reporters, offended by efforts to obstruct and suppress their coverage, were among the first to question the discrepancy.

There is no one narrative that fully explains how and why press coverage of the Vietnam War evolved from supportive to skeptical. Critical coverage may have reflected the "adversary culture" that developed in the 1960s.[42] Although this antagonism was clearest in the youth-oriented counterculture, its base was larger and its focus broader. A significant number of Americans were dissatisfied with their lives and distrustful of the government, even if most did not move to San Francisco's Haight-Ashbury district or try to levitate the Pentagon, as antiwar protesters did in 1967. Journalists felt the stirrings, if not in their own hearts, then in those of whom they covered, and a growing sense of unrest rippled through their reporting and writing.

Another way to view the antiwar coverage is as an ideological negotiation among elites. News outlets' owners and managers, committed to the status quo, try to set boundaries on what is newsworthy and should be covered.[43] In the case of Vietnam reporting, the boundary shifted in 1971 when the *New York Times* published the Pentagon Papers, secret Department of Defense documents chronicling American activity in Vietnam between 1945 and 1967. The material showed that the government had consistently lied about the extent of US involvement. That made the antiwar movement's reports on casualties and losses seem more reliable than the government's lower tallies. Yet even as the press toughened its coverage of the government's line, it did not transgress all borders. Most differentiated between "legitimate" antiwar protesters and those who, like the Reverend Dr. Martin Luther King Jr., extended their critique to include systemic racism and global capitalism.

A related explanation for the shift in coverage is that the media followed rather than led public opinion. It mirrored the initial support for the war until that turned to doubt and then opposition. According to this theory, the media operates within parameters that distinguish among spheres of consensus, legitimate controversy, and deviance.[44] War coverage moved from the sphere of consensus to that of legitimate controversy when the public began questioning the loss of American lives in a distant civil war. But ideological critics such as King and Noam Chomsky, who called the war racist and neocolonial, were relegated to the sphere of deviance and rarely, if ever, quoted in the mainstream press about their opinions.

In fact, the perception of the press's role was as significant as the part it actually played. After the *New York Times* published the Pentagon Papers, the elite media appeared to lead the charge against what appeared to be an ill-conceived campaign. This opening to adversarial reporting affected news content as well as narrative style. Reporters wrote sympathetically, or at least not overly critically, about domestic liberation movements by and for women, Blacks, Chicanos, and gays. They covered love-ins and be-ins, rock concerts, and demonstrations with the same wide-eyed curiosity once directed at debutante balls and Friday night football. The era's "new journalism," narrative nonfiction that was novelistic in tone and detail, lavished effusive descriptions on countercultural activities, from San Francisco's peace-and-love hippies to Manhattan's radical chic fundraisers. But when public opinion about the Aquarian Age curdled—soured by news of Watergate, a reprobate president, an ignominious war, and an oil embargo—many Americans labeled the press as part of the problem.

Although newspapers and broadcast outlets were part of corporate America, most journalists did not identify with their owners' business interests. In the 1970s, at the height of adversarial reporting, reporters found as much fault with American businesses and corporations as they did with the government. Businesses seemed riddled with corruption,[45] at least according to reporters who aggressively pursued stories examining corporate responsibility for environmental hazards and other threats to citizens' health and safety. These investigations—including Monsanto's culpability in health problems caused by Agent Orange and Ford Motor Company's liability for the Pinto's defects—raised public ire. But public opinion was truly enflamed by news that during the 1973 oil embargo and subsequent gas shortages, oil companies profited while Americans waited in interminable gas station lines and suffered in cold, dark homes.

Corporations mounted several defenses against the critical reporting. At one extreme, offending reporters were hounded and discredited. More often, corporations hired public relations firms to tell their side of the story. Business leaders also leaned on publishers and broadcast owners to stifle damaging reports and contributed to efforts to cast the news media as the liberal stronghold some politicians claimed it was. That charge, given credence by books like *The Media Elite*, worried reporters more than it concerned the public. A 1985 Gallup survey found that only 22 percent of the public felt that the press had a liberal bias, and 53 percent wished it were less influenced by "powerful people and organizations."[46]

Was the news media liberal? It depends on whom you ask. Media critic Edward Herman said that the *New York Times* ended adversarial, antibusiness reporting when its stock prices plunged in the 1970s. According to a 1976 *Business Week* article, the paper had "slid precipitously to the left and . . . become stridently antibusiness in tone, ignoring the fact that the *Times* itself is a business—and one with very serious problems." But even before that piece appeared, the paper's management had replaced the executive editor, swapped out the editorial board, and repositioned coverage toward "softer and more advertiser friendly news."[47]

Such moves were not unusual. Once news became a business built on advertising revenues, owners and managers had to respond to commercial pressure.[48] The economic model built to support the corporate media had the power to shape coverage as well. The penny press, dependent on advertisers and a broad base of readers, brought an end to partisan news journals that skewed toward political parties and the subscribers who subsidized them. Nineteenth-century publishers, aware that advertisers brought in more money than readers, sought to please them, whether by spiking negative stories, running ads with false claims, or accepting payoffs for favorable press. Though many of the most egregious practices had ended by the 1930s, surveys in the 1980s found that editors were still concerned that arm-twisting advertisers would undermine their coverage.[49]

News was a business, and the stakes grew higher as industry leaders realized just how profitable a business it was. In 1945, circulation for daily papers rose 5.3 percent over the previous year, a growth record unsurpassed for twenty-five years. Circulation figures, continuing to climb, fueled advertising, which doubled between 1945 and 1949. Trumpeting the health and stability of their industry, publishers gleefully reported double-digit profits. Some even invested a portion of their revenues to update their facilities[50] and increase their staffs. But amid success were troubling signs. When the GIs returned, many news outlets fired the women and elderly men who had reported and edited during the war years and replaced them with young men who expected a bump in salary. Newsprint was in short supply and its prices skyrocketed 70 percent between 1945 and 1948.[51] Unions, too, asked for more money; pay had remained flat during the war, and workers wanted to make up for lost income. Strikes became a regular occurrence during the late 1940s, slowing business and contributing to owners' antiunion stance.

The balance between costs and revenues was a growing problem. By the 1950s, circulation gains stalled, and advertising, increasingly drawn to radio, television, and magazines, leveled off. Newspapers were besieged on all sides. Publishers knew they needed to invest in research and development to improve their technology, but most were reluctant to spend the money. Yet modernizing production could cut costs, and by the end of the decade most newspapers were evaluating a move from multistepped, labor-intensive letterpress printing to quicker and cheaper offset printing. Over the next decade, the technical and design limitations of offset printing were addressed; and photocomposition, which allowed newspapers to electronically set "cold" type on paper rather than using the "hot"-type method that relied on heavy metal plates, became a reality. Some papers were quick to adopt the new methods; others stalled, unwilling to make the investment.

By the mid-1960s, the halcyon days of the press's postwar period seemed long gone. Some newspapers closed or consolidated, while others found ways—cutting costs, breaking unions, buying up other papers—to survive. Those that succeeded did very well; circulation and readership grew and ad space expanded. But rising numbers only told part of the story. The rise in circulation was not keeping pace with population growth, and readership did not extend to the younger generation or to growing immigrant communities. The exodus of young families from cities to suburbs raised a host of additional problems for urban newspapers. How could publishers cover a larger area without hiring more reporters? Could the morning paper arrive before commuters left for the train? And what about all the men who now drove to work? Even if the paper arrived early, they could not read it en route. Would suburban families even care about the issues that the papers covered, or would they want news about their local communities? And what about city-based businesses whose urban customer base had decamped to the suburbs? Suddenly, suburban weeklies were a threat to daily metropolitan papers; as the former gained eyeballs and advertisers, the latter lost both.

In fact, suburban weeklies were far more prosperous than the urban dailies, where frequent strikes hurt business, and consolidations decreased healthy competition. More than four hundred newspapers, mostly metropolitan dailies, closed or merged between 1945 and 1965, but the total number of papers remained constant as suburban ones sprang up.[52] Still, despite such challenges, many publishers were content. Their revenues remained strong despite the obstacles they faced, and few admitted that the biggest hurdle was their own neglect. Many owners put profits above mission, taking money out of the business instead of using it to improve their physical plants or to raise salaries.[53]

Publishers, increasingly likely to be working for corporate chains at a distance from the newsroom, fixated on the business side of the news industry. In 1960, newspaper chains owned 32 percent of all dailies; by 1977, the number had risen to 60 percent.[54] Chains supported the postwar flip in the news-to-ad ratio: at the end of World War II, it was 60:40; 60 percent of the paper was filled with news and 40 percent was taken up by ads. But by the mid-1960s, the ratio had flipped to 40:60, with news trailing ads for space. The concern with profitability was driven by financial demands. By the late 1960s, three of the largest chains—Dow Jones, Times Mirror, and Gannett—had been publicly traded.[55] Like other Wall Street companies, they needed to show rising revenues, which in their case were achieved by cutting costs, eliminating staff, and either raising the ad-to-news ratio or decreasing the number of news pages. Readership and profitability seemed to be linked in inverse proportions. As the former fell between the 1960s and 1980s, the latter rose from single to double digits.[56]

Changing the ratio made marketing sense. In the early days of the penny press, when mass circulation as well as advertising supported the news, publishers sought as many readers as possible. But by the late twentieth century, large advertisers paid for the news, and they wanted an affluent audience.[57] The rise of special sections was one strategy to attract the right readers. In 1976, the *New York Times* launched special Sunday sections for New Jersey and Long Island, and the following year it added inserts for Westchester County and Connecticut. During the same period, the paper also introduced stand-alone feature sections on sports, science, lifestyle, and home.[58]

Eager to expand the right readership, publishers funded a six-year study to investigate the drop in their audience. The Newspaper Research Project, which ran from 1977 to 1983, was an ambitious effort to track Americans' newspaper habits. Researchers conducted telephone interviews with some three thousand newspaper readers and affirmed that certain aspects of modern life, such as commuting and gated communities, made newspaper reading less convenient. But the final report soft-pedaled an even more problematic aspect of modern life: the failure of publishers to invest in either the editorial or the marketing side of the business. Whereas publishers once allotted 10 percent of gross revenues for newsrooms, that figure had become closer to 6 percent by the 1990s. Marketing budgets were even tighter: in the 1980s, few owners directed even 2 percent of their budgets for promotion.[59]

The Newspaper Research Project found that readers liked hard news. But that message was contradicted by a small sample from focus groups that newspaper editors funded to augment the larger project. Ruth Clark, who oversaw the 1979 report *Changing Needs for Changing Readers*, said that subjects wanted "more attention paid to their personal needs, help in understanding and dealing with their own problems in an increasingly complex world, news about their neighborhood, not just the big city and Washington, and advice on what to buy, where to play, how to cope." They also wanted "more help in handling emotional problems, understanding others, feeling good and eating well, having fun, and in general fulfilling oneself" as well as "news about personally helpful subjects like health rather than just the usual heavy fare of politics and government." Besides all that, they wanted more "good news," positive stories that featured "human drama with a happy ending."[60] However, in the 1980s, when Clark's recommendations became standard fare at many newspapers, she backpedaled, claiming that these were meant as additions to rather than replacements for hard news. But her suggestions resonated with advertisers leery of adversarial reporting and publishers eager for easy ways to reinvigorate their product. The result was a more market-driven, softer-edged newspaper.

Clark's report coincided with Ronald Reagan's 1980 presidential campaign. Reagan came to office with strong corporate ties. In 1953, when his movie career stalled, he became host of *General Electric Theater*, a half-hour television program. Soon after, he was traveling to GE plants nationwide to promote the series and the company's products. During his eight-year run, Reagan met some 250,000 GE employees and, according to his biographers, sharpened his communication skills.[61] The experience also deepened the future politician's belief in the free market and his dislike for government regulations.

The timing was propitious. Many of the corporate leaders who supported Reagan's probusiness agenda also were vehemently antimedia. Thanks to their newfound status as Washington insiders, they were well placed to influence publishers.[62] Moreover, some corporations already had burrowed into the newspaper pages: starting in the 1970s, Mobil Oil staked

FIGURE 4. Untitled photo of Ronald Reagan during his *General Electric Theater* years. Courtesy Ronald Reagan Presidential Library and Museum.

out the bottom-right corner of the *New York Times*' op-ed page to present its public policy positions with wry, commonsensical élan. Simply by leasing this prime real estate, it became the era's preeminent corporate voice. The strategy enabled Mobil to "legitimize corporate speech" and "frame the corporate role in democratic processes as no less than *identical* to that of the individual citizen."[63] This was a change with lasting consequences; in 2010, the US Supreme Court legitimated corporate personhood with its decision in *Citizens United v. Federal Election Commission*.

INDUSTRY CHANGES AND EDITORIAL IMPACT: THE 1980S

The 1980s was a landmark decade for American news media. Reagan's probusiness administration led to shifts in industry ownership and news content. At the same time, new technologies increased television's incursion into newspaper territory, forcing publishers to undertake defensive innovations. Yet even as technological and regulatory changes were transforming the industry, the 1980–82 recessions (January–June 1980 and July 1981–November 1982) hastened the pace of change and deepened the effects of commercialization and consolidation.

During his presidency, Reagan made it much easier for media owners to amass monopolies. The renewal time for television station licenses rose from three years to five, and the process almost guaranteed a pass. Instead of limiting businesses to owning no more than seven television stations, they were now allowed to have twelve. (Multiple ownership of AM and FM radio stations similarly expanded.) When large corporations sought to consolidate their media holdings, as with Capital Cities' takeover of ABC in 1985 and GE's acquisition of RCA in 1986, neither the FCC nor the US Department of Justice opposed the moves. A free-market approach superseded regulatory policy that once sought to promote competition and alternate points of view. The 1987 repeal of the Fairness Doctrine, which required broadcasters to air alternate perspectives on controversial issues, was one casualty and a change that enabled conservative talk radio and partisan television news. Media properties increasingly were concentrated among a few large corporations seeking to vertically integrate their holdings. The change was profound: the number of mainstream media outlets shrank, and those that remained were increasingly profit oriented.[64] Ownership was concentrated in fewer and fewer hands. In 1983, twenty companies dominated the news industry. Seven years later, that number had dropped to fourteen.[65] In 2022, just six corporations, with total net worth exceeding $430 billion, ran 90 percent of US media.[66]

As big companies accumulated media properties, they developed economies of scale across multiple platforms. Vertical integration enabled one owner to control book publishing, movie studios, television networks, and newspapers. A company could turn its book into a movie that was promoted on its television shows and featured in its newspapers. As just one cog in a complex media machine, newspapers' success was more precarious than when they were solo properties. At a meeting of newspaper executives in 1979, a year that saw an 18 percent gain in per-share newspaper earnings, a security analyst asked her audience why they were avoiding the challenges facing the industry. A follow-up piece in the *Chicago Tribune* enumerated the problems: declining readership, competition for ads from television and suburban papers, the possibility of an "electronic newspaper," and a looming recession.[67]

Between 1970 and 1982, 141 newspapers either shut down or merged, including large papers in New York, Washington, DC, Minneapolis, Cleveland, and Philadelphia.[68] Home circulation had remained at 62 million for a decade, while the number of American households had risen from 63.4 million to 80.4 million.[69] Yet even as closings and concomitant problems cast a pall over the industry, stock prices for the largest newspaper companies skyrocketed. Amid the 1981 recession, overall earnings on the New York Stock Exchange declined 1.85 percent, but profit on the twelve largest newspaper stocks increased an average of 17.5 percent. (At the extremes, Capital Cities' stock grew 26.4 percent, while that of the *New York Times* rose 2.2 percent.) As the *Boston Globe* noted, "The strong performance of newspaper stocks in relation to stocks of other businesses is nothing new. Since 1971, the index of newspaper stock has risen 340 percent compared to an increase of 63 percent in the New York Stock Exchange Index."[70]

According to industry analysts, among the key factors for the stocks' growth was the industry's "non-competitive environment," which allowed newspaper chains to raise or at least maintain advertising rates during the economic downturn.[71] And notwithstanding large profit margins, many investors still considered newspaper stocks "underpriced," thus valuable for "long-term appreciation."[72] Yet even as some newspaper stocks posted significant gains, others—including afternoon papers and papers in competitive markets—experienced setbacks. Despite the uptick in display ads for retailers and supermarkets, slumps in housing, automobile, and classified ads resulted in employee layoffs and newspaper closings. Twenty-one newspapers folded in 1981, and newspaper staff unemployment doubled between 1981 and 1982. Even highly successful papers such as the *Wall Street Journal* and the *Los Angeles Times* resorted to belt-tightening measures when their classified ads fell by double digits.[73]

This both-and situation resulted in contradictory coverage of the news industry. Even as profits soared for many newspapers, others closed and still others cut back. Was the industry languishing or thriving? And if it was thriving, who were the winners? Corporate owners were doing well, but newspaper employees and the public at large were not sharing in their success. In a November 1982 front-page story, the *Chicago Tribune* fretted over the "diminished role of the press as watchdog of the government" as well as the "arrogance and lack of enterprise on the part of those healthy papers operating without competition."[74] Even in a downbeat economy, the average paper's profit return was 8 percent, and circulation across the board was up. Moreover, with fixed costs for printing and delivery, labor costs steady (on top of several rounds of layoffs and salary freezes), and the price of newsprint down, most newspaper executives predicted that 1983 would be a banner year.[75]

Those predictions seemed sound by the summer of 1983. The top seven publicly held newspaper companies were faring better in the first half of 1983 than they had in the same period a year earlier. At the high end, Times Mirror's profits had grown from $50.3 million to $72.5 million; more modestly, Gannett's numbers had risen from $50.3 million to $52.5 million. According to a leading industry analyst, "The newspaper industry is coming back through a combination of both improving advertising, lower newsprint costs and only modest increases in labor."[76]

THE GAME CHANGER

Amid the industry shakeout, a financially driven process culminating in fewer papers making higher profits, publishers faced a second challenge—this time to professional standards. This new threat upended common assumptions about what constituted daily newspaper journalism. Among the early inklings of this game changer was a July 1981 *Los Angeles Times* article about a newspaper that Gannett planned to launch the following year. Gannett had circulated a prototype of *USA Today*, its proposed national paper, to five thousand "key business, media, government, arts and sports leaders," and many were unimpressed. *USA Today* was a national general-interest newspaper, but its look and feel had more in common with television journalism than with print. Bright and light, filled with briefs, graphs, photos, and fluff, the planned paper won few fans. According to the *Times*, "The vast majority of those polled Tuesday by *The Times* said they would recommend that Gannett scrub the idea."[77] Even Wall Street, which typically esteemed Gannett's attention to the bottom line, was skeptical about *USA Today*'s prospects for success.

There were valid reasons why the venture seemed quixotic. In the early 1980s, few papers had robust national circulations; the technology for simultaneous printings was new and expensive, and the readership was not there. The *Wall Street Journal* had built a national audience because its financial focus superseded regionally distinct political and cultural interests. Moreover, its cutting-edge satellite technology simultaneously delivered the paper to printing plants nationwide. The *Christian Science Monitor* also was national, but its circulation was small, and the *New York Times*' national edition, launched in April 1980, had not significantly expanded beyond the paper's Boston-to-Washington, DC, base.

Like the *Journal*, *USA Today* proposed to use satellite technology, but unlike the *Journal*, the new paper's scope was all encompassing. Both its prototypes included national and international news as well as state news briefs and sections on business and sports. The result, according to an unnamed newspaper executive, was "bland busyness." Two assessments predominated: newspaper people derided the paper's light-and-bright look, and Wall Street questioned its financial feasibility. The two critiques were related. Local advertisers would have little interest in a national newspaper, and national advertisers would have little use for a paper that was "*People* magazine without the salt and spice and excitement."[78] Despite negative reviews—"it's ridiculous," succinctly noted one Wall Street analyst[79]—Allen H. Neuharth, the Gannett chairman and the creative force behind the project, barreled on. Gannett's previous success grew from buying small newspapers, which lacked competitors or published under joint operating agreements, and then cutting expenses to maximize profits. At best, newspaper insiders considered Gannett papers adequate; at worst, they were labeled cash cows.

But Neuharth had a different goal for *USA Today*. He was not aiming to challenge the top tier of journalistic excellence, nor was he simply hoping to make a profit. He wanted to create something new. While some industry insiders opined that a national newspaper had no hope against the burgeoning cable news scene (Cable News Network, or CNN, was launched in June 1980), he judged that increased mobility—growing numbers of Americans traveling for business and pleasure and many moving for work—made a news outlet for the entire nation possible.[80] Neuharth also had a strategy for marketing *USA Today* to advertisers and readers. He planned to target the latter by making the paper available at hotels, motels, airline counters, supermarkets, and fast-food restaurants. He would snag readers with the paper's bite-size news stories and bold use of color.[81] Extrapolating from the September 15, 1982, launch date, Neuharth projected a readership of 1.2 million by the end of 1983 and 2.4 million after five years.[82]

On that date, the *Washington Post*'s small, black-and-white weather map predicted clouds and rain over much of the country. The exact details were hard to assay from the map itself; there were clear and partially blacked-out circles, ropes of triangles, bands of lines, random capital letters, and long columns of information that needed to be decoded before ascertaining that it would be fifty-five degrees and partly cloudy in Bismarck, North Dakota, hot and rainy in Houston, Texas, and warm and humid in the nation's capital.[83] There were no such problems with the new *USA Today* weather map. Filling almost an entire page and printed in ten rainbow colors plus bright white, the map telegraphed regional weather patterns with easy-to-read graphics.[84] The new paper was novel in other ways. Unlike most newspapers with a 60:40 or even a 70:30 ratio of ads to news, *USA Today* flipped the equation to 30:70. Its pages were filled with short articles, crisp photos, tantalizing graphs and charts, news briefs from every state, and late-breaking sports scores.

Rather than the home deliveries that most newspapers relied on to win subscribers, copies of the new Gannett paper were available in strange-looking boxes that some observers said looked more like television sets than street-corner newspaper dispensers. The comparison was apt: *USA Today* was a newspaper for television viewers, a visual feast that was, according to the *Los Angeles Times*, "a slick, quick read—bright, trashy, accessible, well-packaged and, for the most part, determinedly superficial by the best journalistic standards."[85] Amid a flood of stories on the paper's looks, advertising prospects, technological innovations, and financial prospects—Neuharth expected it to break even by 1985—one detail remained unanswered: what had it cost to start up? When asked that question by a *Los Angeles Times* reporter, Neuharth's answer was blunt: "It's none of your damn business.'"[86]

The paper's start-up costs as well as its profit potential dominated initial responses to *USA Today*. Its style—Color! Graphics! Briefs!—also took up many column inches. But Jonathan Yardley, the Pulitzer Prize–winning *Washington Post* essayist, grasped the heart of the matter when he dubbed *USA Today* the newspaper of the future. Yardley described the paper as "a tour de force of packaging and technology," with chilling ramifications for journalism and society.[87] It was, he said, the triumph of perception over reality: news was not what trained journalists deemed it to be but rather what the public perceived it should be.

As an example, Yardley pointed to the paper's initial lead story: the death of Princess Grace of Monaco. Other newspapers carried that sad news, but most led with the assassination of the president-elect of Lebanon. Three months earlier, Israel had invaded Lebanon in an attempt to rout Palestinians hostile to the Jewish state. Before withdrawing, Israel smoothed the way for a Christian head of the Lebanese state, and it was he who was murdered. Two days later, in what was termed a retaliatory attack, a Lebanese Christian militia group killed between 700 and 3,500 mostly Palestinian civilians in Lebanese refugee camps. Surrounding Israeli troops did nothing to stop the slaughter. The Sabra and Shatila massacre would be one of the major news stories of the decade—and a turning point in world opinion of Israel.

Neuharth, however, had "asked around town" and discovered that most people were interested in Princess Grace. If the people wanted Princess Grace, then *USA Today* would give them Princess Grace. Yardley saw this as a significant break from the "cod liver oil" school of journalism. In the new *USA Today* universe, "if a president-elect is killed in Lebanon and no one is interested, then the event is not news." Allowing that his views might be elitist and old-fashioned, Yardley admitted that the new paper might well

THE NATION'S NEWSPAPER

WEDNESDAY, SEPTEMBER 15, 1982

NEWSLINE

WEATHER:

ASSASSINATION:

HIT MAN:

DEATHS:

MERGER:

NATION:

WASHINGTON:

ABROAD:

OPINIONS:

MONEY:

SPORTS:

LIFE:

USA TODAY

Coast-to-coast

News from all 50 states

Weather across the USA

Scoreboard

All sports, all results

Miracle: 327 survive, 55 die

Minnesota passenger's crash photos

America's Princess Grace dies in Monaco

FIGURE 5. Front page of *USA Today*, September 15, 1982.

be a "smasheroo," which greatly influenced the future of journalism. But he wondered whether that influence would be benevolent.[88]

Few others at the time wrote about *USA Today*'s impact on the state of journalism. Some focused on its influence over industry aesthetics: papers scrambled to add color, photos. and graphics; bump up their sports coverage; and improve their weather maps.[89] Still others weighed the new paper's chance at success. The *Wall Street Journal* reported that many local dailies were fending off *USA Today*'s challenges with "more aggressive sales tactics and changes in news treatment, handling and displaying."[90] Sales for *USA Today* rose when the paper debuted in a new region, then dropped. Gannett claimed that its paper was attracting readers, but advertising remained sluggish. Ad count inched up when, after seven months, the company said that *USA Today* had the third-largest US circulation (after the *Wall Street Journal* and the *New York Daily News*), with 1,109,587 readers.[91] Critics countered that Gannett's figures were inflated, and it was not until June 1984, when the results of an accredited audit were released, that the chain's boasts were officially verified. The news earned grudging recognition from Madison Avenue. "I was a skeptic," an advertising executive told the *New York Times*, "but right now I feel much more confident of *USA Today* both as an advertising medium and as a viable product in the marketplace." Wall Street was more reticent. According to one analyst, the audit did not show who the readers were (demographics were important for advertisers as well as for targeting ads) and whether the circulation was stable or simply a reflection of the ups and downs as the paper moved into new regions.[92]

Two years later, the *Washington Post* called *USA Today* "a money losing experiment in publishing a national newspaper" while also reporting that the paper had the break-even number of ad pages as well as a thriving circulation.[93] Neuharth still wasn't saying how much money had been invested in the venture, nor would he state unequivocally that the paper would survive. Yet by 1986, most of the naysayers had been won over. In a comprehensive overview of the "coast-to-coast" trend in newspaper design, *Los Angeles Times* media critic David Shaw described the outsize impact that *USA Today* had on the industry. In addition to quoting several newspaper editors who said as much, Shaw noted, "Although the use of both color and graphics was increasing before the arrival of *USA Today*, the new newspaper clearly accelerated both trends, and many editors concede that *USA Today* forced them to analyze and reevaluate their own approach to news presentation."[94] Two months later, Shaw's colleague Tom Rosenstiel reported that even if *USA Today* was still losing money—some estimates said the company had invested over $400 million thus far—it was "here to stay," according to some Wall Street analysts.[95]

Writing a year later to analyze the paper at its five-year mark, Rosenstiel took a measured tone. Yes, *USA Today* had changed journalism as usual, but all its innovations were in the works elsewhere when the paper launched. Yes, it had survived, but its financial viability was only possible because of its owners' deep pockets. What might be most significant about *USA Today*, Rosenstiel wrote, was "its personality as a newspaper designed for the TV generation, with its hopeful tone, its mixing of entertainment and news and its quick-bit, non-linear way of delivering information."[96]

Neuharth's personal mission was to create a "journalism of hope" as a corrective to the sensationalism and general unpleasantness that were standard fare at other news outlets. Assessing current trends, he was convinced that the public wanted good news delivered in a lively format.[97] What Yardley deemed as pap, Gannett's chairman saw as hope. Yardley's point may have had merit, but Neuharth's formulation mirrored the mood of the times.

The politics of hope—the conviction that life could be better—had driven Ronald Reagan's 1980 election. Four years later, his "Morning in America" reelection slogan signaled a national rebirth of optimism. The president and his handlers liked positive news that projected America's strength, goodness, and godliness. With more news outlets in corporate hands and a public eager for positive change, the time seemed right for Neuharth's journalism of hope. At a reception celebrating the first edition of the new paper, Reagan praised Gannett's achievement: "It's another distant light, another glimmer of hope on the horizon of a world where too often the avid pursuit of the truth is discouraged or suppressed. I speak for everyone in the administration when I say, 'You have our very best wishes, and we'll all be rooting for you.'"[98]

CHAPTER TWO

1973

The Body Politic and the Religious Body

> Going around this country, I have found a great hunger in America for spiritual revival; for a belief that law must be based on a higher law; for a return to traditions and values that we once had.
>
> RONALD REAGAN, Presidential Debate, Baltimore, September 21, 1980

On Monday, January 1, 1973, Americans were more than ready for a new year. A series of calamitous events had darkened the final days of 1972. An earthquake in Nicaragua killed 12,000; the "Christmas bombings" of North Vietnam claimed more than 1,600 lives; 101 people died when an Eastern Airlines passenger jet went down in the Everglades; and then, on New Year's Eve, the Pittsburgh Pirates' star player, Roberto Clemente, died when his plane crashed en route to aiding Nicaraguan survivors.

On the East Coast, the view was grim. Partly cloudy skies held a hint of rain, and New York's paper of record reflected the dreary day. The *New York Times*' front page was a gloomy reminder that so much seemed awry: air raids in North Vietnam and antiwar protests at home; depleted blood supplies in the nation's hospitals; and tighter airline security as a ward against hijackers. Inside the paper were stories about gangland killings in the Bronx, striking workers in Long Island, and renewed calls for environmental controls. A featured columnist, addressing the nation's adversities, wondered what went wrong. "Can a nation grow richer and richer and yet debase the standards of its life and its democratic and moral principles?"[1]

The question echoed the anxiety gripping many Americans as they saw, or thought they saw, their nation in free fall. The belief in American exceptionalism, as either a religious calling or a civic responsibility, had flourished in the post–World War II era. For more than two decades, many Americans felt proud of their democracy and thriving economy. The postwar tide of prosperity had lifted many white families into the middle class;

restrictive housing and university quotas against Jews and Catholics were falling; and civil rights legislation promised to accelerate the slow march to racial equality. But over the past decade, the nation's sense of optimism had waned.

Previously, when the culture shocks of the 1960s threatened to short-circuit national stability, the tumult was ascribed to youthful antics. But the crises of the early 1970s were not as easily dismissed. A futile war, a broken economy, and myriad jolts to family life could not all be blamed on rebellious young people. Neither could the fallout from the June 1972 Watergate break-in, when five Republican operatives illegally entered the Democratic National Committee headquarters and were caught with bugging devices, thousands of dollars in cash, and rolls of film. Their trial, which eventually led to the resignation of President Richard M. Nixon, began on January 8, 1973.

Facing a profound disruption of the status quo, citizens questioned their institutions: Could government be trusted? Was management fair to labor? And why were so many churches more concerned with the here and now than with the hereafter? The seventies was a decade of national reckoning, and 1973 was arguably its most fateful year.[2]

By examining some of the cultural shifts that came to fruition in 1973, this chapter sets the background for Ronald Reagan's 1980 election. Reagan, promising a break with the past, offered a new vision that normalized a conservative social and political agenda and hallowed traditional family values—specifically a self-sufficient, heterosexual unit. Aligned with conservative elements of Protestantism, Catholicism, Mormonism, Judaism, and Islam, Reagan's religious imaginary supported male headship, the belief that men rule the family. It also justified female subordination at a moment when anxieties about women's bodies were social and political flashpoints. The Reagan-era imaginary cast feminists, gays, single parents, and supporters of abortion as personally immoral and a threat to civic society. The upheavals of the seventies help explain why many Americans could accept that judgment.

A NEW ORDER ARISES

The church-and-steeple image of American religion exploded in the 1960s. *Time* magazine worried about the "death of God,"[3] while the civil rights and antiwar movements rallied religious leaders. The Aquarian Age and the Jesus People offered new ways of believing, behaving, and belonging, while Will Herberg's trope of Protestant-Catholic-Jew,[4] the religious foundation for white, postwar civil society, teetered under the weight of shifting demographics. Between 1959 and 2009, membership in the Protestant main line declined by 25 percent, despite significant population growth over the same period.[5] Neo-evangelicalism was on the rise, most significantly among young adults, and many Roman Catholics were seeking a more affective, charismatic faith. Some Black Christians defected to the Nation of Islam; others found meaning in the poetry and protest of the Black Power movement. Young Jews, among others, explored Eastern traditions, and a 1965 law lifting 1920s-era immigration restrictions brought an influx of newcomers and their religions to America's shores.

These religious shifts shaped and were shaped by many of 1973's most significant occurrences. That year, the Supreme Court legalized abortion; the American Psychiatric Association voted to remove homosexuality from its list of disorders; the Vietnam War ended; Native Americans occupied the site of the 1890 Wounded Knee massacre; Blacks were elected as mayors in Atlanta, Detroit, and Los Angeles; Israel won the Yom Kippur War; and OPEC, in retaliation for American aid to the Jewish state, cut off oil supplies to the United States, causing a quadrupling of gas prices.

Social unrest defined the zeitgeist. Many of the year's cultural productions had a noirish spiritual cast. Pink Floyd's *Dark Side of the Moon*, Stephen Sondheim's *A Little Night Music*, Bernardo Bertolucci's *Last Tango in Paris*, Thomas Pynchon's *Gravity's Rainbow*, and Toni Morrison's *Sula* plumbed the essence of human nature, testing the boundaries of agency and acceptance, alterity and convergence, compassion and callousness. Even death elicited more than the usual degree of mourning as the loss of icons, including Pablo Picasso, Pearl Buck, J. R. R. Tolkien, Jeanette Rankin, Arna Bontemps, Lyndon B. Johnson, and David Ben-Gurion, seemed like a cosmic demarcation of a passing era.

The tumult and confusion of the times are well documented. Much of the dislocation, though not apparent then, resulted from a transforming global economy, including a shift in the United States from heavy manufacturing to information and service industries.[6] The impact of a new social and economic order, powered by factory closings, birth control pills, and two-income households, excited some but troubled others. Many Americans worried about the safety of their daughters, the future of their sons, the status of stay-at-home wives and mothers, and the authority of husbands and fathers.

The year's upheavals had a significant impact on gender issues, troubling many of the faithful and their moral certitudes. The birth control pill had detached sex from reproduction, giving women the same freedom as men to enjoy sexual activity for its own sake. The 1970 publication of *Women and Their Bodies: A Course* (later retitled *Our Bodies, Ourselves*) took women's autonomy a step further. The widely distributed booklet, initially self-published by the Boston Women's Health Collective, received wide attention, thanks to its inclusion in the first edition of *The Whole Earth Catalog*. *Our Bodies, Ourselves* taught thousands of young women not only about the workings of their reproductive systems and genitalia but also about their role in the American political economy. Linking women's health, or the lack thereof, to politics and capitalism, the authors urged readers to take control of their own well-being.[7] And while the import of this idea seemed at the time to have little resonance with most business and political leaders, religious conservatives understood the threat—especially as the notion of women's agency and independence, and the ensuing challenge to patriarchy and the family, percolated through the mainstream.

THE FEMALE BODY AND THE FAMILY UNIT

The ad for *Goodbye, Columbus*, the 1969 film adaptation of Philip Roth's celebrated novella about sex, love, and social status, was elegantly understated: a single red rose with the tagline "Every father's daughter is a virgin." The old-fashioned sentiment may have doomed the film among feminists, but it reflected an outlook shared by many American parents. Similarly mirroring real life were the movie's depictions of its young characters discussing premarital sex and birth control. Its straightforward take on the "sexual revolution" made *Goodbye, Columbus* "the trendiest (or the most trendy) movie of the year so far . . . the must-see, controversial, surpassingly contemporary picture of the moment."[8]

Movies like *Goodbye, Columbus* and *Bob & Carol & Ted & Alice*, a well-received film about extramarital relationships, represented Hollywood's version of changing gender and family roles, but the actual effect of the sexual revolution was both less dramatic and more extensive. A decade earlier, Brenda Patimkin, the lustrous heroine of *Goodbye, Columbus*, could not have debated the merits of birth control pills versus a diaphragm. Approved for contraceptive use in 1960, the pill was restricted to married women—and not permitted in every state. But two Supreme Court decisions made birth control widely available, affecting the lives of millions of Americans. In *Griswold v. Connecticut*, seven justices struck down a rarely used state law that violated the due process clause of the Fourteenth Amendment protecting "the right to marital privacy." As a result, the 1965 decision invalidated an 1879 statute that forbade the use of contraceptives among married couples.

Seven years later, in 1972, the court further extended the notion of privacy in *Eisenstadt v. Baird*. Under Massachusetts state law, only medical

FIGURE 6. Ali MacGraw starred in the 1969 movie *Goodbye, Columbus*. One tagline for the movie, released during an era of increased sexual experimentation outside marriage, was, "Every father's daughter is a virgin." Goodbye, Columbus

professionals could distribute contraceptives and then only to married people. When birth control crusader Bill Baird lectured at Boston University on the right to sexual privacy, he was arrested for displaying contraceptive devices and giving a condom and contraceptive foam to a young, single woman. The Massachusetts State Supreme Court ruled that while it was permissible to describe and demonstrate birth control devices, it was illegal to give them to unmarried individuals. Baird served three months in prison before being vindicated by the US Supreme Court. The justices, reviewing the law's original intent "to defend the sanctity of the home and thus to engender in the State and the nation a virile and virtuous race of men and women," opted instead to defend individual privacy from "governmental intrusion" in a decision as fundamental as bearing a child.[9] As the ruling followed the 1971 adoption of the Twenty-Sixth Amendment, which lowered the federal voting age from twenty-one to eighteen, most states also lowered the age of majority (the age at which an individual is considered an adult), further increasing the number of women who could legally use birth control.

The Supreme Court decisions legalized adult use of the pill, but millions of women, married or not, had used contraceptives even before *Griswold* or *Eisenstadt* was adjudicated. During the decade before *Roe v. Wade*, the pill's growing popularity and its impact on female identity and autonomy helped redefine women's attitudes to their bodies, their partners, and their futures. The results inspired trends and phenomena ranging from egalitarian marriage and feminist theology to women's erotica and an increase in female college graduates. Correspondingly, the accessibility of reliable oral contraception made the goals of the women's movement more realistic. In 1961, President John F. Kennedy established the Presidential Commission on the Status of Women to address inequalities in the labor force. Five years later, with its final report in hand, the National Organization for Women was launched. NOW's objective was "to bring women into the full participation in the mainstream of American society now assuming all the privileges and responsibilities thereof in truly equal partnership with men."[10]

Seeking "a civil rights movement" for women, the organization's founders pledged to abolish sex discrimination, secure equality of education and opportunity, and challenge "the traditional assumption that a woman has to choose between marriage and motherhood, on the one hand, and serious participation in industry or the professions on the other."[11] These were not new concerns. During World War II, many women had experienced an expanded degree of personal and financial independence due to work opportunities formerly reserved for men. But when the GIs returned home, an idealized vision of the nuclear family with a stay-at-home mom justified the rollback of women's professional gains. In 1963, Betty Friedan documented the "problem that has no name," the malaise of white, educated middle- and upper-class housewives, in her best seller *The Feminine Mystique*. Three years later as NOW's first president, Friedan wed a positive agenda of social equality to a blunt critique of homemaking—an analysis that incited critics even as NOW and its detractors overlooked the different conditions affecting poor and working-class women as well as women of color.

Many privileged young women were dissatisfied with traditional female roles, but they did not attend NOW meetings with their mothers. Rather, they flocked to the burgeoning counterculture, a social movement birthed in a marijuana-laced, psychedelic haze of rock music, antiwar protest, and Romantic utopianism. Throughout the early months of 1967, word spread that something strange and wonderful was happening in San Francisco's Haight-Ashbury district. Young people were inaugurating a new order of peace, along with free food, free drugs, and free love.

Come summer, some one hundred thousand people—including many high school and college students—descended on the Haight. They believed that a cultural revolution was in the making as well as a stoned good time. Images from the Summer of Love feature lithe young women bedecked with flowers while their hirsute partners palmed a joint. Despite promises of paradise, the 198-acre district could not accommodate the large ingathering of hippies, stoners, and flower children. The steady drain on the neighborhood's infrastructure strained the love and soured the music. News photos of kid-bashing cops and waifs huddled on street corners replaced shots of scantily clad chicks with lazy smiles. But images of daughters and sometimes mothers gone wild resurfaced over the next few years. Reworked to play into fears of sexual permissiveness, they fueled the religiously based defense of the family as well as prurient ad campaigns for movies such as *Barbarella*, *The Graduate*, and a new, nubile adaptation of *Romeo and Juliet*.

FIGURE 7. Summer of Love, San Francisco, 1967. Dennis L. Maness Summer of Love, San Francisco History Center, San Francisco Public Library.

The media stoked the scare; it was good copy. In 1970, *Time* magazine opined on the American family's uncertain future, beginning with a bleak assessment from the recently concluded White House Conference on Children and Youth: "America's families are in trouble—trouble so deep and pervasive as to threaten the future of our nation." The article ominously noted that the divorce rate was up and the birthrate down, offering four reasons for the family's imminent demise. Near the top of the list was the changing role of women. "'Put very simply,' says Cornell Political Sociologist Andrew Hacker, 'the major changes in the family in recent years, and the problems of the future, are both summed up in one word: women.'"[12]

If mothers were a source of concern, daughters were even more so. Moms, at least, were going to work; daughters were sneaking off to have sex. "Youth's sexual revolution is not just franker talk and greater openness," said a 1972 story in *Time*. "More teenagers, and especially younger ones, are apparently having intercourse, at least occasionally." The proof? A 1953 survey found 23 percent of white female respondents had premarital intercourse by the time they turned twenty-one; a similar study in 1972 saw the number rise to 40 percent by age twenty. According to the magazine, the side effects were devastating. In addition to shame, heartbreak, and unwanted pregnancies, increased sexual activity set off an epidemic of venereal disease: "after the ordinary cold, syphilis and gonorrhea are the most common infectious diseases among young people."[13] When sorting out reasons for the new "permissiveness," the article found fault with "dolls with breasts," incompetent clergy, ineffectual families, and peer pressure. "My virginity was such a burden to me that I just wanted to get rid of it,"[14] *Time* quoted a junior at the University of Vermont telling a sex counselor.

Two films, one at the beginning of 1973 and the other at the end of the year, reflected ongoing angst about families, sex, and out-of-control female bodies. In January, *Last Tango in Paris* premiered, starring Marlon Brando as a cuckolded widower drawn to rough, anonymous sex with a much younger woman.[15] Although Brando's character, a seedy hotel owner, is past his prime, his partner is a nubile twenty-something beauty. Written and directed by Bernardo Bertolucci, the movie, which broke the five-dollar admission barrier for legitimate films, was "a sensation and a scandal" in Europe at the time of its American release.[16]

Critics debated whether Bertolucci had made a soulful meditation on the meaning of life or a sophomoric sex film. Multipage spreads in weekly newsmagazines and television talk shows debated whether the film was art or pornography. Some pundits tried to explain why scenes of rape, sodomy, and sadomasochism were justified, but folks at home weren't buying it. After the publication of an in-depth feature on *Last Tango*, one *Newsweek* reader wrote the editor, "What a waste of seven pages!" Penned another, "*Newsweek* is presumably a magazine for all the family. What do I do with this issue that shows two views of illicit intercourse?"[17]

In a *Christian Century* editorial, James Wall said the hoopla about the film was a marketing coup. "As a social phenomenon, *Tango* was created by the media. . . . The magazines benefit because sex on the cover sells magazines, just as sex on the marquee sells tickets."[18] Wall had a point; audiences weren't coming for the movie's thin plot. While house hunting in Paris, Paul (Brando) meets Jeanne (Maria Schneider) in a vacant apartment and the two begin an affair. At Paul's insistence, they don't exchange names and they barely talk; their only interaction is uninhibited sexual intercourse. But an unexpected metamorphosis occurs. Rediscovering his ability to love, Paul breaks his silence and confesses feelings for Jeanne. She bolts, and when he pursues her she shoots him. Victim turned victimizer, Jeanne embodies the fearful subtext of the sexual revolution.

Equally disturbing was the physical domination of an even younger woman, Regan MacNeil (Linda Blair), in *The Exorcist*. Released on December 26, the movie was an adaptation of a best-selling horror novel about demonic possession. In this film and in *Last Tango*, an older male (Regan's demon appears as masculine) physically dominates a fatherless girl (Jeanne's father is dead, and Regan's mother is divorced). Salvation depends on the violent sacrifice of a wounded healer. Paul in *Last Tango* is transformed from exploiter to martyr. In *The Exorcist*, Father Damien Karras (Jason Miller) calls the demon from Regan's body into his own and leaps out a window to destroy it. Just as Paul in *Last Tango* is grieving a recent death (his wife's suicide), so Karras has experienced a dark night of the soul, triggered by the loss of his mother. *The Exorcist*, like *Last Tango*, chronicles a desperate man's psychological journey to wholeness. Recovery entails the recognition of love as well as self-sacrifice in service to a female body.

In between the screening of Paul's murder and Karras's death, real-world events echoed the fears about women and families that both movies addressed. On January 22, 1973, when the Supreme Court ruled that a woman could terminate a first-trimester pregnancy, the issue of abortion became, in some quarters, emblematic of the out-of-control woman, the failing family, and the permissive society. From the standpoint of the Supreme Court and many contemporaneous commentators, the decision followed from *Griswold* and *Eisenstadt*: sexual and reproductive matters were private and should be free from governmental intrusions. Many secular and religious commentators saw the ruling as a controversial but ultimately conservative outcome that safeguarded the rights of the individual. "It is a sensible decision,"[19] said an anonymous *Los Angeles Times* column.

Echoed the *Wall Street Journal*, “We think the court struck a reasonable balance on an exceedingly difficult question.”[20] Most presciently from the *Chicago Tribune*, “The court’s majority on this question (7–2) is decisively large, but we don’t think we have heard the last of this matter.”[21]

Critics and headline writers said the decision amounted to “abortion on demand.” In fact, the ruling was anything but a wholesale validation of abortion. Rather, it enabled a woman, with her physician’s consent, to

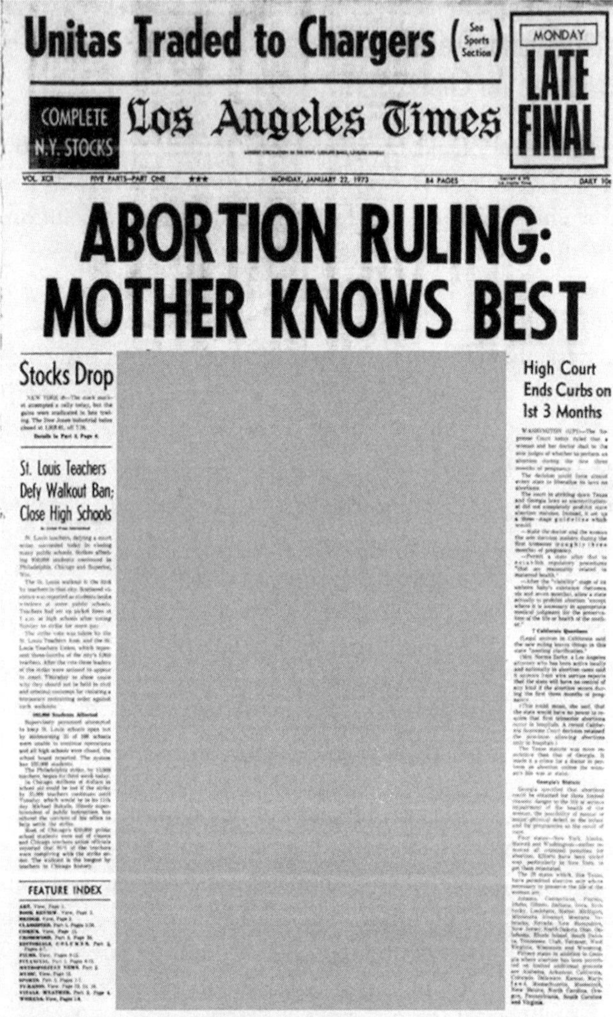

Unitas Traded to Chargers (See Sports Section)

MONDAY

LATE FINAL

COMPLETE N.Y. STOCKS

Los Angeles Times

MONDAY, JANUARY 22, 1973

ABORTION RULING: MOTHER KNOWS BEST

Stocks Drop

St. Louis Teachers Defy Walkout Ban; Close High Schools

FEATURE INDEX

High Court Ends Curbs on 1st 3 Months

FIGURE 8. Banner headline from the *Los Angeles Times* on the day that the US Supreme Court’s decision on *Roe v. Wade* legalized abortion. Copyright © 1973. Los Angeles Times. Used with permission.

end a pregnancy during the first three months. In the second trimester, the state could "regulate" procedures in light of the mother's health, and in the third trimester the state could forbid them entirely—except in extreme cases to protect the mother's life or health. Many editorialists as well as political and religious leaders praised the compromise, which was based on the justices' understanding of fetal viability. But the opportunity to stoke the controversy was too tempting for many media outlets. In an otherwise balanced summary of the issues, *Time* headlined its piece "Abortion on Demand,"[22] and other secular news publications followed suit.

The religious press registered a variety of opinions on *Roe v. Wade*. The Protestant mainline's flagship magazine, the *Christian Century*, supported the ruling as a "fortuitous juxtaposition of an idea whose time has come and a time to which an idea has come."[23] An unnamed editorial writer discerned the moral dilemma at the heart of the issue but noted that every woman had to negotiate it for herself. Opinions varied among evangelicals. *Christianity Today*, whose readership was evangelical, reported a divide among conservative Protestant leaders.[24] Several Southern Baptist leaders including the Reverend W. A. Criswell—pastor at First Baptist Church in Dallas and a hero of the denomination's fundamentalist wing—approved of the decision. Criswell's position reflected both a conservative political perspective as well as the Baptist view that favored individual privacy, limited government, and church-state separation. Several years later, when his denomination embraced the religious Right's agenda, Criswell became an ardent opponent of abortion.

Christianity Today noted that some Southern Baptists shared Criswell's positive opinion of the ruling, but its own view was different. An editorial condemned the decision, because it "explicitly rejected Christian moral teaching." Readers were warned to "accustom themselves to the thought that the American state no longer supports, in any meaningful sense, the laws of God."[25] *Newsweek* also reported that the staunchest opposition came from Roman Catholics. New York's Terence Cardinal Cooke called it "horrifying," while Philadelphia's John Cardinal Krol said it was "an unspeakable tragedy for the nation." A California lawyer, representing lay disapproval, avowed, "We'll go over the grey heads of these seven old men."[26]

This new militancy was surprising, since Catholics typically eschewed taking sides in social controversies and political conflict. (Individual Catholics were active in the civil rights and antiwar movements, but their positions did not elicit wide support from coreligionists.) Evangelicals who had historically decried Catholics as papists and heretics now contemplated bridge building in service to a greater good.

Abortion cleaved the conservative movement, dividing secularists from

2 ★★★★ DAILY NEWS, TUESDAY, JANUARY 23, 1973

Top Court Throws Out Abortion Bans

By JEFFREY ANTEVIL

Washington, Jan. 22 (NEWS Bureau) — The Supreme Court ruled in a historic decision today that it is entirely up to a woman and her doctor to decide whether she will have an abortion during the first six months of pregnancy.

The 7-to-2 decision, in an opinion written by Justice Harry A. Blackmun, in effect overturns laws in 46 states which permit abortions only under such conditions as when the mother's life or health is in danger. Blackmun said there are three separate periods in a pregnancy, and during these a woman's "right of privacy" may be increasingly restricted by a state:

- During the first three months, the decision on whether to end a pregnancy is up to a woman and her physician, with no state interference permissible.
- During the second three months—until the baby is capable of "meaningful life outside the mother's womb"—state regulation is limited to such matters as who may perform an abortion and in what kind of facility.
- During the final three months, the state's interest in protecting a "viable fetus" gives it the power to "go so far to proscribe abortion except when it is necessary to preserve the life or health of the mother."

There were seven separate opinions, totaling 110 pages; these included dissents by Justice Byron R. White and William H. Rehnquist. The ruling followed nearly two years of deliberations by the high court on what Blackmun called a "sensitive and emotional" issue.

Although the court dealt directly with laws in Texas and Georgia, all but four other states—New York, Alaska, Hawaii, and Washington—impose similar restrictions on abortion. Efforts have been going on in those four, particularly in New York, to get criminal penalties reinstated.

The Texas law, similar to those in 29 other states including New Jersey and Connecticut, made it a crime to end a pregnancy at any stage except to save the mother's live. Georgia was one of 16 states with more liberal laws permitting abortions on limited grounds, such as danger to the life or health of the mother, cases of rape, or the possibility of mental or physical defects in the offspring.

A Matter of Debate

Georgia's statute also stipulated that an abortion could be performed only in a state-accredited hospital and with the approval of a hospital staff abortion committee and two outside physicians. Blackmun said all three procedural conditions were unconstitutional.

Based primarily on a qualified right of privacy, Blackmun's opinion appeared to reject the claim by "right to life" groups and other abortion foes that a fetus is a person and thus entitled to the same constitutional rights as other Americans.

He said the use of the word "person" in the Constitution applied only after birth, but he added that the courts need not resolve the question of when life begins "when those trained in the respective disciplines of medicine, philosophy and theology are unable to arrive at any consensus."

President Nixon, in a letter to New York's Cardinal Cooke last year and in other statements, has come out strongly against an unrestricted right to abortions such as that provided by New York's law. But only Rehnquist of Nixon's four Supreme Court appointees dissented from today's ruling.

Rehnquist wrote:

"The decision . . . partakes more of judicial legislation than it does of a determination of the intent of the drafters of the 14th Amendment" (which guarantees

(Continued on page 30, col. 1)

Cooke Calls Ruling 'Tragic'

By ROGER WETHERINGTON

Cardinal Cooke bitterly assailed the Supreme Court's decision on abortion laws yesterday as the "shocking," "horrifying" and "tragic" act of judges usurping the powers of state legislatures.

But abortion advocates reacted warmly to the court decision. "A triumph," said birth control crusader Bill Baird. Dr. Alan F. Guttmacher, president of the Planned Parenthood Federation of America, called it "a wise and courageous stroke for the right to privacy and for the protection of a woman's physical and emotional health."

Cooke, in one of his strongest public statements, charged that the court majority "have made themselves a 'super legislature.'"

"How many millions of children prior to their birth will never live to see the light of day because of the shocking action of the majority of the United States Supreme Court today?" the cardinal asked.

'Good News,' Says Chase

"Whatever their legal rationale, seven men have made a tragic utilitarian judgment regarding who shall live and who shall die," he said.

City Health Services Administrator Gordon Chase called it "good news" but warned New Yorkers to resist any efforts to weaken New York's liberal law.

The immediate impact of the law in New York, as well as New Jersey and Connecticut, was unclear.

Edward Golden, chairman of New York State Right to Life, which nearly succeeded in getting the liberal law repealed last year, called a "moratorium" on his group's lobbying campaign.

But Golden emphasized that "we're not disbanding." After studying the decision, he said, his group will announce some "course of action." He said he did not know whether the effort would be directed toward reducing the

(Continued on page 57 col. 1)

Cardinal Cooke: "Shocking."

FIGURE 9. Roman Catholic clergy, including Cardinal Terence Cooke, the archbishop of New York, opposed the Supreme Court decision legalizing abortion.

true believers. In the ensuing struggle, which the latter won, the rest of the country was pulled to the right. Among conservative Christians, *Roe v. Wade* represented the apotheosis of the women's movement and its danger to the family. Religious patriarchs, true believers in male headship, decried the murder of unborn life but also sought control of women's bodies, especially their sexuality. In truth, the seven Supreme Court justices who decided the ruling were neither gender pioneers nor social progressives. Rather, they understood themselves to be building on previous decisions restricting governmental intrusion into the home and sexual matters. But subsequent events changed the frame of the discussion from a defense of personal privacy to a call for national morality and, concomitantly, a debate on whether women had control over their own bodies. The decision also foreshadowed a converging interest in religion and politics among religious conservatives and mainstream journalists.

Would *Roe v. Wade* have been as contentious if other factors did not seem to be undermining the nation's well-being? At a moment when Americans felt militarily vulnerable, beset by social change, and stung by rising inflation, perceived challenges to the family may have had added significance. Ending abortion on demand became a conservative rallying cry not only for personal morality and traditional families but also for the soul of America.

As if to highlight why promoting traditional values was imperative, just days before the *Roe v. Wade* ruling PBS rolled out *An American Family*, a twelve-part documentary. The series was unlike anything previously seen on television. Its scope was unprecedented: twelve episodes culled from three hundred hours of film at a cost of $1.2 million. Producer Craig Gilbert, inspired by anthropologists Margaret Mead and Oscar Lewis, wanted to document "how the enormous technological, social and cultural changes of the past half century have affected the family life of an American family."[27] Gilbert spent months looking for the right family to film, and the household he finally chose was both *an* American family and *the* American family.

At first sight, the Louds—Bill, Pat, and their five children—seemed golden. The family's image, "toothpaste-bright affluence, California-style,"[28] embodied the American dream: a hilltop home in Santa Barbara that included a recording studio, pool, horse, two cats, three dogs, and four cars. But once in focus, the Louds displayed a shocking level of dysfunctionality. Lies, silence, and misdirection constituted the familial core. Bill drank, Pat dithered, and the children lacked personal discipline. Credit cards propped up appearances. Pat tolerated Bill's infidelities, and no one discussed their eldest son's homosexuality—even when he took up residence alongside artist Andy Warhol's transgressive crew in New York City's notorious Chelsea Hotel.

The unflattering portrait of the Louds reflected the problematic state of many American families. Divorces and female-headed households were on the rise. In one out of six homes, fathers were absent or unemployed. The number of women having first babies outside marriage had doubled from 5 percent in the 1950s to 11 percent in the early 1970s, and nearly half of all marriages ended in divorce.[29] The Louds put a white, upper-middle-class face on the statistics that had prompted reports, commissions, and recommendations on the foundering American family. The media attributed the problem to cultural changes: sexual permissiveness, feminism, and abortion had exacted a heavy price on family stability. The not-so-subtle sexism that wound through many news narratives blamed the women's movement for the breakdown of the family and subsequent national woes.

MEN AT WORK AND HOME

On January 22, the day that the *Roe v. Wade* decision was announced, former president Lyndon B. Johnson died. A day later, President Richard M. Nixon told the world that the Vietnam War had been won. "Ironically, Mr. Johnson died in what appeared to be the waning days of the Vietnam war," noted the *New York Times* obituary. "The man who won election in 1964 to a full term as President with the greatest voting majority ever accorded to a candidate was transformed by that war into a leader of a divided nation."[30] The divided nation was weary; depending on one's reckoning, the Vietnam conflict had lasted between twelve and twenty years. By 1973, many Americans had been worn down by setbacks, body bags, and antiwar demonstrations. Television had brought the fighting into their homes, and *Tet*, *My Lai*, and *the Hanoi Hilton* were part of their vocabulary. One million Vietnamese were dead, three hundred thousand Americans wounded, and fifty-six thousand Americans killed, with the US military effort costing $140 billion.[31]

After the 1968 election, Nixon, in pursuit of a viable exit strategy, began redefining the US mission in Vietnam. America's objective became "peace with honor," and its goal was to bring home its prisoners of war. Between the government's pull and the media's push, the POWs assumed center stage in the national drama. Portrayed as courageous soldiers ennobled through imprisonment and torture, they transformed the conflict's script from a dispiriting tale of a superpower ensnared in a debilitating guerilla war to the saga of brave fighters held captive by a ruthless enemy.[32] Although the narrative threw a redemptive gloss on the war's toll, the subdued reaction to news of its end belied the success of the government's spin. As the *Washington Post* noted, "There was no World War II-style jubilation in the [Times Square] streets below, nor any talk of triumph either from Americans who waged the Vietnam war or those who opposed it. Except for the church bells, it seemed to be ending, as it began, quietly and, in many homes, unnoticed."[33]

But newspaper editorialists were unwilling to conclude the war as quietly as their readers seemed to want, and many penned strong words for the occasion. "In the context of what the greatest military power the world has ever seen has done to a tiny Asian nation there can be no talk of peace with honor," the *Saint Louis Post-Dispatch* fulminated.[34] Opined the *Boston Globe*, "Triumph can have no part in our grateful relief at the ending of conflict in which, most Americans now agree, we should have never taken part."[35] On the other side of the country, the *Los Angeles Times* wondered what was actually gained: "It would seem that the future of Indochina is not significantly different with this peace than under the Geneva peace agreements of 1954, and that its people are irreparably worse for the mutilation, devastation and carnage of the war."[36] Similarly, the *Chicago Daily News* rued the impact on US policy: "The plain fact is that the

United States, having been the chief agent of destruction, bears the chief moral responsibility. For the still longer range there are great lessons to be soberly digested and applied to our role in the world. We have a decade long demonstration of the futility of the armed approach to international problems."[37] But Americans eager for the war to end were not necessarily ready for a moral reckoning.

The POWs were supposed to bridge the gulf between what the war was and what it could be; a chronicle of valor rather than a record of failure. The men returned to cheering crowds and effusive press coverage, but trouble soon arose. The lost years were not just measures in time but gauges of a cultural chasm that separated the world they left from the one they found. After almost nine years in captivity, Lieutenant Commander Everett Alvarez Jr. learned that his wife had divorced him and that his sister had opposed the war. Homecoming for him and many others was not the

FIGURE 10. POW wives at Naval Air Station Miramar awaiting husbands who were released on February 12, 1973. Courtesy US National Archives and Records Administration.

joyful reunion they anticipated.[38] Even families that remained intact had adjustment issues, as Lieutenant Colonel Ken North discovered in conversations with his four daughters: "'We've had dinner discussions where the girls used such vivid language that I was at a loss how to clean it up,' he jokes. His eleven-year-old lectures him on Women's Liberation. 'She tells me how she is a person and has to be able to express herself,' he said in disbelief. In prison, he took a vow that he would never let long-haired boys into his house. Now, he admits, 'well they've come and they've stayed.'"[39]

Despite the government's intention that the POWs serve as the cast of an American success story, accounts of their homecoming fed concerns about a crisis in American masculinity. Social changes left some wondering how to protect their status now that African Americans, gays, and women demanded the same privileges that were formerly the domain of white men only. Further, the economic climate was endangering white men's financial power. Well-paying factory jobs were disappearing, and more women were working outside the home. At the same time, the US economy, accustomed to steady growth in the postwar years, braked hard in the 1970s.

Among the many reasons for the economic slowdown were two that were not well understood at the time. One was a tectonic realignment as jobs in manufacturing and heavy industry shifted to services and information. The other was the evolution of national corporations into global conglomerates. But at the time, the downturn was ascribed to more proximate causes: the nation was paying a steep bill for LBJ's Great Society programs, and the Vietnam War was expensive. Nixon's decision not to raise taxes exacerbated the problem. By the mid-1970s, the gross national product's annual 4 percent increase had dropped to below 2 percent, and unemployment had doubled. The actual value of after-tax pay fell, but prices and interest rates kept climbing. Pundits called the problem stagflation—the unanticipated conjunction of stagnant business activity, rising inflation, and increased unemployment.

Between 1971 and 1973, Nixon tried a variety of measures to boost the economy, including wage-price freezes, mandatory price controls, and devaluation of the dollar. He also took the dollar off the gold standard and allowed it to "float," losing, at one point, 15 percent of its value.[40] The devaluations sent ripples through the economy, upsetting the international balance of trade, depressing stock prices, and driving up the cost for food and basic commodities. In March, when consumers threatened to boycott meat, Nixon imposed price controls.

The impact of rising food prices was accompanied by a growing oil shortage. Up through the mid-twentieth century, the United States drew from its own oil supplies to fuel the economy. Cheap domestic oil, supplemented by inexpensive imported petroleum, made possible the American dream. That dream, incarnate in big cars, shiny appliances, and brand-new homes, required 6 percent of the world's population to consume one-third of the world's energy. But as domestic demand for energy increased, America's oil reserves decreased; in 1948, the United States produced almost two-thirds of the world's oil, but by 1972 that number was down to less than 25 percent.[41]

By then, Americans had become dependent on oil-rich Middle Eastern nations. These countries, coming into their own after decades of colonial control over their governments and oil fields, saw petroleum exports as a way to raise money and exert political muscle. The Organization of Petroleum Exporting Countries (OPEC), a paper tiger during its first decade, now determined how much oil would be produced and what it would cost. Both decisions hit Americans at the pump. But American oil companies also played a role in the shortage. Eager to boost profits, the oil industry reduced domestic oil exploration and development, invested in Middle Eastern oil companies, and maintained an import quota system to cut supplies and inflate prices.

The strategy benefited the industry but hurt consumers. During the 1972–73 winter months, homes were cold and gas prices were high. Some factories and schools, unable to afford heating, were forced to close.[42] Previously, Nixon had resisted calls for governmental intervention, assuming the market would correct itself—and, if not, American know-how would find a solution to the problem. (At the time, the prospect of nuclear energy looked promising.) But in April 1973, the president told Congress, "If present trends continue unchecked we could face a genuine energy crisis."[43] Proposing to both "minimize shortages" and spur development of new energy sources, he outlined a range of interventions that included implementing fees on imported oil, increasing offshore drilling, incentivizing the production of natural gas, building the Alaska pipeline, and supporting nuclear energy.[44]

But Nixon's pronouncements had little effect on American pocketbooks. With an inflation rate of 9.4 percent, basic commodities were increasingly expensive. Food costs were particularly worrisome. On April 1, consumer groups announced a weeklong meat boycott to force down prices.[45] Grassroots backing for the boycott included tenants' groups and block associations as well as informal networks of housewives and working women. Women helped organize the protest, and nationwide, 25 percent of all consumers participated.[46] From the Mid-Atlantic region alone, more than half a million shoppers sent their grocery receipts to the White House.[47]

The news media, ever gender conscious, framed the meat boycott as a women's issue, whereas protests against rising gas prices were reported to be led by men. Thus, Nixon's mid-boycott choice to serve beef at a state dinner was a political snub with symbolic resonance; there was no crisis of masculinity in his home. Moreover, his decision to freeze prices at their height, one of the spurs for the boycott, was contrarian as well as counterproductive. But the most pressing concern at the White House—growing public attention to the Watergate break-in—exemplified the challenge to male authority, threatening even the most powerful of men.

WATERGATE AND ITS AFTERMATH

On January 8—two weeks before the president's announcement of "peace with honor" in Vietnam—the Watergate burglars went on trial. The seven defendants were charged with breaking into the Democratic National Committee's Washington, DC, headquarters the previous summer. At first, the break-in was dismissed as a botched but random crime. But the previous fall, *Washington Post* journalists Carl Bernstein and Bob Woodward had learned that the burglars, who were attempting to place hidden listening devices in the DNC office, were part of a "massive campaign of political spying and espionage conducted on behalf of President Nixon's re-election and directed by officials of the White House and the Committee for the Re-election of the President."[48] Woodward and Bernstein called their source Deep Throat, a wink at the year's most talked-about pornographic movie. The name also was a nod to the new sexual permissiveness while also intimating anxiety about women's public sexuality.

As disturbing as the news was of the break-in, it had not derailed the Nixon juggernaut, which swept the 1972 election with over 60 percent of the vote. Yet just two months later, the Watergate burglars, now known to be working for the Committee for the Re-election of the President (CREEP, as it was popularly called), were convicted. One subsequently admitted to perjury, confessing that the cover-up conspiracy extended to the White House. The Democrats, skeptical of the Nixon administration's willingness to admit to wrongdoing, empaneled a Senate committee to investigate whether any campaign laws had been abrogated. Senator Sam Ervin, a North Carolina Democrat, convened hearings in May. But before then, Nixon, eager to stanch the affair, announced that four of his top aides—including Attorney General John Mitchell—had participated in the ruse. The men resigned, and Eliot Richardson, Mitchell's replacement, immediately appointed a special prosecutor to look into Watergate.

Widespread interest in the case convinced Ervin's committee to televise its proceedings. Gavel-to-gavel coverage, rotating daily among the three major networks, provided the public with a ringside seat for the most controversial congressional investigation since the 1954 Army-McCarthy hearings. More than 80 percent of American households[49] watched what *Variety* called "the hottest daytime soap opera."[50] In the same way that the Loud family had exposed the dysfunction underlying many American families, the Watergate hearings illumined the dark corners of America's government, including John Mitchell's claim that the possibility of a McGovern presidency justified illicit campaign activities and the admission of the president's deputy assistant, Alexander Butterfield, that Nixon set up voice-activated tape recorders in White House offices.[51]

The existence of secret tapes shocked not just the public but also many members of the president's inner circle. But shock was not the same as surprise: Americans were familiar with what the news media called Nixon's history of "dirty tricks."[52] The Watergate hearings revealed White House involvement in wiretapping, slush funds, and favors for financial support, along with the existence of an "enemies list" and plans to harass reporters as well as political opponents. The most astonishing aspect of the proceedings was also the most prosaic: Nixon's bland, buttoned-down men—whom the *Washington Post* had valorized earlier that winter as "all work and no frills"—damning themselves in uninflected monotones.[53]

Though broadcast in color, the Watergate hearings seemed to be in black and white, the suits and ties relics from an earlier era. Nixon's "scrupulously disciplined" subordinates sharply contrasted with the family pop bands, shaggy teens, and single working women who normally populated the television landscape. But the hearings were compelling in a way that few other shows were. Anticipating the popularity of reality TV, they brought the frisson of individual fault and group failure into America's homes. A similar sense of outrage, horror, and fascination had transfixed viewers ten years earlier when Jack Ruby shot Lee Harvey Oswald. But that fuzzy scene of a light-suited man firing into a prisoner's belly lasted only seconds; the Ervin hearings went on for 319 hours. Coverage was continuous. If a broadcast was missed, there were recaps on the nightly news. If the nightly news was turned off, the morning newspapers had updates. Columnist Mary McCarthy, traveling around the country, reported, "In every city I arrived at, the local papers were full of Watergate; regardless of their politics and of pressure, if any, from their advertisers, they were keeping their readers in touch with the most minor episodes in this fantastic crime serial."[54]

Telling and retelling the story compelled Americans to accept its implications: the presidency was imploding before their eyes. During the dog days of summer, executive authority seemed to melt under the camera's steadfast gaze. When Nixon refused to hand over the tapes, arguing that executive privilege meant serving a "higher law," rumblings of impeachment swept through Congress. Two out of three Americans believed the president's "ability to govern had been severely damaged," and 60 percent assumed he knew about the cover-up.[55]

Nixon's slow march to resignation began several months later. On Saturday, October 20, special Watergate prosecutor Archibald Cox (whom Richardson had appointed to investigate the cover-up) rejected Nixon's proposed compromise to provide written summaries of the secret tapes, which Senator John Stennis would verify. Enraged, Nixon ordered Richardson to fire Cox, but the attorney general, who had assured Cox he would have a free hand with the investigation, resigned, as did his deputy, William Ruckelshaus. At last, Nixon persuaded Robert Bork, the solicitor general, to dismiss Cox—the final link in a chain of events the press dubbed the Saturday Night Massacre.[56]

Nixon's high-handed machinations hardened public opinion against him. Angry calls and telegrams swamped the White House and Congress. Before that fateful Saturday night, roughly a quarter of Americans thought Nixon should be "impeached and compelled to leave the presidency."[57] Afterward, their number rose to 33 percent. Despite the public's unhappiness with the president, many saw an even deeper problem, and almost half doubted that his leaving office "would have any fundamental effect on how fast things improve."[58] For many Americans, the desired improvement was not just a matter of governance. As disturbing as Watergate was, many citizens had an even more pressing concern: the collapse of the economy.

Over the summer of 1973, the political drama had diverted the public's attention from an array of social changes and cultural milestones. Domestically, the courts mandated busing to desegregate northern schools, and the draft gave way to an all-volunteer army. But even Americans who failed to notice that *Jesus Christ Superstar* had closed on Broadway or that Secretariat had won the Triple Crown could not miss the impact of inflation and historically high oil prices. Nor could they avoid news of the war in the Middle East that had begun on the holiest day of the Jewish calendar.

The Yom Kippur War started on October 6 when Syria and Egypt launched a surprise attack against Israel. Initially, the Arab states made significant headway, moving to recapture the Sinai Peninsula and the Golan Heights, both of which Israel had conquered during the 1967 Six-Day War. Israel's heavy losses stunned not only Golda Meir's government but also Nixon and his new secretary of state, Henry Kissinger. Both men assumed that American military support for Israel as well as the alleged strength of the small country's military and intelligence gathering rendered it invincible. Instead, they found themselves desperate for a solution that satisfied contradictory US policy goals: supporting Israel and buying oil from the Arab states of the Persian Gulf.

Nixon, concluding that the United States could not allow Israel to lose, sent arms shipments to the beleaguered nation. America would not use direct force, but it did provide 22,395 tons of military supplies, including tanks and ammunition, to its ally.[59] In retaliation, Arab oil-producing nations announced a cutback in oil production and a subsequent embargo against the United States. In addition, OPEC raised prices by 70 percent. Taken together, the price hike, embargo, and production cutbacks sparked fears of shortages among American consumers even though there was no real reason for worry, given domestic and other international suppliers. However, on November 9, when Nixon sought to reassure the nation, he made things worse. Noting the impending energy crisis, he asked Americans to lower their thermostats, reduce speed limits, and cut back on air travel. But rather than conserving energy, Americans began stockpiling resources, their desire to safeguard themselves compounding the problem.

Neither domestic nor international crises halted the Democrats' investigation into Watergate and the pileup of incriminating information. Nixon held on for another nine months while the case against him grew stronger and public support weaker. At the end of July 1974, the House Judiciary Committee prepared three articles of impeachment, and the Supreme Court ruled that he had to turn over the secret Watergate tapes. Among other damning revelations, the transcripts disclosed that the president had instructed his subordinates to stop the FBI's investigation into the scandal. Several days later, Nixon resigned, retreating to his home in California.

Even if Watergate had not ended the Nixon presidency, his second term most likely would have been marked by turmoil. The social and economic convulsions that defined the 1970s defied easy solutions. Neither of his successors, Presidents Gerald Ford and Jimmy Carter, was able to stem the tide of lost jobs, rising prices, and waning international prestige. The Vietnam War and the OPEC oil embargo revealed America's weakness in the international arena, and domestically, many viewed the sexual revolution as an assault on the American family. Taken together, these circumstances strained the nation's unity almost to the breaking point.

E PLURIBUS UNUM

Despite the political and economic turmoil in 1973, Americans did not make common cause. Tempers flared in long gas station lines, and consumers filled their pantries with little thought about their neighbors' welfare. Intergroup tensions also ran high. Were television audiences laughing at or with Archie Bunker, the ranting racist at the center of *All in the Family*, the nation's top-ranked show from 1971 to 1979? Archie gave cultural cover, as well as a liberal imprimatur, to nasty stereotypes. A working-class antihero, his grievances were directed not at the system that perpetuated economic inequality but at "others"—so-called fags, hebes, spades, gooks, and wops—who seemed better at gaming it. Norman Lear, the series' politically liberal creator, picked up on a post-60s trend that pitted interest and identity groups against one another. Whether the otherness was racial, religious, ethnic, political, or based in class or gender, it led to rivalries over access to resources. Nixon's successful 1968 campaign was built on this divide-and-conquer premise. His "Southern strategy" went after Dixiecrats embittered by the civil rights agenda, and his subsequent mustering of a "silent majority" drafted blue-collar conservatives who, like Archie Bunker, resented Blacks, women, Latinos, hippies, and welfare cheats who seemed to have hijacked their country.

The distance between us and them was signaled early in 1973 when the *New York Times* ran a four-part series on the South Bronx. The paper described the neighborhood as "a foreign country where fear is the overriding emotion in a landscape of despair," a desolate cityscape fit only for gangs, drug pushers, and wild dogs.[60] After chronicling the housing, economic, educational, and medical woes of the predominantly Black and Latino community—and noting state and federal resistance to providing additional funds for rebuilding—the reporter sought answers from the era's wise men. Robert Moses, architect of the massive building projects that were, in large part, the cause of local blight, expressed no sympathy for his victims. "You must concede that this Bronx slum and others in Brooklyn and Manhattan are irreparable," he said. "They are beyond rebuilding, tinkering and restoring. They must be leveled to the ground."[61]

A similar sentiment, albeit in a very different context, was evoked by a protest at Wounded Knee, South Dakota. On February 27, several hundred Native American activists occupied the site where US troops had massacred their forefathers in 1890. The demonstrators were protesting corrupt tribal leaders as well as the US government's unwillingness to grant them self-determination, which resulted in economic hardships.[62] Initially, public opinion sided with the proponents of Red Power.[63] But a standoff with federal troops that dragged on for seventy-one days—punctuated by shootouts and casualties—eroded that support.

Florida Democrat James Haley, who chaired the House committee overseeing Indian affairs, told the *Los Angeles Times*, "I've done as much for the Indians as any man in history. I don't know about AIM [the American Indian Movement] but I know these people at Wounded Knee are wrong."[64] The *Times* along with the rest of the national media had ballyhooed the story, helping keep it alive. But even as the press exploited AIM for headline fodder, the activists, savvy about sound bites and photo ops, used the media to publicize their cause. The public, however, was over it.

Similarly to Native Americans, many Chicanos, or Mexican Americans, saw themselves as members of an indigenous culture that white America had impoverished and marginalized. Beginning in the 1960s and building on earlier campaigns, young leaders in the southwestern states organized Mexicans around political and economic issues. Early wins by La Raza Unida, the Brown Berets, and the United Farmworkers Union buoyed supporters of the movement, as did successful campaigns against degrading stereotypes, such as advertisements featuring the Frito Bandito. But the movement's unity was splintered by internal conflicts over its ultimate goals: was the aim to assimilate into the majority Anglo culture, or was it to retain ethnic and community values? Discord also arose among Chicanas, who complained that their voices were not part of the leadership, and setbacks in the political and legal arenas stalled the movement's agenda.

In 1968, Nixon reached out to Spanish-speaking constituencies and won 36 percent of their vote. But his friendship was short lived when he moved to close government agencies, including the Office of Economic Opportunity, designated to assist them and other low-income groups. Correspondingly, a 1973 Supreme Court case reified the financial inequities plaguing public education. Five years earlier, a group of Chicano families in San Antonio had sued the Texas School Board under the equal protection clause of the Fourteenth Amendment. Contending that education was a fundamental right, they maintained that Texas's method of school financing, which used local property taxes to fund public education, discriminated against poor communities. A wealthy Anglo neighborhood could spend $594 per pupil, while a Mexican American district raised only $358. In March 1973, the Supreme Court ruled that education was "not among the rights afforded explicit protection under our federal Constitution," nor, according to Justice Lewis Powell, was it afforded "implicit protection." But Thurgood Marshall, one of four dissenting justices, lamented that the decision was "a retreat from our historic commitment to equality of educational opportunity."[65]

Two months later, another landmark educational ruling went Marshall's way. In *Keyes v. Denver School District No. 1*, seven justices deemed the Denver school system segregated and ordered the city to rectify the situation.[66] The decision was the latest in a series of judicial and legislative mandates seeking to achieve racial parity through equal access to voting, jobs, education, and public accommodations. Over the decade, African Americans had made significant gains: many improved their economic standing, others moved into the middle class, and still others broke through longtime professional barriers to become business executives, elected officials, and religious leaders in predominantly white sectors.

The Denver decision was historic: northern and western states needed to comply with the federal mandate for desegregation. Over the next decade, whites in urban areas from New York to California abandoned the public schools as well as neighborhoods where middle-class Blacks had moved. White flight devastated cities and swelled private school enrollment, seeding a new movement of private Christian academies. As a result, education and housing remained largely segregated, and when the economy languished, Blacks were hardest hit. By the early 1970s, many African Americans were questioning the integrationist model, and Black nationalism, percolating through urban communities, made dashikis, soul food, Afros, and funk markers of Black pride.

Identity politics, an expression of minorities' mixed success at attaining the benefits of the majority, helped spark a countermovement, the "Southernization" of white America. A de facto white power movement, it was as much an unintended consequence of the civil rights movement as it was a result of population shifts, economic restructuring, and renewed religiosity.[67] The trend represented two realities: the South was becoming as urbanized and industrialized as the rest of the country, and at the same time the rest of the country was adopting southern values, especially evangelicalism, as southerners and their churches migrated beyond the Bible Belt.[68] The upshot was a conservative tide propelled by the rise of the Sun Belt, the westward push of the Southern Baptist Convention, the growth of the defense and service industries, and the Republicans' successful Southern strategy.

An anomalous mix of tradition and modernity, best embodied by Southern California's Orange County evangelical aerospace engineers, this new movement was "not a rural 'remnant' of the displaced and maladapted but a gathering around principles that were found to be relevant in the most modern of communities."[69] Those principles, including advanced market capitalism, would seem to put adherents' earthly ambitions at odds with the faith that gave constancy to their lives. Instead, it strengthened a form of Christianity that saw religion, market capitalism, and nationalism as the bedrock American identity.[70]

Most of the mainstream news media missed this rising religious tide. Since *Time*'s declaration eight years earlier that God was dead, elite journalists focused more on colorful, if marginal, groups—Jesus People, cults, and communes, as we will see in the next chapter—than on institutional shifts and theological realignments. Mainline Protestantism was on a downward trajectory, but that was old news. Some historians even argued that the main line's demise dated back to the Great Depression, when a lack of vision diminished its vitality.[71]

In 1973, more than forty years after the stock market crash, Catholic historian John Tracy Ellis saw a similar crisis facing his own church. Ellis ascribed the problem not to internal forces (some of his coreligionists blamed changes set in motion by the Second Vatican Council) but rather to "the cultural and social forces that, willy-nilly, condition Catholics' daily lives." He called out "the communications media and the institutions that serve as their transmitters," but his article on Catholic anxiety focused on the diminution of religious commitment in higher education—a problem reflecting the twin perils of acculturation and secularization.[72] According to the *New York Times*, some conservative churches were having the same troubles as liberal ones. Only Pentecostals and groups with "vigorous programs of proselytism" were growing.[73]

This general unease may have been why Key 73, an ecumenical evangelistic campaign, had seemed to be such a good idea. The national outreach effort united evangelicals with mainline Protestants and forty-three Roman Catholic dioceses. The plan was to emphasize the evangelical nature of Christianity by providing a range of ways to commit oneself and convert others.

Despite the Catholic hierarchy's support, the crusade languished on the ground. Fund-raising stalled, fundamentalists criticized Catholic participation, and Jews decried the goal of "calling our continent to Christ."[74] The latter led to so much bad publicity that several evangelical leaders were compelled to start a dialogue with their Jewish counterparts. But even as religious organizations seemed to sputter and stall, Americans found new paths for transcendence and community. Writing in October 1973, religion scholar Martin Marty predicted that the future of American religion would be shaped "by the generation of the 1970s."[75] But unlike Jesus People and TMers (followers of Transcendental Meditation), members of suburban churches, Black congregations, and Jewish *havurot* (small fellowship groups) did not draw headlines when they wove religious particularity and experiential questing into their communities. Even as pundits and observers predicted that religion was another victim of the times, Marty noted that many Americans sought spiritual "ballast," existential security in an anxious age.

By the end of the year, the signs of change had seared the body politic as well as local communities and individual lives. The three often entwined as the nation's problems reverberated in the daily lives of its citizens. It wasn't just high prices at the supermarket and long lines at the gas pump; the impact could be seen in many ways and in many places. In Los Angeles, which received almost half its oil from Arab states, households cut back 10 percent on their energy consumption. On Christmas weekend, the city was "a shadow of its normal radiant self," its lights even lower than they had been during World War II.[76]

Due east in the heartland, a Middle American family expressed puzzlement and concern. Sonda and Harold "Curt" Curtis of Galesburg, Illinois, were bewildered by Watergate, confused by the energy crisis, and shocked by Vice President Agnew's resignation. (Accused of political corruption, Agnew resigned in October 1973.) "'It's been one thing after another,' said Sonda, a cosmetologist and mother of two. 'You just wonder what the coming year is going to be.' Her husband, an insurance salesman, Episcopal vestryman, and Republican, was more philosophical: 'I think there is a lot of uneasiness right now. But I for some reason have a lot of faith that our problems in some way will be solved.'"[77]

In Washington, DC, residents of a working-class neighborhood said 1973 was the worst year in recent memory. Crime was up, prices were high, and the government could not be trusted. According to Nellie Chase, a nursing assistant with three daughters, "'It was a horrible year, with shortages of everything, even toilet paper,' she went on, finally coming to the point her daughters wanted her to make, 'The most important thing is Watergate,' to which, she said, she believed the shortages and other problems are related."[78]

On New Year's Day 1974, an unsigned *New York Times* editorial predicted that fundamental shifts were under way: "This New Year's Day, symbolized by dimmed lights, chilly rooms and empty gasoline tanks, ushers in a new era of enforced—if only relative—austerity."[79] The *Washington Post* was even more foreboding. According to columnist Jack Anderson, the United States had entered middle age. "For the first time, Americans have begun to look backward," he noted. "There is a growing apprehension that we have reached the end of a golden age."[80]

CHAPTER THREE
An American Religious Imaginary

> I've always believed that this blessed land was set apart in a special way, that some divine plan placed this great continent here between the oceans to be found by people from every corner of the Earth who had a special love for freedom and the courage to uproot themselves, leave homeland and friends, to come to a strange land.
>
> PRESIDENT RONALD REAGAN, Spirit of America Rally, Atlanta, January 26, 1984

In May 1983, *Archie Bunker's Place* went dark, and television's blue-collar avatar—like millions of his countrymen—was out of work. For twelve years as America's most notorious curmudgeon, Archie Bunker had voiced the anger and frustration of his fellow citizens over social and economic turmoil. Racist, sexist, and suspicious of almost everyone outside his white, ethnic, working-class corner of Queens, New York, Archie loved his country and championed family, hard work, and religion. (An infrequent churchgoer, he nevertheless quoted scripture to make a point.)

Archie supported Ronald Reagan, and Ronald Reagan sought the votes of Americans like Archie—working-class white Democrats, unsettled by the social changes of the 1960s. Reagan offered hope and a return to security: a prosperous economy, a strong military, and a nation right with God. Many citizens still clung to that hope, even though the American dream remained elusive. Like Archie, they believed that the dream was real, even if their own hopes were unfulfilled. In this unsettling time of economic crisis, Reagan articulated a new religious imaginary, which, spread through mainstream news outlets and countercultural Christian media, reshaped Americans' understanding of their personal and civic responsibilities. The acceptance of—or at least acquiescence to—this vision of nation and citizenship shifted the nation's political center to the right. This chapter looks at the evolving religious milieu that helped make those changes possible.

A BRIEF HISTORY OF AMERICAN RELIGIONS

For readers unfamiliar with American religions, some background will help explain how various strands align. For most of the nineteenth century, evangelicalism was the dominant form of American Protestantism among whites and Blacks. Protestantism was culturally ascendant because its history was believed to be entwined with American history, it was the largest faith in the nation, and elites in all spheres of society were adherents. Many white Protestants also converted their slaves, and free Blacks often started their own Protestant denominations. Roman Catholicism was considered un-American because of that church's hierarchal structure and theology, and other faiths, such as Judaism, were too small to signify.[1]

Nineteenth-century American evangelicals believed that the Bible was God's literal word and that salvation occurred when Christians welcomed Jesus into their hearts as their personal savior. Sharing Jesus's saving message with the world was their primary mission. Before the Civil War, many thought they could usher in the Second Coming by spreading the gospel and reforming society. Consequently, some became missionaries to foreign lands while others worked to end slavery at home or to aid the poor, among other causes.

But the Civil War caused widespread death and disillusionment, and many evangelicals reassessed their ability to improve society. At the same time, scientific discoveries, biblical scholarship, and a heightened appreciation of world religions threatened Christian convictions, particularly among educated and cosmopolitan white believers. Responding to the times, new forms of religiosity took root in the last decades of the nineteenth century and the early years of the twentieth. Some white Protestants became religious liberals, adopting a laissez-faire approach to doctrine and faith. Instead of viewing sin as an individual problem, some of these religious liberals considered it a systemic evil. Rather than call for personal repentance, they pressed for political, social, and economic changes to alleviate poverty and reform society. Heralded as the Social Gospel, this version of reformist Christianity found support not only among mainstream Protestants but also from members of the Progressive movement and muckraking journalists. Their shared perspective—a desire for a more just political system, a recognition of communal responsibility, and a belief in a loving and benevolent God—was the basis for a religious imaginary that would eventually enable President Franklin D. Roosevelt to justify the New Deal and the US entrance into World War II.

But religious liberals were not the only breakaways from the antebellum Christian consensus. Others, who became known as fundamentalists, took a hard line on religious orthodoxy and biblical literalism. Their focus was on saving as many souls as possible before Jesus returned, which could be today, tomorrow, or decades away. They homed in on their own communities, strengthening fundamentalist schools, churches, and other organizations. Still other Protestants believed that the Holy Spirit had endowed them with special gifts, such as speaking in foreign or unknown tongues, prophesying, and healing the sick. Pentecostals, as these Christians were called, used what they called gifts of the Spirit to spread God's Word.

Another popular religious alternative beginning in the late nineteenth century was the New Thought movement, which took Christian and non-Christian forms. New Thought was a metaphysical religion, and its different branches shared a belief in the power of the mind to shape and change physical reality. Many adherents believed that physical health, material wealth, and spiritual well-being were available through proper mental training—that is, positive thinking that could align the individual's mind with the cosmic oneness and thus banish negativity, sickness, and sin. Such beliefs resonated with Pentecostals, who trusted Jesus to save their souls, heal their bodies, and protect them from evil. Beginning in the early twentieth century, Pentecostal and later some evangelical churches began teaching that complete faith in God, especially when expressed through tithing, would yield spiritual, physical, and material blessings. This came to be known as the prosperity gospel, and it grew increasingly popular as the century progressed. A transactional form of Christianity, the prosperity gospel sanctified success and glorified its material manifestations. It appealed to Americans regardless of race, region, or socioeconomic background.

In the 1920s, conservative religious, business, and political leaders worried that the godless, antidemocratic forces of the 1917 communist revolution in Russia were a threat to the American way of life. In response, they funded popular media, aimed at conservative churches, which extolled the sanctity of free markets and the grace of material success. By the 1950s, many of these ideas had crossed into the mainstream, fueling Republican senator Joseph McCarthy's crusade against domestic communists. Around the same time, neo-evangelicals, who split off from fundamentalists after World War II, sought connections with the larger society. Their first goal was to save sinners, but they also enjoyed the postwar accoutrements that accompanied the new consumer culture. The emergence of Christian media, products, and providers reflected this desire for material goods and services. Innovative parachurch ministries to college students, young adults, and athletes signaled the neo-evangelicals' commitment to reach an unsaved world. Youth missionaries experimented with contemporaneous cultural forms, including rock music, coffeehouses, and "alternative" print media. Their goal was to reach unchurched youth as well as to retain churched teens curious about the "new cool"[2] and eager to experiment with the trappings of the counterculture.

By the 1970s, a new youth culture, along with the seeds of a new religious imaginary—one that hallowed individualism and materialism with a whiff of utopianism—had taken root among white baby boomers who sought meaning and purpose for their lives. These were not runaways or hippies. Rather, they were Protestant, Catholic, Jewish, and even nonreligious teens and young adults alienated by the older generation's "straight" lives and the banality of suburbia. Even so, many had no desire for a truly alternate lifestyle. They liked material comforts, but they worried whether they would be able to afford them. Many of their fathers had lost their jobs, others settled for lower-paying positions, and still others were on unemployment.

Well-compensated blue-collar workers were especially hard hit as factories closed or moved offshore, and family tensions were exacerbated as the Vietnam War helped stoke a generational divide. Calls by racial, gender, and ethnic groups to end white male privilege added to the economic and cultural blows hitting once comfortable homes. In such a confused and uncertain world, many baby boomers believed that authenticity, the truth that stemmed from personal experience, was their only touchstone.[3] Self-styling through music, clothes, speech, and behavior offered one path to authenticity, and faith was another. "The times they are a-changin',"[4] prophesied the generation's poet laureate, and young people prepared.

SPIRITUAL AUTHENTICITY AND RELIGIOUS SALVATION IN THE 1960S AND 1970S

The search for authenticity and an openness to change added to the spiritual effervescence of the 1960s. Contrary to some theologians' declarations, God was anything but dead.[5] Rather, current incarnations thrived in small communes, ashrams, and intentional communities. For their part, Christian leaders found success building pop-culture bridges to the young, despite concerns that becoming too culturally relevant would dilute the church's message. Prescient pastors saw that psychedelia and sexual openness were less ends in themselves than steps on a quest for meaning that, at its core, was neither nihilistic nor self-abnegating.

Scholars and journalists have chronicled the remarkable spectrum of cults and new religious movements that flourished during this era.[6] Touting new ways to live the Christian message, self-proclaimed spiritual leaders such as Jim Jones, Elizabeth Prophet, and Moses Berg organized acolytes into small, highly structured, quasi-Christian communities. Other seekers, enamored of Eastern modes of enlightenment, meditated at home and abroad with masters including the Maharishi Mahesh Yogi, Chögyam Trungpa, and Swami Satchidananda. Whether Christian, New Age, or Eastern in their worldview, devoted followers joined groups with a charismatic authority figure, a comprehensive behavioral code, and a communal approach to work, family, and finances.

Rejecting their parents' religiosity, many found spiritual guides whose highly structured, tightly bounded communities were even more restrictive than those they had fled.[7] Many leaders required total commitment, demanding a more faithful existence in separatist communes or peripatetic communities than was possible in the outside world. Whether followers of Charles Manson or Maharaj-ji, so-called cult members made headlines, but many more young people stayed home, spurring change from inside their congregations. Influenced by the counterculture and its emphasis on personal freedom, authenticity, and self-fulfillment, they embodied the turn to "expressive individualism," which sociologist Robert Bellah documented in *Habits of the Heart*.[8] Yearning for a personal, affective spirituality, these youth sought experiential practices that provided religious certainties in their own idiom.

Praising God with drums and guitars felt "authentic," the generational coin of the realm. Some young Jews turned to Messianic Judaism or Eastern meditation, but others revitalized Jewish ritual in small groups called *havurot*. Some Roman Catholic youth experimented with evangelical and Asian practices, but others liked the folk masses and vernacular liturgy recently sanctioned by the Second Vatican Council. Other Catholic and mainline Protestant youth made their way to evangelical and charismatic congregations, where lively music and born-again experiences felt compelling and vital. A statistically small number of African American youth joined countercultural religions, while others explored Islam, Black nationalism, and Black cultural movements. A majority, like their white counterparts, remained in established churches.

For all these groups, consumerism played a central role in establishing authenticity and providing self-expression. Whether wearing dashikis or granny dresses, listening to the Grateful Dead or Marvin Gaye, young people discovered that consumer products rooted them in communities of meaning and signaled their identity to outsiders. The countercultural new cool, marketed as the youth culture, ironically became a commodity-based rebellion against conformity and bourgeois values. Hippiedom was bought and sold at head shops, record stores, and Army-Navy outlets' racks of jeans and peacoats. Commodified youth culture turned the hippies' touchstones—authenticity, self-expression, and even spirituality—into merchandise.

Two streams of baby boomers had a significant impact on American Christianity. One was made up of young people who stayed in their home churches but were eager to integrate the new cool into their worship life.[9] The other included the hippies and hangers-on who fled to Haight-Ashbury, the Sunset Strip, and other youth meccas. Together, these two groups formed the basis of "one of the most significant national movements of the postwar period."[10] It started in 1965 when Ted Wise, "a dope-smoking Sausalito sail maker," found God and set out to save young stoners like himself.[11]

Within a few years, Wise and other young ministers were tending to hippies, druggies, and similarly lost souls from Cleveland to Berkeley. Underground Christian newspapers and coffeehouses attracted those whom the street preachers missed.[12] Outreaches like these succeeded because by the late 1960s, the impulse fueling the counterculture quest for enlightenment was seeking new frontiers of meaning and experience. Many young adults were ready to swap sex and drugs for an authentic religious high. The result was an individualistic, experiential, evangelistic faith, and its followers were called Jesus freaks.

Amid this flux and fervor, established evangelical leaders like Bill Bright and Billy Graham reached out to the Jesus People, an alternate name for the Jesus freaks. The "straight" leaders' imprimatur spurred local congregations to accept the scraggly strangers whose attitude and appearance seemed at odds with Middle America. Both Bright and Graham were deeply committed to youth evangelism: Bright through his Campus Crusade for Christ outreach and Graham through the Billy Graham Evangelistic Association, a parachurch ministry with a strong youth following.[13] Convinced that the Jesus People were the start of a national revival, Graham purposefully sought them out during his 1971 crusades. His enthusiasm, as well as the mainstream popularity of folk and rock music, encouraged local pastors to experiment with youth-oriented music, dress, and lingo. As they had done in the past, evangelicals adopted the modes and media of popular culture to reach their target audience. At the same time, churched teens, eager to be part of the youth-oriented zeitgeist, could remain in the fold.

Graham encouraged this convergence of Jesus People and "Jesus kids," Christian youth who liked the new cool—that is, the counterculture's material trappings. Doing his part, he signed on as honorary chairman of

FIGURE 11. Revs. Bill Bright and Billy Graham holding the Explo '72 program. Explo '72 Photos. Cru Archives, Campus Crusade for Christ, Inc. Used with permission.

Explo '72, Bill Bright's "religious Woodstock" that took place at the Dallas Cotton Bowl. Among the eighty thousand attendees were some Jesus People but many more Jesus kids eager to give old-time religion a modern spin. The *New York Times* described the meeting as "the largest and most conspicuous public outpouring thus far of the Jesus Movement, which has revived interest in fundamentalist Christianity among young people across the country."[14]

Many of the young people attending were "neatly-dressed, well-mannered high school and college students still sympathetic to middle class values."[15] They happily sat through a nine-hour rock festival and seemed equally content with the "patriotic and establishment overtones" that ran through the crusade's sermons and speeches.[16] Catching the significance of what this new group meant for the Jesus movement, a *Newsday* reporter wrote, "Most recently the movement has built along solid middle class lines. Waiting in the wings was a sizeable corps of Sunday School regulars, raised by devout Protestants to obey authority and honor America, whose fundamentalist faith previously earned them more embarrassment than respect from their peers. When some of the hippest elements started embracing their faith these more conventional Jesus people emerged proudly from their relative obscurity to join the cause."[17]

Crusades like Explo '72 and similar concert-type worship experiences brought popular culture and its youthful adherents, including future vice president Mike Pence—then a Catholic and a Democrat—into the heart of American evangelicalism. There was and would continue to be a stream of traditional religious conservatives coming through evangelical and fundamentalist seminaries, congregations, and parachurch organizations. But the inclusion of the Jesus People and outreach to the Jesus kids expanded church rolls beyond what might have been expected during this tumultuous period. The movement spread out from California, and within a few years, some observers said its greatest strength was in the Midwest.[18]

The Jesus People exemplified the expressive individualist turn of the 1960s and 1970s. Despite their of-the-moment gear, believers found comfort in a fundamentalist faith that promised eternal life and unconditional love. Predisposed to supernaturalism, their beliefs easily accommodated

FIGURE 12. Rev. Billy Graham preaching at Explo '72. Explo '72 Photos. Cru Archives, Campus Crusade for Christ, Inc. Used with permission.

the Virgin Birth and bodily resurrection as well as biblical inerrancy and an imminent Armageddon. Assured that the Second Coming was about to happen, many expected "signs and wonders," miraculous manifestations that would convince skeptics to repent. Jesus People found homes in evangelical and even fundamentalist churches as well as Pentecostal and charismatic congregations, bridging divides created by differing theologies. This unexpected mingling among Jesus People, evangelical youth, and straight churchgoers had a noteworthy outcome: doctrinal barriers that divided evangelicals and Pentecostals, Protestants and Catholics, and mainliners and evangelicals lowered, paving the way for Reagan's religious coalition in the 1980s.

Los Angeles was a particularly active recruitment center for counterculture converts. By 1970, more than one hundred Christian nightclubs and coffeehouses operated in Southern California.[19] Chuck Smith pioneered a surge of independent congregations when he started one of the most successful new churches in nearby Costa Mesa. Smith had been a minister in the Foursquare Church, a Pentecostal denomination begun by Aimee Semple McPherson, but he sidelined sectarian commitments when naming his new pastorate Calvary Chapel. In explaining the decision to become nondenominational, Smith later wrote, "You know the beautiful thing about being called Calvary Chapel? People don't know where you really stand. . . . When you're marketing something, you want the largest market appeal possible."[20] At his family's prodding. he invited what he considered to be unkempt hippies to church, and they soon brought their friends. Within a few years, Calvary Chapel had grown from several dozen to several thousand members. Teenagers also flocked to the church, since the newcomers' style reflected modern youth culture. To accommodate the rocketing membership, Smith mentored young men to start Calvary Chapels at home and abroad.

Smith's experience was not unusual; not only did Calvary Chapels take root worldwide, but similarly youth-friendly congregations spread out from Southern California, sending offshoots coast to coast. Jesus People transformed established churches with youth-oriented music, spirit-filled Pentecostal-style worship, and a commitment to evangelism. At the same time, many of these young adults were learning from the leading Christian teachers of their generation.

Francis Schaeffer, a conservative Presbyterian, had captivated many Christian youth when he toured American churches, campuses, and Bible schools in the mid-1960s. After World War II, Schaeffer had left the United States to start L'Abri, a Christian community in Switzerland. Returning home with a message aimed at young people, he preached about "infinite possibilities for human creativity by liberating the individual from naturalistic philosophy and the technocratic lifestyle that [it] had imposed upon society."[21] In other words, an increasingly technological society was stifling the creative possibilities inherent in Christianity. Schaeffer's defense of expressive individualism resonated with young adults, as did his call to ground one's actions in scripture. Authenticity meant holding on to biblical teachings even when they clashed with cultural norms and secular laws. For instance, Schaeffer was an early and ardent foe of the 1973 US Supreme Court *Roe v. Wade* decision that legalized abortion. He challenged young Christians to take up the pro-life banner as an expression of biblical morality that defied secular humanist expediency.

Hal Lindsey was similarly influential among Christian youth. During the 1960s, Lindsey worked with Campus Crusade for Christ in Southern California. Alarmed by current events, he penned *The Late, Great Planet Earth* (1970), an easy-to-read exposition of dispensationalist premillennialism, a theology predicting that the Second Coming was about to occur. Lindsey's best seller and an eponymous movie made a strong case for Christians to love Jews, support Israel, fight communism, and be ready for the Rapture, when believers would ascend bodily to heaven.

By the mid- to late 1970s, many Jesus People were swapping ribbed tees for rep ties. Approaching the age of thirty, the seemingly once and forever teens and young adults were turning into parents, professionals, and homeowners. Along with the Jesus Kids, these new suburbanites provided a membership boom for new paradigm churches, conservative congregations that highlighted cultural currency and charismatic gifts.[22] Others slipped into more mainstream evangelical congregations or prosperity churches. Still others helped build a new movement of nondenominational "seeker churches," such as Willow Creek Community Church in South Barrington, Illinois.[23]

As these ministries expanded and began addressing social and political issues, their growing membership cleaved to the right side of the burgeoning culture wars. The Jesus People and the Jesus kids had become the foot soldiers of the religious Right.[24] Their comfortable lives were filled with the material benefits they'd once rejected. But their faith was unchanged, and its conservative fervor was reflected in their allegiance to right-wing views. By the early 1980s, their ranks would be part of a loose coalition of evangelicals, conservative Catholics, Mormons, and Orthodox Jews organizing against abortion.

Over the next two decades, this generational cohort provided a groundswell of support for faith-based family values—including opposition to the Equal Rights Amendment and gay marriage as well as backing for limited government, lower taxes, Second Amendment rights, a strong military, and a "greater" Israel encompassing the territories taken in the 1967 and 1973 wars. Many of these former Jesus Freaks and Jesus kids also became ardent Reagan supporters; his religious imaginary was an expression of their own.

BUILDING THE REAGAN COALITION

After 1964, the challenge facing political newcomer Ronald Reagan was to unite diverse, conservative strands of the electorate under a common banner. Arizona senator Barry Goldwater had been the Republican Party's choice as its 1964 presidential candidate, but his nomination signaled a rift between its hard-line conservatives and the moderates who preferred New York governor Nelson Rockefeller. Republican strategists hoped to win over southern and working-class Democrats, whose party loyalty had been strained by the Kennedy and Johnson administrations' support for civil rights. Conservative southern Democrats liked Goldwater's avowal of states' rights as well as his opposition to federal legislation and executive decisions that forced desegregation on local communities. Moreover, polls showed that the white working class in the Northeast and Midwest were concerned about Blacks taking their jobs, moving into their neighborhoods, and attending their schools. Goldwater's promise not to push desegregation appealed to them too.

Hard-line conservatives never swerved in their support for the senator. Further, Goldwater's campaign slogan, "In Your Heart You Know He's Right," resonated with evangelicals, and his pledge of "extremism in the face of liberty" seemed an appropriate response to the Red Scare. Yet the hard work of his backers, including Young Americans for Freedom, church groups, and small businessmen, proved no match for press ridicule and Wall Street jitters. Nor could Goldwater compete with President Johnson's promises of lower taxes, a Great Society, and a quick victory in the Vietnam War.

Johnson's overwhelming 61 to 39 percent win at the polls may have looked like a full-throated rejection of conservatism, but true believers saw the rout more as a beginning than an end. The movement's leaders agreed that a less polarizing candidate could expand far beyond the fledgling bloc that Goldwater had built. Likewise, the movement's rank and file, their hopes whetted by the race, agreed that a better spokesman would bring more supporters to the cause. Both perceived a potential champion in Ronald Reagan, a divorced, formerly liberal Hollywood actor turned General Electric pitchman who showed an aptitude for politics. Campaigning for Goldwater, Reagan was poised and polished, projecting an easy-going warmth. His casual, relaxed manner and broad smile made the Arizona senator's positions seem less extreme to a wide audience.

Goldwater's resounding defeat was a boon for Reagan; his star was on the rise. In January 1966 at the urging of his bicoastal base, he entered the race for California's governorship, opposing incumbent governor Edmund "Pat" Brown. Reagan's bid for the top spot in Sacramento was a bellwether for the Democrats' subsequent fall from national power. His campaign positioned him as a candidate committed to the American dream but unwilling to use big government to achieve it. His message resonated with Americans eager to believe in the saving graces of hard work and self-reliance. They may have liked the idea of a "great society" that provided affordable education, a social safety net, and opportunity for all, but they worried about how to pay for it. Moreover, the tension between individual rights and communal responsibilities was an ongoing Protestant legacy, and many voters did not want social welfare benefits to increase their taxes or equal opportunity programs to jeopardize their own prospects. In this climate, conservative calls for slower, decentralized change were a welcome alternative to what seemed like costly government attempts at social engineering.

Californians liked Reagan's political message, and his religious testimony sealed the deal. For another politician without his genial, charismatic personality, Reagan's divorce, his Hollywood connections, and his history as a union president would have been deal breakers among religious conservatives. But his straightforward articulation of his born-again faith made him a viable option for all but the most die-hard fundamentalist voters. Before running for office, Reagan had joined the conservative Bel Air Presbyterian Church in Los Angeles and befriended California's evangelical leadership. In a 1967 interview after his successful gubernatorial campaign, he told the *Oakland Tribune*, "I can't conceive of anyone trying to meet the problems we face today without help from God."[25]

With a steel will sheathed in a sunny smile, Reagan's identity as a Christian cold warrior ensured his success among grassroots evangelicals, free-market enthusiasts, and Goldwater's anticommunist supporters. But this coalition might not have been enough if events leading up to the election had not convinced many California Democrats that their party's liberal agenda had failed. Social upheavals, staged first by student activists leading Berkeley's Free Speech Movement during 1964–65 and then by protesters in Watts in 1965, were vivid demonstrations of what happened when liberalism promised more than it could deliver. Many Californians were upset when Berkeley students ran amok; their demands for free speech appeared to outstrip their respect for civil society. In Watts, an altercation between the police and the local community, made desperate by poverty and unemployment, sparked six days of civil unrest that claimed thirty-four lives, cost millions in property damages, and left a lasting scar on the city's soul.

Fairly or not, incumbent governor Edmund "Pat" Brown's administration was blamed for the disturbances. During his two terms as governor, Brown championed many of the big-government solutions that defined New Deal liberalism. He tried to end racial discrimination in housing, mandate equal opportunity in employment, and make higher education available to all the state's residents. But he also ran up a large deficit. Reagan, campaigning for fiscal responsibility, law and order, and traditional values, beat Brown in a solid victory, which was mirrored in several national races that year. Democrats still controlled Congress, but in 1966 Republicans "gained 47 House seats, three Senate seats, eight governorships, and 557 state legislative seats."[26] Republican wins in the South presaged the strategy that would help the GOP capture five of the next six presidential elections. The Democrats would remain in power for another two years, but Johnson's dream of the Great Society was over.

After eight years in Sacramento, Reagan's next challenge was to take the coalition strategy that had worked in California and build it into a national platform for a presidential run. Religious voters were key. A network of clergy, evangelical educators, parachurch ministries, and Christian anticommunist groups connected Southern California's conservative churchgoers with like-minded believers across the South. In the emergent Sun Belt, the swath of states from Florida to the West Coast, Southern California's evangelicals held a preeminent place, set apart by their wealth and activism. As early as the 1950s, Los Angeles–area evangelicals had been engaged in local politics, a step that many of their coreligionists would forego for another two decades. Accustomed to cultural quiescence, some Sun Belt evangelicals focused on the hereafter rather than the here and now. Others, living close to the poverty line, had little time for activities beyond basic survival. But Californians' prosperity made it possible to organize for civic change. Moreover, West Coast evangelicals did not cling to custom in the same way their coreligionists did elsewhere. Californians were constantly reinventing themselves, and the state's evangelicals were no different.

Among these reinventions was a willingness to collaborate with those who did not share their exact same beliefs. In the 1960s and early 1970s, interreligious coalition building was suspect among white evangelicals in other regions. But Californians saw the benefit of building partnerships around common problems. Whether it was opposing secularism in the public schools, communists at the UN, or sexual permissiveness in the media, evangelicals organized alongside Roman Catholics and Black Protestants when it was expedient. Many California evangelicals also accepted support from members of the new charismatic movement that began in 1960 at a Van Nuys Episcopal church. The movement swept through Catholic and mainline churches, attracting evangelicals whose congregations did not tolerate spiritual gifts such as speaking in tongues and faith healing.

Evangelical leaders such as Billy Graham, George Benson, and Jerry Falwell were frequent visitors to the Golden State. By delivering news and encouragement across the Sun Belt, they strengthened regional networks of religious faith and social activism. As mentioned above, Graham's willingness to embrace the Jesus People heralded a rising generation of young leaders. Even if they did church differently from their parents, they shared their elders' faith in democracy, freedom, and capitalism. Their political influence would only grow.

The years between the late 1960s and the mid-1980s were key for the emergence of a new conservative movement. One strand, neoconservatism, argued that the United States needed a strong military and an aggressive foreign policy. This militant internationalist focus would have been anathema to an earlier generation of conservatives, whose ideological predilection was a unilateral libertarianism. But neoconservatives, many of whom were Jews and previously liberal, were aligned with conservativism's shifting focus, particularly the growing importance of the evangelicals' worldview. Many Protestant conservatives, casting the Soviet Union as the Antichrist's wingman, anticipated an imminent end-time scenario. Central to the plot was the recently established state of Israel, which evangelicals saw as a divine sign that the end was near. Their Zionism converged with that of many American Jews, and while most neoconservatives rejected evangelical theology, they welcomed Christian support for the Jewish state.

Another strand in the new political alignment comprised economic and free-market conservatives who had been appalled by what they perceived as Roosevelt's Bolshevik agenda. During and after his presidency, their campaigns touted free enterprise and critiqued the New Deal, arguing that business was better positioned than the federal government to aid citizens. Some who backed these efforts embodied the interlocking strands of business, politics, and religion. The Pew brothers, who donated millions to bring others into the conservative fold, epitomized this nexus. In the early twentieth century their father, Joseph Newton Pew, rose from tilling the family farm to heading Sun Oil Company. A devout Presbyterian and staunch Republican, the Pew paterfamilias taught his children to esteem hard work, self-reliance, and their evangelical faith. His sons, Joseph Jr. and J. Howard, inherited not only his company but also his religious compass. J. Howard, the more activist of the two brothers, donated to mainstream conservative institutions such as the Republican Party, Grove City College, and *Christianity Today*. But he also contributed to right-wing groups, including the John Birch Society; the Christian Freedom Foundation, which sought to Christianize the United States; and the Presbyterian Lay Committee, a fundamentalist caucus within the Presbyterian Church.

Nonevangelicals made up a third strand of mid-twentieth-century conservatism. Apprehending the importance of a robust right-wing intelligentsia, William J. Baroody Sr. helped shape the American Enterprise Institute into a preeminent think tank for policy and strategy during the 1950s and 1960s. In 1955, William F. Buckley Jr. founded the *National Review*, a magazine that would serve as an intellectual hub for the growing conservative movement.[27] Baroody and Buckley were Roman Catholics, but both found allies among evangelicals, signaling a retreat from conservative Protestants' long-standing hostility to so-called papists. The new alliance further isolated fundamentalists, who distrusted Catholics and whose inability to form political coalitions with members of other religions doomed their efficacy until Jerry Falwell's Moral Majority provided a big tent for Jewish and Christian right-wingers.

Anti-Catholicism had been axiomatic for evangelicals, fundamentalists, and even some Protestant mainliners, who viewed the pope and his church's theology as a threat to soul competency, the belief that each individual alone is accountable to God. These Protestants also believed that the hierarchal and centralized Catholic Church was incompatible with democracy and a free-market economy. But in the postwar era, Catholic and evangelical conservatives found common cause in their shared commitments to biblically based morality, anticommunism, free markets, and divine sovereignty over worldly affairs. Orthodox Jews who shared a similar outlook also found a place in the conservative movement. At the very time that Will Herberg was explicating the "triple melting pot" that blended America's Protestants, Catholics, and Jews into civically productive and interconnected social groups, alliances between conservatives within these faith traditions were seeking ways to renew civil society through religious interventions.[28]

Buckley's vision of elite, top-down conservative influence was as crucial to the emerging right-wing consensus as grassroots movement building had been in the 1930s and 1940s. Conservative ideas spread through church bulletins and farm magazines and discussed in Bible studies and community forums had nurtured local networks of pastors and working people.

By the 1950s, these alliances had united against communism and for small government and market capitalism. Emboldened by America's global stature, some groups waged local campaigns, such as the Los Angeles–area parents who protested public school education that, in their view, was "too soft on Communism."[29] Others supported regional institutions that nurtured local leaders. In Searcy, Arkansas, George Benson, president of Harding University, developed a curriculum to train the next generation of Christian businessmen. The model attracted national support and replication, and it played an important role in modeling Christian entrepreneurialism and corporate anticommunism for capitalists of Walmart founder Sam Walton's generation.[30]

Although there were overlaps among political, economic, and religious conservatives, their agendas did not always coincide. When they made common cause in the late 1970s, each wanted to preserve core principles. Evangelicals needed assurance that the movement centered on God. Their goal was to translate the divine plan into legislation and social policy that ended abortion, strengthened families, and returned prayer to public schools, among other issues. But rank-and-file religious conservatives were predominantly white Protestants, and their leaders knew that their movement needed a wider base. They needed Roman Catholics, Orthodox Jews, and nonwhite evangelicals with a similar worldview. Members of these groups, similar to white evangelicals, viewed conservatives' political and economic aims in a religious frame.

Evangelical Christianity, emphasizing the individual's relationship with Jesus and the need to personally experience salvation, provided a template for the importance of individualism and individual rights. The only brake on individual freedom was violating (selective) biblical precepts, which was why—in their reading of scriptural verses such as "Before I formed you in the womb, I knew you" (Jer. 1:4–5)—abortion was wrong. Conservative Protestants rallied like-minded members of other faiths who agreed that the sanctity of each person demanded an end to abortion. By trading theological specificity for a shared acknowledgment of biblical truth and an effective social movement, conservatives across the religious spectrum joined forces.

As evangelicals flexed their political muscle on the economy and the importance of fighting communism, they also took strong stands on hot-button social issues, initiating what became known as culture wars.[31] As we saw in the previous chapter, between 1960 and 1980, cultural changes shook centuries-old notions of gender authority. The birth control pill revolutionized women's relationship to their bodies, ending the link between procreation and recreational sex. Women could pursue careers and make

FIGURE 13. Right to Life protests in front of the White House and the Capitol on January 23, 1978. Courtesy of the Library of Congress.

their own decisions on whether or when to start a family. Conservative Christians, alarmed by this prospect, organized in support of traditional gender and family norms, and by the late 1970s abortion, homosexuality, and feminism had become lightning-rod issues. Under the banner of family values, religious leaders and local conservative activists launched campaigns against the Equal Rights Amendment, Planned Parenthood, and gay rights. In defense of Christianity, they promoted their own religious values, and their campaigns became battles in a culture war covered fervently by the news media. These right-wing beliefs, along with the social and political principles of neoconservatives, libertarians, and Buckley conservatives, would successfully mesh with Reagan's religious imaginary.

ESTABLISHING REAGAN'S RELIGIOUS IMAGINARY

A religious imaginary expresses a commonsensical, collective understanding of what matters and why. It accomplishes this by integrating metaphysical truths, ethical norms, and civic virtues into the core convictions and salient images defining a good citizen and a good society. In turn, these notions are expressed as a lived religion, the ways in which people enact ultimate concerns in their daily activities. These can range from preparing a Sabbath meal to confronting a cyberbully to participating in a Bible study group to voting. Daily activities both reflect and strengthen a religious imaginary; engaging in the activity reinforces the conviction, and the conviction gives meaning to the activity.[32]

During the Reagan era, the specifics of the nation's predominant religious imaginary shifted. Rooted in white Protestantism, the imaginary stipulates that America is special to God. Although other religious imaginaries reflect the theology and worldview of their faith groups' relationship to the United States, the social, cultural, and political dominance of white Protestantism gives its imaginary preeminence. That's why Catholics, Jews, Hindus, Buddhists, Muslims, and even nonbelievers can have their own religious worldview yet also accept the confluence of religion, politics, and economics that defines the white Protestant imaginary.

Reagan did not set out to shift the religious imaginary; the very term likely would have puzzled him. But his core convictions, which contrasted with the principles that had guided the country since Franklin D. Roosevelt's New Deal, resonated with many Americans. Reagan put their fears, hopes, and desires into words. Those words, circulated by the news media, became tangible, and their expression—in everyday life as well as in governmental policies—altered how many Americans understood their civic identity and personal responsibilities. Reviving the conservative vision of Barry Goldwater's 1964 presidential campaign, Reagan called for less government and more individual accountability. Once elected, he converted these ideas into neoliberal policies. Ideologically, neoliberalism was a departure from the welfare liberalism espoused by Democrats since Roosevelt's New Deal. Both ideologies support individual liberty and freedom, but the latter accepts restraints, such as regulations on business and a strong central government, to ensure the greatest good for the greatest number of citizens. Neoliberalism, in the name of maximizing individual freedom, advocates limited federal power and an unfettered marketplace, without concern for the greatest good for the greatest number of citizens.

As a lived religion, or set of everyday practices for meaning making, neoliberalism is expressed through the logic and practices of the market. Under Reagan, these political and economic practices overlapped with expanding segments of American religion—specifically, conservative evangelicalism and the prosperity gospel.[33] Decades before Reagan's election, conservative Christian pastors and businessmen had asserted the connections among democracy, Christianity, and capitalism.[34] Now the American president was singing the same tune while the news media circulated the lyrics.

The Reaganite religious imaginary rested on two convictions that were part of a conservative Protestant worldview: America is an exceptional country because it is God's chosen nation, and God wants Americans to be free. The former validated America's role as a world leader, and the latter confirmed the sanctity of the individual, made in God's image, as a free agent. Over the centuries, successive generations shaped the divine covenant to reflect and to be reflected in the political and social currents of their day. Specifically, the Protestant religious imaginary has moved between poles of collective responsibility and of self-reliance. While the fundamentals of American identity remain the same—godly people doing God's work in God's country—public opinion and government policy mirrored changing perspectives on the philosophical and practical framework of a good and godly society. The Protestant imaginary, the shared framework for this virtuous society, has been communicated through news and entertainment media, textbooks and sermons, laws and legal rulings. It is embedded in daily life and manifested in everyday decisions ranging from hanging the flag on the Fourth of July, to promoting or opposing school prayer, to sending care packages to troops overseas.

Reagan and his supporters believed that America had lost its way: a bloated federal bureaucracy inhibited political freedom; an expanding welfare state choked the economy; government entitlements thwarted individual accountability; and secular humanism suppressed religion's role in public life. Left unchecked, these trends would lead to communism, according to the Reaganites. In their view, a new paradigm was needed to secure Americans' material freedom and to safeguard their spiritual well-being. Even as they acknowledged their country's distinctiveness, Reaganites were less concerned with its citizens' collective welfare than with the individual's ability to live as freely as possible. This notion of self-reliance, based in equal parts on an Emersonian belief in the sanctity and integrity of the individual and on the Protestant conviction of "the priesthood of all believers," lies at the heart of the Reagan-era religious imaginary. Its highest expression was the formation of virtuous citizen-consumers, each in God's image, participating in a democracy that sustains free markets and unregulated capitalism. Reagan expressed this worldview in the idiom of evangelical Protestantism, but his emphasis on personal freedom and economic gain attracted Christians across the theological spectrum as well as members of other faiths and even nonbelievers.

The linkage of political, economic, and religious allegiances is a long-standing American trope. The Jacksonian era's commitment to political democracy, individual salvation, and an imminent Kingdom of God, the Gilded Age's fascination with Andrew Carnegie's philanthropic beliefs outlined in his essay "The Gospel of Wealth," and the Progressives' articulation of the Social Gospel all expressed Americans' desire to align their civic project with a higher calling. In the 1970s, the vision inspired by the Social

Gospel and enacted through the welfare state and plans for the Great Society succumbed to the Vietnam War, economic decline, political scandal, and social upheaval. But in the next decade, Reagan linked spiritual values to economic success, social stability, and military strength. In a religiously diverse yet secular society, the new formulation was both more and less explicitly Christian than earlier iterations. Reagan put evangelical particularism in service to universal goals, speaking directly to religious conservatives with a message that also held wide appeal. Evangelicals heard a message of faith-based politics, but nonevangelicals heard a candidate promise to "make America great."

The success of Reagan's Protestant imaginary depended on its spread through tabloids and magazines, and its reiteration on large screens and small. It was voiced in bingo halls and book clubs, in schoolrooms and boardrooms, and in churches and civic groups. Reagan spoke in an evangelical Christian register, but his message of free people living in an exceptional nation resonated with many Americans. The religious imaginary embraced core evangelical tenets, but it also spoke to men and women who cared more about money and markets than about school prayer or safeguarding traditional families. And as it penetrated newsrooms from the 1980s on, the imaginary became central to many of the stories that explained and organized everyday life.

In the predigital era, reading the morning newspaper—or listening to a morning radio or television show—was a secular ritual. Repeated daily, it oriented news consumers to their world. By telling them what they needed to know, news outlets defined and structured a collective reality, creating "imagined communities"—masses of people who, though they might never meet, were nevertheless connected by shared narratives of what mattered and why.[35]

Leaders seek to rally these imagined communities, and Reagan excelled at it. Once he had access to the mainstream press, his deeply felt assumptions about meaning, purpose, and identity—that is, his religious imaginary—were woven into the news. Tweaking public opinion by normalizing these narratives, the media played a role in the rise of the religious Right, the emergence of a "new" patriotism, and an ambivalent recognition that "greed is good," the mantra of Gordon Gekko, the rapacious investor in the 1987 movie *Wall Street*. By helping set the nation's vision and values, Reagan's Protestant imaginary, relayed by the media, shaped the lived religion of the American people.

I have posited a Protestant religious imaginary that alternates between two poles. During the twentieth century, one of these gave rise to a Social Gospel–inflected welfare state, while the other culminated in a spiritualized neoliberalism. Just as the Social Gospel, a product of liberal Protestantism, had provided a religious frame for the New Deal and the subsequent rise of the welfare state, so conservative evangelicalism supplied a vocabulary and worldview for neoliberalism. During the Reagan era, conservative white evangelicals seized the cultural moment, obscuring the political moderation and social progressivism of other white and many Black coreligionists. As a result, *evangelical* became a synonym for white conservatives committed to having their religious beliefs dominate the public square and determine public policy. The story of why and how this happened hinges on the connections among the baby boomers' spiritual seeking, a new kind of evangelicalism, the Reagan-era religious imaginary, the rise of evangelical mass media, and the mainstream news media.

EVANGELICAL MEDIA AND THE RELIGIOUS IMAGINARY

Media is central to religion, key to teaching and disseminating its message. For Christians, tasked with spreading the "good news" that God saves sinners, media is paramount—starting with Paul's First Letter to the Thessalonians and continuing to the Trinity Broadcasting Network, which in 2022 deployed seventy satellites worldwide. In between Paul's epistles and a global satellite network, American evangelicals embraced each technological innovation as it arose: printing unprecedented numbers of Bibles and tracts in the 1820s, making religious movies in the 1890s, pioneering Christian radio in the 1920s, turning to television in the 1950s, and moving online in the 1990s.[36]

American evangelicals' primary message is salvation through Jesus, and they understand that some political ideologies are more amenable to religion than others. In the 1920s and 1930s, many conservative Christians found common cause with business moguls who shared their antipathy to and fear of communism. After the 1917 Russian Revolution and the subsequent establishment of a communist regime, many Americans considered the Soviet republic a threat to democracy, capitalism, and religion. Corporate leaders and conservative Christians agreed that a communist takeover would lead to the shuttering of American churches and an end to free markets. In 1933, when President Franklin D. Roosevelt rolled out the New Deal, many conservatives believed that the Red takeover had begun. Christians, often funded by captains of industry, used whatever means possible—magazines, church bulletins, and radio programs—to broadcast their alarm. Communism was a multifaceted assault on America's divine blessing of freedom, and from the 1920s on, Christian conservatives used pulpit, print, and radio to get that message out.

The message was louder in some media than in others. Radio ministries, wary of provoking a backlash against extremism, were most circumspect. In the 1930s, Father Charles Coughlin, a Roman Catholic priest, broadcast inflammatory rants praising fascists and denouncing Jews. Concerned about his influence on thirty million listeners, the Catholic hierarchy, the National Association of Broadcasters, and the federal government all took steps to end his radio show. Their success was not lost on other religious broadcasters, who throughout the 1940s were patriotic but, unlike Coughlin, neither overtly political nor rabidly polemical. That changed when Carl McIntyre, a well-known fundamentalist firebrand, launched *The Twentieth Century Reformation Hour* in 1955. McIntyre believed that Christians were called to be politically active. An able propagandist, he started a Christian newspaper in 1936 and promoted networking among like-minded clergy and laity through nationwide councils and conferences. Radio provided him with the widest platform to preach on the evils of communism and the welfare state and on the merits of free-market capitalism and a strong American military. McIntyre had an audience of twenty million when his partisan right-wing views were challenged under the Federal Communications Commission's Fairness Doctrine. He lost the fight and forfeited his radio license, but he continued to distribute his program.[37]

In the 1950s, when televisions began appearing in American households, religious broadcasting was part of the mix. Evangelicals had to pay for airtime, while mainline Protestant denominations were given free access for "public service" educational and inspirational programming. But as the new medium became more popular and financially profitable, federal rules on public service programming changed. Networks opted to sell time to religious groups rather than give it away. Fundamentalists and evangelicals, already raising money as part of their programming, eagerly bought airtime. Later, when cable television provided new possibilities for reaching a national audience, conservative Christians were early adopters. In 1976, Ted Turner's superstation, Cable News Network (CNN), was the first to use satellite technology, which allowed it to broadcast nationwide. A year later, Pat Robertson's Christian Broadcast Network became the second. That same year, evangelicals were responsible for 92 percent of religious television programming.[38] By the early 1980s, there were more than 220 religious television stations and three round-the-clock Christian networks.[39] While many of these were focused on worship, preaching, and Bible study, their message also included commentary on the issues of the day, including the (submissive) role of women, homosexuality, and legalized abortion.

Two teleministries were especially successful at building their audiences and using donor support to start auxiliary political organizations.[40] (Christian Voice, a third group formed at the time, did not achieve as much visibility as the other two.) The Moral Majority and the Christian Coalition, launched by Jerry Falwell and Pat Robertson, respectively, became hubs for the religious Right. Both men felt strongly about the social and political implications of Christian faith. Several other televangelists, while not as consistently partisan, also were clear about their opposition to abortion, homosexuality, and feminism as well as their support for traditional families, prayer in school, a strong military, and Israel's security. In 1980, electing Reagan as president became a religious crusade for many televangelists. After the election, pollsters were split on whether the evangelical vote was determinative, but leaders of the religious Right insisted that their followers had swayed the results.

The question of the televangelists' influence was linked to another unreliable statistic: just how big was the audience for televangelism? Jerry Falwell claimed that his program attracted twenty-five million viewers, and a 1981 Gallup survey indicated that as many as seventy-one million Americans had watched religious programming over the course of one week.[41] But scholars and religious moderates contended that actual viewership was significantly lower and that evangelicals' impact on the 1980 election was not decisive.

In 1980, the Ad Hoc Committee on Religious Television Research, which included a wide range of religious organizations, decided to get the facts. They commissioned scholars at the University of Pennsylvania's Annenberg School of Communication and pollsters from the Gallup Organization to survey the audience for televangelism. The researchers discovered that the audience was "far smaller" (between seven million and nine million watching fifteen minutes or more per week) than televangelists claimed and that programming tended to reinforce existing beliefs rather than convert viewers to new ones.

A striking finding was the existence of two distinct television audiences. Those watching religious television were more "conservative and restrictive," while the audience for mainstream programming was "politically moderate." The two groups rarely saw each other's shows, and the study's authors noted the growing chasm between them. Viewers of religious programming disliked mainstream television because of its positive depictions of secular values, and since they consciously avoided watching it, conservative Christians were immune to its effect on "values, attitudes and behavior."[42] The two groups were being socialized differently, but the study's authors did not speculate on what this polarization signified or where it could lead.

Years before Ronald Reagan dreamed of being president, fundamentalist and evangelical media had circulated a religious imaginary similar to his own. Tens of millions of Americans who read Christian newspapers, listened to Christian radio, and watched Christian television knew that God blessed America with freedom. They also knew that God wanted traditional patriarchal families, limited government, free markets, a strong Israel, and an end to government interference in religion. But even as popular Christian media spread the message among rank-and-file churchgoers, a new cadre of religious leaders were mounting a campaign to bring their message to the entire nation.

The story of how Billy Graham, Harold Ockenga, and Carl Henry, among others, built institutions that brought evangelicals into the political and cultural mainstream is well known in Christian circles. In fact, the tale is more complicated than the conventional narrative of religious hardliners who, after several decades of political quiescence and sectarian institution building, decided to participate in the culture at large. Many fundamentalists, for instance Carl McIntyre, had been outspoken about religion and politics since the 1930s. But beginning in the late 1940s, a group of younger men, more irenic and pragmatic than McIntyre, founded key organizations to spur conversations with religious moderates as well as the general public. Chief among these institutions were a religious network, a professional association, a seminary, and a magazine—specifically, the National Association of Evangelicals, the National Religious Broadcasters, Fuller Theological Seminary, and *Christianity Today*.

Billy Graham envisioned *Christianity Today* as the evangelical counterpart to the *Christian Century*, the weekly flagship publication for mainline Christians. Just as the *Century* helped shape the theological worldview of its readership—influential clergy and lay leaders who set the tone for Protestant engagement with the secular world—so *Christianity Today* would establish the voice and priorities for a new generation of evangelical leadership. Graham and his fellow founders, including his father-in-law Nelson Bell and Harold Ockenga, had ambitious goals for the publication. They wanted to legitimate evangelicalism, establish a conservative Christian power base, and shape the future of the nation. In this last goal, they were joined by men like J. Howard Pew, the conservative businessman who, retired from the helm of Sun Oil, was committed to curbing the leftward drift of the nation's churches and government.

Pew rarely intervened in *Christianity Today*'s editorial decisions, because its editors shared his estimation of faith, freedom, and free enterprise. When Graham initially sought Pew's backing, he had told him, "[CT] is the greatest possible investment an American businessman can make in the Kingdom of God at this moment."[43] Graham's prediction appeared to come true. In its first year, the magazine's circulation rose to 120,000—significantly higher than the *Christian Century*'s base of 40,000. Like the *Century*, most of *Christianity Today*'s readers were clergy and lay elite. They were keen on applying evangelical principles for the betterment of society: criticizing labor unions and the welfare system, and praising limited government and free enterprise. Communism was a perennial target, and years before the Moral Majority's embrace of family values, the magazine extolled heterosexual marriage, male headship, and chastity outside marriage.

Christianity Today played a significant role in the evangelical media ecosystem. In the same way that radio preachers and televangelists reached millions of Christians, the weekly periodical targeted conservative religious leaders, especially congregational ministers. Behind the various outlets' affirmation of individual freedom, best expressed through democracy, capitalism, and religious liberty, was a shared understanding that America is an exceptional country because it is God's chosen nation. This was the core message of Reagan's religious imaginary, which posited a covenant between God and his chosen people that grants the divine gift of freedom in exchange for the establishment of a good and godly society. Of course, the specifics of a good and godly society shift over time, shaping and shaped by the social, political, and economic currents of each era. In the late twentieth century, such a shift occurred when America's manufacturing-based national economy gave way to a global, high-tech service economy. The social contract that for more than a generation presumed that a good society took care of its people—an idea that religious and political conservatives had attacked for decades—became suspect to many whose material security was threatened by job loss and inflation and whose sense of cultural superiority was challenged by social upheavals.

Reagan did not formulate a new religious imaginary. In fact, his core convictions echoed the same worldview that religious conservatives had held for decades. But when he became president, his faith in this religious imaginary had a significant impact on the nation. Invoking his worldview in speeches and interviews, it was normalized through subsequent news narratives. These stories rarely noted the religious convictions that shaped Reagan's perspective. But those familiar with the conservative Christian worldview that linked God's blessing to individual responsibility agreed with the president on the importance of welfare reform, US military dominance, and traditional family values. For decades, the religious imaginary that Reagan mainstreamed through the secular news media had circulated through right-wing corporate, political, educational, and religious media. But Reagan and his team packaged it in images and language that outsiders could understand and affirm, even as religious conservatives heard the message differently.

PART TWO

Reporting Reagan's Imaginary

CHAPTER FOUR

Evil Empires

Communism and AIDS

An America that is militarily and economically strong is not enough. The world must see an America that is morally strong with a creed and a vision. This is what has led us to dare and achieve. For us, values count.

PRESIDENT RONALD REAGAN, New York City, December 12, 1983

The 1983 theme for the annual Tournament of Roses Parade in Pasadena, California, was "Rejoice," and several floats used religious motifs for their tableaux. A giant Jesus won the award for best thematic representation, and "The Arrival of Rebekah," with scantily clad male "slaves" accompanying the biblical heroine as she met her bridegroom, was a spectator favorite. A floral representation of Saint George slaying the dragon won the award for the most beautiful float, and for millions of viewers watching nationwide, the saint's triumph was a hopeful sign that their adversities might be vanquished too.[1]

But the real dragon that needed slaying that January morning was not a mythological fire-breathing monster but the threat of financial disaster. According to the *Los Angeles Times*, California was experiencing "its worst series of economic setbacks in four decades": layoffs devastated not only statewide construction and manufacturing but also the high-tech and service industries, including the once-booming aerospace sector.[2] Agriculture, California's biggest industry, was likewise beset by problems that included falling prices, tumbling exports, and bad weather. The only economic metric on a steady rise was unemployment, which some economists predicted could climb to 12 percent. Neither the economists nor the state's hard-pressed citizens saw reasons for hope. Still, as bad as it was in California, much of the United States was in even worse shape. The nation's gross national product had fallen by almost 02.5 percent in 1982, the largest drop-off in the postwar era.[3] Housing starts were at their lowest since 1946,[4] and twelve million people were out of work—the unemployment rate hovered at 10.4 percent.[5]

Parade Grand Marshal Merlin Olsen, a football star turned actor and sports broadcaster, may have had these statistics in mind when he told a *Los Angeles Times* reporter that "Rejoice" was the right message for this New Year's Day pageant. "For many people watching, 1982 was a year they want to put behind them," he said. "It's important to start this year with fresh dreams and enthusiasm."[6]

President Ronald Reagan could not have said it better. Two years into his first term, he needed Americans to believe in a bright future, but even his silver-screen smile could not chase the dark clouds cast by the recession. By mid-January, his job approval rating would fall to 35 percent, an all-time low.[7] His proposals to cut income taxes and social spending while tightening the money supply and increasing the military budget had not produced the positive results he had predicted. In fact, the economy was so bad and Reagan's image so tarnished that the president's advisors were desperate to provide a compelling case for his continued leadership.

Reagan, with help from his proxies, would make that case in speeches and interviews throughout the year, grafting his vision of America's role and mission onto current events and making it central to the year's news stories. In his capacity as newsmaker-in-chief, his message was broadcast every time reporters quoted or paraphrased him, every time editorial writers panned or praised him, and every time columnists debated his plans and policies. Through repetition, Reagan's vision, his version of a religious imaginary, was mainstreamed. But the vision would only take hold—that is, a majority of Americans would accept or at least accede to it—if his proposals appeared to work. By the end of 1983, that seemed to be the case: the economy had turned around and the United States had improved its international standing. For the first time in more than a decade, many citizens felt that their lives were getting better and that the country was on the right track. Feeling more secure than they had since the 1960s, white Americans in particular judged the Reagan Revolution to be a success.

At the heart of that revolution was the president's vision of America's global role. He believed that good, in a religious sense, was embodied by the United States, a country that God had blessed with freedom. Evil was manifested by the Soviet Union, a regime that suppressed freedom. Reagan's certainty of a cosmic clash between these worldviews led him to introduce religiously tinged terms into what had previously been the mainstream's largely secular sociopolitical debate. By pitting the "good" United States against the "evil" Soviet Union, Reagan transformed a political conflict into a religious crusade. With mounting Manichaean fervor, his allies from the religious Right likewise cast public health concerns about the AIDS epidemic as a confrontation with domestic evil. Their decisions about the language and framing of the issue helped contextualize social and political problems as moral choices at the heart of a divine plan. Subsequent coverage repeated this language and framing, amplifying religious and moral perspectives through sourcing, story organization, and writing style, particularly evident in the overheated prose favored by newsmagazines.

Establishing baseline good and evil was fundamental to Reagan's rebooted religious imaginary. A black-and-white worldview appealed to Americans weary of the ethical gradations of gray, which had proliferated since the 1960s. Structural changes spurred by an increasingly global high-tech and service economy would have been difficult to navigate at the best of times. Now, after ten years of international setbacks and domestic instability, the center no longer held. The worldview favoring big government, Keynesian economics, and religious moderation that had dominated the decades from FDR to LBJ seemed tapped out. Reagan seized this opportunity to prioritize individual freedom over the common good, Christian conservatism rather than religious moderation, and clear notions of good and evil instead of the gray areas of moral relativism.

These principles were familiar to many white evangelicals. As the previous chapter demonstrated, religious leaders and conservative businessmen had long used Christian media to commend the merits of limited government and a free-market economy to farmers, workers, and other laypeople. After World War II, growing numbers of Christian media outlets featured not only sermons and inspirational stories but also religious slants on news and public policy. Ideas fundamental to the Reaganite imaginary freedom, personal responsibility, and American exceptionalism—suffused broadcasts and publications. These same outlets portrayed communism as the embodiment of evil, with its all-powerful state, centralized economy, and prohibition on religion.

As this chapter will explain, Reagan's integration of secular news narratives and evangelical media messages gave additional dynamism to a religious imaginary in which moral issues shaped political, economic, and social policies. That this moral stance accompanied policies that enhanced the nation's economy made it palatable even for voters who disagreed with Reagan's vision.

COURTING EVANGELICALS

Modern presidents, at least since Franklin D. Roosevelt, have drawn on religious imagery, language, and themes to promote their agendas.[8] But most drew on a generic, mainline Protestantism that presumed all forms of religion—particularly Protestantism, Catholicism, and Judaism—were equally good. Eisenhower famously exemplified this inclusivity when he said, "Our form of government has no sense unless it is founded in a deeply felt religious faith, and I don't care what it is."[9] Religion and patriotism were two sides of the American coin, as Eisenhower demonstrated when he signed bills adding "under God" to the Pledge of Allegiance and "In God We Trust" to the currency, and a steadfast public religiosity distinguished the United States from other Western countries. But early in his presidential campaign, Reagan signaled his support for a particular religious group with a specific political agenda. Drawing on the "Southern strategy" that had boosted Nixon's 1972 reelection campaign, Reagan targeted white Christians below the Mason-Dixon line. His first campaign stop after securing the GOP nomination was the Neshoba, Mississippi, County Fair, seven miles from where three civil rights activists had been slain just sixteen years earlier. To balance the scales, Reagan followed that trip with visits to African American communities in the North. But a few weeks later, the candidate was in Dallas directly appealing to fifteen thousand mostly white religious conservatives. "I know you can't endorse me," he told them, the Reverend Jerry Falwell onstage with him. "But I want you to know that I endorse you and what you are doing."[10]

In the early 1980s, reporters at major metropolitan newspapers introduced readers to this new cadre of political "crusaders." In the third installment of a four-part series on the rise of "ultraconservative evangelical Christians," Dudley Clendinen, the *New York Times*' Atlanta bureau chief, ascribed the group's ascendancy to the influence of southern television evangelists (also called televangelists), such as Jerry Falwell and Pat Robertson, in league with Beltway conservatives.[11] The latter group, including political operatives Richard Viguerie, Paul Weyrich, and Edward McAteer, previously campaigned to protect tax exemptions for segregated Christian schools. In addition, they linked free enterprise to Christianity, but their current "pro-family" agenda centered on registering religious voters offended by "abortion on demand," homosexuality, and the ban on prayer in public schools.

Reagan and Falwell had a particularly deep history and many shared commitments. By the late 1970s, Falwell was stumping cross country for a variety of conservative causes, including Dade County, Florida, to support entertainer Anita Bryant's campaign against gay rights. During frequent trips to Southern California, where he copastored a church in Orange County, Falwell advocated for a strong Israel and strengthening ties with Christian Zionists. And in 1979, with a small push from Weyrich and other Beltway conservatives, he started the Moral Majority, a grassroots coalition for religious conservatives who wanted their faith to influence government policies and public life. The organization was similar to Christian Voice, a California-based group begun a year earlier. Both welcomed members—including Protestants, Roman Catholics, Mormons, Jews, and even libertarian atheists—who were historically suspicious of each other if not openly hostile. The Moral Majority stressed the commonalities among these disaffected Americans, tapping into widespread discontent over what they perceived to be the rise of secular humanism and the diminution of religious values. The organization sought to educate and organize members concerning political matters, particularly "culture war" issues: abortion, homosexuality, and family values. Although not explicitly stated, the movement also upheld the cultural supremacy of white Christians and of male headship, or biblically sanctioned patriarchy.

The new movement grew rapidly. Within its first year, it had raised $1.5 million and recruited two million members.[12] Since it was tax exempt, the Moral Majority could not endorse candidates, but it could encourage churches to sponsor voter registration, disseminate voting guides, and discuss issues. Planting chapters nationwide, the Moral Majority may have had as many as six million members at its height by the early 1980s. In 1980, when Reagan asked Falwell for help with his presidential campaign, the Virginia fundamentalist lent Robert Billings, the Moral Majority's executive director, to the effort. Falwell also hosted the candidate in Lynchburg, his ministry's headquarters, and used his television program to promote Republican issues and exhort supporters to register new voters. Reagan received 61 percent of the evangelical vote in 1980, up from the 50 percent that Gerald Ford received in 1976.[13] Yet even at the time, some observers questioned the evangelical impact on Reagan's 1980 win. For example, the Moral Majority claimed it brought in four million votes for Reagan that year, but pollsters and pundits at the time put the number closer to two million.[14]

Falwell's identification with Reagan helped the preacher's standing with the press.[15] Reporters who watched Reagan woo the Christian Right coalition and its leaders saw Falwell as first among equals, and his invitation to the White House just two days after the inauguration confirmed their speculation. The meeting between the president, Falwell, and several other pastors occurred on the eighth anniversary of the *Roe v. Wade* Supreme

Court decision. In the two years following that meeting, Falwell would emerge as the religious Right's preeminent spokesman, heading a movement whose standing had risen because of its purported political leverage and its leaders' ties to the president. Falwell's grassroots movement, television ministry, and links to the White House positioned him to be a formidable political influence, but he succeeded because he understood power, politics, and the news media. Reporters wanted colorful quotes, and politicians needed surrogates who knew when to punch and when to parry. Just as Reagan used Falwell to bolster his religious bona fides, so, too, the minister used the president to signal his political clout. Their mutual interests and shared narrative, a forceful articulation of God's role in national affairs, made their overlapping religious imaginaries a staple of the mainstream press.

Through his associations with Falwell and other highly visible religious leaders, Reagan courted conservative white evangelicals during the 1980 campaign.[16] Repeatedly asked about "family issues," his answers left "conservative activists secure in their feeling that he [was] one of them." In addition to supporting the pro-life position and tuition tax credits for Christian schools, the candidate routinely lamented "the erosion of the American family,"[17] noting that prayers were forbidden in public schools, but sex education was authorized. Even worse, minors could seek abortions without parental consent. Some journalists implied that Reagan, ever the actor, was playing to the crowd, but others recalled religious allusions earlier in his political career. For example, covering Reagan's unsuccessful bid for the 1976 Republican presidential nomination, *Washington Post* reporter Paul Hendrickson wrote that the candidate described his grief-stricken supporters as "Americans . . . who wanted Washington to be a 'shining city on a hill.'" Later, recollecting his concession speech, Reagan said, "They were just standing there, thousands of them. With tears streaming down their faces. And . . . I couldn't bear the thought of them going out of that hotel so unhappy and maybe turned-off simply because I had lost. And then I thought of John Winthrop, in 1630, off the coast of Massachusetts, in his tiny Arabella [*sic*], saying that someday, 'We shall be a city on a hill.' [Winthrop] didn't say 'shining.' I added that."[18]

Indeed, Reagan may have believed that the city on a hill was shiny. "Progress in products goes hand in hand with providing progress in the human values that enrich the lives of us all," he said in one of the hundreds of speeches he gave to General Electric employees nationwide in the 1950s and 1960s.[19] He used these speaking engagements as opportunities to decry governmental intrusion in the nation's businesses as well as in the lives of its citizens. If asked, he also shared his strong anticommunist sentiments and opposition to the New Deal, which he thought had expanded the state at the expense of free enterprise. He also disparaged containment—the Cold War policy of restraining the Soviet Union—because it sought to limit rather than defeat communism.

Reagan's GE addresses focused on freedom, a gift, he believed, that God gave America. He did not harp on the connection in his talks for the company, but he was explicit at places such as Eureka College, his alma mater. Addressing the class of 1957, Reagan warned students about the socialist threat to the nation: "This irreconcilable conflict is between those who believe in the sanctity of individual freedom and those who believe in the supremacy of the state."[20] For him, politics had a religious dimension that was his lifelong lodestar. According to one of his biographers, "[Reagan] quotes Scripture, remembers Bible stories from his childhood days in the Christian Church, and regards Christ as his personal savior and as a hero of history."[21]

When he ran for governor of California, Reagan capitalized on his Christian commitments, making it known that he had had a born-again experience. Confirming press reports of his "spiritual conversion" in a 1967 interview, he said, "I can't conceive of anyone trying to meet the problems we face today without help from God. I have spent more time in prayer these past few weeks than I have in any previous period I recall."[22] Seventeen years later, during the first 1984 presidential debate, he took issue with the term *born-again*, but he affirmed his deep-seated beliefs.[23]

Over the years, Reagan frequently cited his mother's faith, his matriculation at Eureka, a Christian college, and his baptism after reading *That Printer of Udell's*, a 1903 inspirational novel, as the wellsprings of his religious commitment.[24] In the mid- to late 1960s, Reagan was an active participant in Southern California's evangelical network. He belonged to Bel Air Presbyterian Church and fellowshipped with Christian luminaries such as entertainer Pat Boone, Pentecostal pastor Harald Bredesen, and two-time football All-American Donn Moomaw, Bel Air's minister. These religious friends grasped the former movie star's political potential. During a 1970 prayer meeting at Reagan's Sacramento home, George Otis, a businessman and evangelical leader, surprised participants by prophesizing that if Reagan followed God's call, he would end up in the White House.[25]

How much did the 1980s press corps know about Reagan's spiritual journey? Did reporters consider it newsworthy? Despite widespread interest in the actor turned politician, the news media rarely, if ever, probed the president's personal religious life and practice. Few accounts detailed his immersion in Southern California's evangelical community, much less his lifelong relationship to Christianity. (Some reporters, however,

FIGURE 14. Undated photograph of Ronald Reagan and his mother, Nelle Wilson Reagan. Courtesy Ronald Reagan Presidential Library and Museum.

did question why he rarely attended worship services after moving to the White House.)[26] Instead, journalists explored how his faith served his political objectives, thereby following a long-standing media practice of covering religion instrumentally, focusing on its political effectiveness in wooing constituencies, rather than on its substantive impact as a deeply held conviction providing meaning, identity, and purpose.

Contemporaneous reporting, centered on Reagan's rapport with evangelical audiences, also noted when the president disappointed his religious constituency, including his selection of George H. W. Bush as a running mate, his nomination of Sandra Day O'Connor to the Supreme Court, and his unsuccessful attempts to end abortion, reinstitute school prayer, and legislate family values. By 1983, his limited achievements on core issues had prompted a growing number of evangelical leaders to openly question whether to support his bid for reelection. According to Howard

Phillips, head of the Conservative Caucus, "All they've done is throw us a few bones to keep the dogs from biting their heels."[27] A year later, the midterm election showed what happened when white conservative voters stayed home. The Democrats gained twenty-seven seats in the House of Representatives and one in the Senate.

White House staffers worked on several fronts to improve Reagan's standing with religious voters. Morton Blackwell, the president's liaison to conservative groups, told the *Boston Globe* that the president and his surrogates, including Interior Secretary James Watt and Vice President Bush, were reassuring constituents at small events and large gatherings. (Watt's religious conservatism was well known and a source of controversy due to its influence on his environmental policies.)[28] Blackwell also noted that Reagan's pledge to fix the economy dominated his first two years in office, but he would focus on social initiatives in his second term. But not all right-wingers bought the excuses. Some pressed for cuts in domestic spending and a harder line with communist insurgents in Latin America. Others wondered whether the president was sufficiently committed to their issues.[29] Richard Viguerie, one of the architects of the religious Right, was among the doubters. "The President has always been good at giving conservatives their rhetoric," he said. "It remains to be seen if the White House staff will stay the President's course and fight for these issues."[30]

REAGAN AND THE "EVIL EMPIRE"

This, then, was the context for the president's March 8, 1983, speech to the National Association of Evangelicals in Orlando, Florida. His advisors wanted the address to reassure religious conservatives that he had neither forgotten their issues nor abandoned them. But Reagan, focused on the global struggle against communism, was determined to rally ministers to oppose a nuclear freeze.[31] The freeze movement, which coalesced in the early 1980s, was an international response to the growing threat of nuclear war posed by the very public US-Soviet nuclear arms race. In 1982, its American supporters organized the largest-ever domestic demonstration. Almost one million people convened in New York City's Central Park to support a weapons ban. Throughout the year, local municipalities as well as ten states passed freeze resolutions, calling on the government to stop "testing, production, and deployment of nuclear weapons and of missiles, and new aircraft designed primarily to deliver nuclear weapons."[32] As much as 74 percent of the country agreed with the freeze's goals, but the president did not share their opinion.[33] Despite his abhorrence of nuclear weapons and long-standing fear of nuclear war, Reagan argued that a

FIGURE 15. President Ronald Reagan at the National Association of Evangelicals, March 8, 1983. Courtesy Ronald Reagan Presidential Library and Museum.

freeze would put the United States at a disadvantage relative to the Soviet Union. He was convinced that the Soviets could not be trusted to uphold a weapons ban even if the West did. His policy, therefore, was peace through strength, and his strategy was increased defense spending.

Recent scholarship suggests that Reagan was neither as naive nor as doctrinaire as many of his contemporaries believed.[34] But in 1983, his opponents considered him an irresponsible warmonger whose defense spending and plans to position medium-range missiles in Europe inched the planet closer to extinction. Adding to the problem, the arms buildup coincided, as we have seen, with the worst economic slump in the postwar period. Unemployment was at a record high while manufacturing capacity and the real gross national product fell to a historic low.[35] Increased military spending also reduced the domestic budget, another obstacle to Reagan's reelection. As the president's approval rating plummeted,[36] news stories speculated that the former host of *Death Valley Days* soon would ride off into the sunset.

Support for a nuclear freeze made surprising bedfellows: Main Street, Wall Street, and labor unions kept company with a cross section of Baptists, Methodists, Presbyterians, Episcopalians, Jews, and Roman Catholics. Even evangelicals supported the freeze by a three-to-one margin.[37] Determined to peel off Catholics and white evangelicals, the White House decided to use conservative social issues as a wedge.[38] But on the morning that Reagan left for Orlando, four thousand freeze activists arrived in Washington, DC, to lobby congressional leaders. That very day, the House Foreign Affairs Committee was considering a nonbinding resolution calling on the president to negotiate an immediate nuclear freeze. (It passed by twenty-seven votes to nine.) Earlier in the week, the National Conference of Catholic Bishops released the third draft of a planned pastoral letter that sought to "curb," which was later changed to "halt," the spread of nuclear weapons. Reagan's speech needed to succeed on two fronts: promoting peace through strength and reinvigorating support for his 1984 campaign.

The press corps traveling with the president did not expect the Orlando appearance to be a major address; rather, they anticipated a quasi-stump speech to a sectarian audience. But Reagan's "Evil Empire" speech, as the thirty-two-minute talk came to be known, has claimed a special place in presidential annals. Historian Henry Steele Commager called it "the worst presidential speech in American history,"[39] and rhetoric scholar G. Thomas Goodnight deemed it "one of the most curious addresses in modern American history."[40] The speech is significant for its intermingling themes of military strength, economic prosperity, religious conservatism, and divine destiny. It reaffirmed the primacy of religion to American identity and detailed its consequent obligations: "There is sin and evil in the world, and we're enjoined by Scripture and the Lord Jesus to oppose it with all our might."[41] Even as Reagan professed the need for the United States to embrace conservative social issues, such as ending abortion and restoring school prayer, he took the larger step of placing America's national and international mission in the context of good and evil, sin and salvation.

Most of the press corps viewed the address as a salvo against the freeze movement, albeit couched in an oddly moralistic framework. In fact, the reporters and the evangelical audience heard two different speeches. Reagan's evangelical listeners brought a different frame of reference to the "Evil Empire" speech, which began with three explicitly religious allusions. The president told the assembled ministers that their welcome "warmed my heart," a nod to the eighteenth-century British evangelist John Wesley, the founder of Methodism. Wesley had felt his heart "strangely warmed" when listening to Martin Luther's preface to a Pauline passage on "the change which God works in the heart through faith in Christ."[42] Reagan's listeners likely recognized and appreciated this historic reference to Christian conviction. Next, the president thanked pastors for their prayers and affirmed his own prayer practice. Concluding the opening section, he told a joke about a minister and a politician receiving their just rewards in heaven. When the former is shown to a modest room and the latter is installed in a mansion, Saint Peter explains, "You're the first politician who ever made it [here]."[43]

After appreciative laughter, Reagan segued into his main point: the deep bond between God and the American nation. He clarified that there were indeed "a great many, God-fearing, dedicated noble men and women in public life, present company included." Next came the crux of his message, two sentences that telegraphed the essence of American exceptionalism: "We need your help to keep us ever mindful of the ideas and the principles that brought us into the public arena in the first place. The basis of those ideals and principles is a commitment to freedom and personal liberty that, itself, is grounded in the much deeper realization that freedom prospers only where the blessings of God are avidly sought and humbly accepted."[44]

Making a case for America's "goodness" and tying it to the nation's godliness, Reagan stated several of his administration's achievements, including mandating federally funded clinics to notify parents when underage daughters sought an abortion; introducing a constitutional amendment to restore prayer in public schools; backing legislation to protect freedom of religious speech in public schools; and urging Congress to support the Hyde Amendment, which placed restrictions on federally funded abortions. Turning to the international scene, he stated that the Soviet Union, a nation whose government denied God, could not be trusted: "Yes, let us pray for the salvation of all of those who live in that totalitarian darkness—pray they will discover the joy of knowing God. But until they do, let us be aware that while they preach the supremacy of the state, declare its omnipotence over individual man, and predict its eventual domination of all peoples on the Earth, they are the focus of evil in the modern world."[45]

Modern presidents typically did not evoke the language of fire-and-brimstone preachers, and in the days following the speech, many editorial writers decried Reagan's words. His remarks were "illegitimate," his view "smug," and his message a summon to "jihad."[46] But the very words that nettled editorialists struck a chord with millions of Americans whose faith in God and country had been tested during the previous decade. For these men and women, Reagan's explicit recognition of America's divine standing was good news, and the National Association of Evangelicals reported that churches nationwide were ordering video copies of the speech and that Christian television stations were broadcasting it. Whether or not the speech changed evangelical minds about nuclear weapons is difficult to assess. Two months later, when the NAE asked Gallup to poll its membership, the results were contradictory. A large majority (77 percent) supported an immediate freeze, but a significant majority (61 percent) backed the president's handling of "the nuclear arms situation."[47]

In the immediate aftermath of the speech, print reporters, needing a news hook for their daily stories, homed in on the president's denunciation of the freeze as a "dangerous fraud." Many also noted his alliterative judgment of the Soviet Union as an "evil empire." Reagan's strong and surprising language was newsworthy in an era when most leaders criticized other nations on political grounds, not metaphysical ones. As the Associated Press summed up for millions of newspaper readers, "Reagan asked church leaders to spread his anti-freeze message from their pulpits because the United States and the Soviet Union are locked 'in a struggle between right and wrong, good and evil.'"[48]

Print coverage juxtaposed Reagan's remarks to protests at the Capitol and the House committee's support for a freeze resolution. Reading the speech as political theater, Juan Williams of the *Washington Post* said it was a "double-edged campaign for the defense budget and against a freeze" as well as a bid "to reenergize his conservative base." At the article's conclusion, Williams noted the president's objection to the freeze on moral grounds, quoting his language of good and evil in the last paragraph.[49] Williams's perspective was widespread. Many television reporters "characterized the address as a work of political propaganda that appealed to evangelical Christians."[50] These reporters heard the president's call for support and quoted his evocation of the United States' divinely ordained destiny, but few unpacked the political or cultural significance of casting an international problem in transcendent terms.

The freeze topped daily news coverage, because it was a controversy that pitted the president against a majority of the American people. Trained to organize stories around news values such as conflict, relevance, timeliness, and continuity, reporters listened for new twists on familiar themes, and for them *evil empire* was a suggestive term, conjuring images of ancient Babylon or the recent blockbuster *Star Wars*. With a reelection campaign looming, Reagan's outreach to the NAE was noteworthy, since many conservative white evangelicals were pro-freeze. But the explanation necessary to contextualize all three points—freeze update, religious language, and constituency wooing—required too much space, time, and context for a daily print or broadcast story. Reporters heard the president's call for support, although his choice to couch it in a vision of America's divinely ordained destiny was unlikely to be mentioned, much less highlighted in their news pieces. But editorialists and opinion writers, following up on the news, attacked the president's perspective, and by focusing their readers' attention on his religious language, they inadvertently helped mainstream his message.

The "Evil Empire" speech affected the president's media coverage going forward. Reagan's linking of religious faith to national strength, foundational tenets of the religious Right, became a dominant news motif throughout the year. Many of his subsequent speeches mentioned God and American destiny. Coverage and public discussion followed suit. Even when Reagan did not specifically refer to religion or morality, he invoked religious virtues, such as personal responsibility and love of country, which informed his policy initiatives whether welfare reform, tax cuts, or defense measures. By applying normative notions of good and evil to political discourse, the "Evil Empire" speech helped recalibrate the American religious imaginary.

That speech condemned the freeze movement, but it also articulated a religious vision: America is great because America is good. Being good meant opposing evil, which in the modern world was communism. Reagan's articulation of a religious imaginary knit together new realities of globalization and nuclear annihilation with older notions of American exceptionalism and muscular Christianity, a linkage of faith and manly vigor. The speech dominated the news cycle, and editorialists, by attacking Reagan's argument, kept the president's views in front of the public. Disseminated by the secular news media as well as many religious outlets, Reagan's explication of citizenship provided a moral compass that pointed Americans to their divine purpose.

REAGAN'S COLD WAR ESCALATION

Reagan's "Evil Empire" speech did not occur in a vacuum, even if its explicitly religious overtones surprised many listeners outside the evangelical world. It followed several decades of well-documented anticommunist fervor. Reagan had first encountered the communist menace during his time in Hollywood. At the start of his career, he was, in his own words, a "near-hopeless hemophiliac liberal."[51] But in the late 1940s, as president of the Screen Actors Guild and a union leader, he became enmeshed in a labor dispute that he believed had been fomented by communists. The experience catalyzed his subsequent journey from Democratic liberalism to hard-line conservatism.

By the time Reagan gave the "Evil Empire" speech in March 1983, he had already signaled that the Cold War might be re-escalating. In his State of the Union address two months prior, he saluted the United States as the leader of the free world, a beacon of strength and democracy. He also reiterated previous calls for world peace, asking the new Soviet government—in November of 1982, Yuri Andropov had replaced Leonid Brezhnev—to make arms reduction a priority.[52] From the Soviets' perspective, Reagan's actions belied his call for peace. After more than a decade of detente, the Cold War and the continuing arms race reignited as each side saw subterfuge in the other's maneuverings. Failed disarmament talks, provocative war games, inflamed rhetoric, and strategic blunders marked relations between the superpowers throughout 1983. Fearing the worst, citizens worldwide held demonstrations protesting the nuclear shadow cast by intransigent Soviet and US leaders. As a United Nations delegate told the *New York Times* later in the year, "We do not want to see further deterioration in the East-West dialogue nor a rupture of the discussions on disarmament and other issues."[53] The problem lay in large part with Reagan and Andropov, who were, each in his own way, deeply suspicious of the other's intentions.

For several years and notwithstanding détente, the Kremlin had supported insurgencies in Africa, Latin America, and the Middle East. It also publicized plans to target a significant number of nuclear warheads at NATO members, even as it promised to limit its numbers of nuclear launchers under the SALT II treaty, the result of the 1969–79 Strategic Arms Limitation Talks. In response, Reagan announced plans to place American missiles in Europe, even as his negotiators sought to cap or curtail such weaponry. But because American proposals would have reduced the Soviet stockpile more drastically than their own, the Russians walked out of the talks.

After arms negotiations broke down in November 1982, each side privately stewed in its own mix of paranoid misgivings. The Soviets harbored suspicions of a surprise American strike. In addition to Reagan's tough talk and his increased military budget, they were concerned about a rise in "U.S.-led naval and air operations, including psychological missions," close to their borders.[54] Comparing Reagan to Hitler, Russian leaders publicly accused the American president of fanning the flames of war while privately assuming he would attack when they least expected it, as Hitler had in 1941. Their anxiety was fueled by a host of domestic and international troubles. The Russian army was bogged down in Afghanistan, Cuba was an economic drain, and the United States was actively challenging Marxist and pro-Soviet regimes in Africa and Latin America. Domestically, the news was no better. The economy was sluggish, Eastern European satellite states were growing restive, and the USSR's scientific and technological edge over the United States had evaporated.

On the US side of the Cold War, avid anticommunism and the need for a strong military were conservative articles of faith, and Reagan supported both. After detente, Soviet leaders had initially assumed that hard-line American rhetoric was more for domestic consumption than an expression of realpolitik. But Reagan meant what he said and backed his words with actions. His description of the USSR as an "evil empire" was not empty bombast when buttressed by the $1.6 trillion allocation for a military buildup that followed. Reagan believed that Soviet behavior justified extending US defense. This was even more apparent two weeks later, when he delivered his "Star Wars" speech on March 23, 1983. Reagan proposed a Strategic Defense Initiative (SDI), a space-based, antiballistic missile defense system to safeguard the United States against Soviet attack.[55] Several of the president's advisors were taken aback by the proposed system, which "appealed to Reagan's dreamy fascination with technological gimmickry, his cinematic science-fiction imaginings of immobilizing the enemy and ushering in world peace, and his frustration at what he saw as one-sided efforts to restrain American military superiority."[56] Most important, Reagan believed that the system's revolutionary capabilities would deter Soviet plans for launching a first strike against the United States.

The Soviets did not see things the same way. Andropov publicly rebuked Reagan for designing SDI as a way to launch a nuclear war. Providing the news media with "unprecedented" specific information about US nuclear capabilities, the Russian leader warned the world that a nuclear showdown was imminent.[57] In reality, America did not have the technology to build the SDI, and many in Reagan's inner circle thought the proposal was unrealistic and only served to further destabilize East-West relations. Their intuition appeared correct. The Soviets, worried that their military capacity was falling far behind the United States', were increasingly desperate. Without the technical ability or financial resources to compete in the arms race, their tenure as a superpower would soon end.

Mutual suspicion took a heavy toll several months later when the Russian military shot down Korean Air Lines Flight 007 on September 1. The passenger jet had mistakenly flown off course and into Soviet airspace. The Soviet military assumed it was a spy plane, and its error cost 269 civilian lives. Reagan immediately denounced the Soviets, even though American intelligence and military leaders concluded that the action had been a mistake. But the Soviets exacerbated the problem by waiting more than a week to provide an explanation. When Andropov did address the tragedy, four weeks after it occurred, he blamed the United States for sending a spy plane over the border and condemned Reagan's subsequent tough talk and accusations.[58]

Later in September, Andropov announced that it would be impossible to pursue better relations with the Reagan administration. Within weeks, warheads from the United States were en route to its NATO allies, as promised earlier in the year. The brinksmanship displayed by the superpowers pushed antinuclear sentiment to new heights worldwide. That fall, anticipating the deployment of US weapons, some three million people demonstrated in Western Europe, with especially large turnouts in London, the Hague, and West Berlin. But perhaps the most poignant "protests" were those of a young girl and a Hollywood executive.

Almost a year earlier, in December 1982, a ten-year-old from Maine had asked Yuri Andropov if he were going to start a nuclear war with the United States. Samantha Smith had written at the urging of her mother, who, questioned by Samantha about US-Soviet relations and the threat to peace, had suggested she go to the source for answers. Four months later, Andropov replied, assuring the child that he, too, wanted peace and inviting her to visit his country. Samantha and her parents went to the Soviet Union the following summer, and she was impressed by the warmth and generosity of its people. (Andropov, who was ill at the time, was unable to meet her.) Many Americans were charmed by press coverage of the youngster and supported her decision to visit their enemy on a peacemaking mission. Others carped that she was a pawn in the Soviets' propaganda war to soften Americans' resistance to communism. But the tide of opinion flowed both ways. Samantha was a revelation to Russians, whose deep misgivings about the United States and its capitalist system had been fostered by state propaganda.[59] Her friendliness and curiosity, which were communicated by international press coverage of her story, touched the hearts of the Russian people.

A Hollywood mogul undertook a very different type of initiative. ABC executive Brandon Stoddard decided that the US-Soviet nuclear impasse presented an opportunity for educational entertainment, much the same way that *Silkwood*, a film about nuclear contamination made during his tenure, had educated viewers about the need for nuclear power plant safety. Stoddard's made-for-television movie *The Day After* dramatized the effects of a Russian nuclear strike on Lawrence, Kansas—a university town that also housed nuclear weapons silos. The program focused on the human aftermath of the tragedy. In the weeks preceding the broadcast in November 1983, commentators debated the movie's worth: would it normalize nuclear weapons, turn America pacifist, or sensationalize Armageddon?

To offset pundits' mounting panic about the broadcast, viewer guides were widely distributed. After the movie aired, newsman Ted Koppel hosted a studio discussion with Secretary of State George Shultz, former secretaries Henry Kissinger and Robert McNamara, General Brent Scowcroft,

The Washington Post STYLE

Friday, November 18, 1983

The Arts/Television/Classified C1

The Body Bonanza

At the Fitness Forum, Wonders & Warnings

By Curt Suplee

America is muscling in on a tougher tomorrow.

That's the word from the White House Symposium on Physical Fitness and Sports Medicine, which ended here yesterday. For two days a conspicuously lean-waisted, ruddy-faced and smokeless throng of 800 medical and athletic professionals converged on the Mayflower Hotel to share the latest developments in physiology, training and therapy.

The result was a beef-tech bonanza. As a clatter of classical jaw-busters like *osteoporosis* and *amenorrhea* shared the air with the sweaty Saxonisms of *snatch lifts, split jerks* and *power-cleans*, participants got the word on: new national interest in resistance exercise and muscle strength to counter the burgeoning spate of sports injuries; pregnant weight lifters and other issues in sports gynecology; a revolutionary technique for healing torn tendons and ligaments using surgically embedded electrodes; lifesaving exercise programs for elderly women; and a computer-driven exercise machine that makes Robbie the Robot look like a waffle iron.

And they learned that despite the med-biz breakthroughs, the *national* prognosis is mixed: After a decade of the fitness boom, *many* Americans, it seems, are exercising too much, too little or too late.

Item: Future Jock syndrome is torturing our tots. "We're seeing injuries now in kids that 15 years ago we'd only see in male college scholarship athletes," says symposium chairman Dr. Bernard Cahill, an orthopedic surgeon from Peoria, Ill. "Tendinitis in a 6-year-old kid, or a stress fracture of the tibia in a 7-year-old girl! In the past 10 years we've seen an accelerated inclination to get young athletes into intensive training"—through a profusion of gymnastics, weight lifting, *swimming*

See FITNESS, C4, Col. 1

Glenn Swengros of President's Council for Physical Fitness leads exercises during break

TV Preview

Nightmare For a Small Planet

ABC's 'The Day After': Convincing Catastrophe

Seeking solace amid the devastation

By Tom Shales

WHO should watch it? Everyone should watch it. Who will be able to forget it? No one will be able to forget it.

Indeed, it could be argued that not to watch "The Day After," the ABC film about nuclear holocaust, would be a socially irresponsible act, considering the public fuss that has preceded the broadcast and the fact that the program itself has achieved the status of an "issue."

Thus it probably should be watched not so much because it is some sort of towering achievement in television (though achievement, of sorts, it is), but because after listening to all the back-and-forth on it, people ought to see the subject of the debate and make up their own damn minds. The film airs Sunday night at 8 on Channel 7 and will be followed, at 10:15, by a special edition of "Viewpoint," with Ted Koppel, that will discuss the film and the unholy topic of nuclear war.

As has rarely happened in television history, a work of fiction has achieved the urgency and magnitude of live coverage of a national crisis. One can imagine an ABC engineer quivering slightly as he presses the button on Sunday night that will send the film into millions and millions of American homes. Despite some predictions to the contrary, those homes and the psyches in them are certain to survive it. Nor will the republic likely perish from exposure to this highly convincing nightmare.

Those lobbying for and against the film seem to think it will send many of those who see it scurrying into the too-eager arms of the nuclear freeze movement, or that it will spread a "War of the Worlds" panic through the land, as if ABC were shouting "Fire!" in a crowded country. The actual impact will probably be less dramatic but more profound—a pervasive shading of popular attitudes toward nuclear weaponry in general and the Reagan administration's New Brinkmanship in particular—because the film forces

See THE DAY AFTER, C8, Col. 1

Jason Robards as a tormented surgeon

Survivors face the wreckage

By Henry Mitchell

Any Day

Lincoln, Mozart and The Mysteries of Art

I shall not explain either Lincoln or "Cosi fan tutte," but for years I have thought before dozing off on great matters such as the central mystery of art.

Lincoln's Gettysburg Address was delivered 120 years ago tomorrow and is a fair sample of words that are more splendid than their surface shows. He twice uses the word "devotion" even though he knew better than any other American president the danger of words longer than two syllables. No other president understood so well the grandeur of monosyllables, yet here he rumbles along with "devotion" twice in one sentence.

He also begins with the archaic, and really silly when you think of it, opening phrase, "Four score and seven years ago," which was risky beyond measure. In the first place it did not make any difference whatever whether it was 87 or 88 or 89 years ago, and to give a date that emphasis carried the danger of seeming simply foolish.

There are a couple of other places in the talk in which the words seem (for a writer of Lincoln's great skill) weak or ill-chosen; for example, "portion," ("a portion of this field") and the unseemly emphasis on the weak prepositions, "of," "by" and "for."

These kinds of word usage almost always weaken the thought. They usually produce a dismal response.

The question is why, since any fool can see the Lincoln address is a masterpiece, something so obvious and indeed trite is suddenly not

See ANY DAY, C13, Col. 1

Gary D., Talking Up a Frenzy

By Jacqueline Trescott

Four moments in the life of Washington's most controversial deejay, Gary D.:

- Caller: "What do you think of mixed marriages?" D.: "All marriages should be mixed, a girl and a boy."
- Caller: "You hit on a good point there. You say we have working mothers, working fathers, people who have the kids and they don't want to take the time with them, man." D.: "Any woman gets pregnant, she has a commitment to carry the baby to term, and that's not nine months, partner. That's 21 years."
- D.: "I'm going to pull out all the stops. Let me tell you this, every time you bite down on a Nestle's Crunch bar, you are supporting poor little babies with a bottle stuck in their mouths, instead of their mother's breast. Amen and allelula."
- D.: "Do you deserve to be heard, sir? You come down here, boy, you yellow-bellied, egg-sucking dog, bed-wetter pinko-commie."

In six weeks, these comments from Gary D., the 48-year-old morning disc jockey at WPKX-FM (105.9), the underdog of Washing-

See GARY D., C3, Col. 1

INSIDE STYLE

Style Plus: Kids and 'The Day After,' C5.

Arts: Ray Anthony/ Radio column, C7.

Evaluating diet books: TV Preview, C10.

Magazine upheld in copyright dispute, C14.

NBC's 'Yellow Rose' gets full season, C14.

FIGURE 16. Many newspapers urged viewers to watch *The Day After*, an ABC special movie on the impact of nuclear war on an American city. The looming mushroom cloud graphically depicted the devastation caused by nuclear weapons.

conservative pundit William F. Buckley Jr., Holocaust survivor and author Elie Wiesel, and scientist and popular cosmologist Carl Sagan on the issues that the movie raised.[60] Shultz tried to explain the administration's policy, Kissinger lamented the movie's simplicity, and Buckley argued for nuclear deterrence—a strategy that the movie seemingly discredited. Echoing Buckley, other conservatives denounced *The Day After* as anti-American and misleading. Yet Reagan, who had watched the movie before it was aired, was profoundly moved by it.[61] Writing in his diary, he noted, "It's very effective & left me greatly depressed. . . . My own reaction was one of our having to do all we can to have a deterrent & to see there is never a nuclear war."[62] The president was not alone: one hundred million people watched *The Day After*, one of the biggest television audiences of all time, and many were shocked by what they saw.[63]

All these events in one year—Reagan's "Evil Empire" speech, the administration's call for a Strategic Defense Initiative, the escalating Cold War, the KAL tragedy, and the broadcast of *The Day After*—had a deep impact on public opinion. While in the early months of 1983, most Americans backed the nuclear freeze that Reagan opposed—including 64 percent of white Protestants who went to church weekly—the tide had begun to shift.[64] Reagan consistently linked conservative social positions to a strong defense and argued that a nuclear freeze enabled an evil empire; his attempt at rhetorical jujitsu used the force of one position to disarm another. His message eventually prevailed. Polls in late 1985 found that between 58 and 78 percent of respondents favored the development of Reagan's Strategic Defense Initiative.[65] Moreover, 83 percent agreed that "the United States should wait to reduce its nuclear arsenal until the Soviets also cut back."[66] Two of Reagan's 1983 speeches—the first demonizing the Soviet Union and the second pledging to use American technology to thwart its evil designs—played a significant role in shifting the terms of the nuclear arms debate and reflected the new religious imaginary at work.

THE "GAY PLAGUE"

Reagan's foreign policy agenda was straightforward: it was dominated by his loathing of communism and the Soviet Union as well as his confidence in the power of an idealized American exceptionalism. But his domestic programs were forced to grapple with multiple issues raised by the changing American family, including the impact of feminism, the rise in households headed by single women, the legalization of abortion, and the increased visibility of gays and lesbians.

The gay community's struggle for accurate and balanced media coverage had begun in the 1950s and 1960s, when "homosexuals" were invisible in the news except for stories describing their "pathology." In 1967, a violent police crackdown at the Black Cat Tavern, a gay bar in Los Angeles, barely registered beyond local media.[67] Two years later, when police and gays clashed during the Stonewall riots in New York's Greenwich Village, the press paid scant attention. Most of the city's newspapers initially ran briefs on the protests, and a longer article in the *Village Voice*, an alt-weekly, mocked the demonstrators.[68]

But four years later, when the American Psychiatric Association withdrew its classification of homosexuality as a mental illness, the decision was widely reported. Other victories made news too: a growing number of cities added "sexual orientation" to their antidiscrimination laws, and more public figures "came out," openly acknowledging their homosexuality. By the end of the 1970s, many reporters, encouraged to write about this "new" constituency, had profiled a community with its own mores, music, and fashion as well as an uninhibited sexual scene. This mainstreaming of gay life spurred one of the early battles over gay rights. In 1977, entertainer Anita Bryant rallied Dade County, Florida, church folks to "Save Our Children" by repealing an antidiscrimination ordinance that protected homosexuals.

Over the next several years, opposition to homosexuality and to gay rights became, along with the promotion of traditional family values and antiabortion legislation, the issues that defined the culture wars, the social and cultural dimensions of the right wing's political crusade. Sociologist James D. Hunter popularized the term in his 1991 book *Culture Wars: The Struggle to Define America*, but real-life confrontations had begun much earlier. In the 1960s, religious conservatives' anger over Supreme Court decisions on school prayer, birth control, and abortion along with their estrangement from the "Sixties' lifestyle" (especially "women's lib," long-haired males, and extramarital sex) became the basis for 1970s Christian protest movements, such as Christian Voice and the Moral Majority. Then in 1978, when an Internal Revenue Service ruling targeted tax-exempt private elementary and secondary schools as potentially discriminatory—an issue for mostly white Christian schools—grassroots political protest began in earnest.[69] In the early 1980s, with Beltway support and at the televangelists' urging, these conservatives launched noisy battles against liberal strongholds. They picketed abortion clinics, took over district school boards, and ran for local offices.

As they would with any story, reporters covering the culture wars sought to provide balance, long considered a hallmark of professional journalism. That meant that every stated opinion required a rebuttal, and both sides carried equal weight, even if one side's statements were false, inaccurate, or unfair. Reporters covering a protest at an abortion clinic needed to balance a client or provider citing female health, legal protection, and freedom of choice with a demonstrator broaching God, the Bible, and dead babies. The stories did triple duty: reporters obtained strong but balanced quotes; protesters reached a broad segment of the public with their message; and many news consumers, unfamiliar with conservative religious positions, were either appalled yet entertained by the believers' zeal or found themselves in agreement with the antiabortion demonstrators. Publishers could point to criticism from both extremes as evidence of the media's impartial reporting.

Journalists, drawn to televangelists' pithy sound bites, mainstreamed their perspective. The Reverends Jerry Falwell and Pat Robertson were press favorites, because they were media savvy and politically astute. While Falwell oversaw his teleministry and the Moral Majority, Robertson headed the Christian Broadcasting Network and anchored its flagship news and magazine show, *The 700 Club*. Reporters, either ignorant about religion or lacking the space to provide context, rarely questioned the ministers' comments. When Falwell and Robertson said that feminists or "abortionists" or homosexuals flouted biblical teachings, journalists seldom asked to which biblical teachings they were referring, nor did they contextualize the ones referenced. Likewise, reporters did not inquire whether evangelicals sanctioned other biblical credos in support of slavery, polygamy, and stoning disobedient children.

Although cases of AIDS may have surfaced in the 1960s and 1970s, the disease was not reported on until 1981.[70] At that time, the majority of American Christians, including Roman Catholics, evangelicals, Mormons, members of historically Black churches, and mainline Protestants, believed that the Bible not only forbade homosexuality but also strongly condemned it. Such attitudes may help explain why a mysterious cancer that afflicted gay men did not initially strike mainstream journalists as newsworthy. When physician Lawrence Mass wrote about it for the *New York Native*, a small gay newspaper, the disease did not even have a name. Several weeks later, the Centers for Disease Control and Prevention (CDC) in Atlanta reported an outbreak of a rare cancer among a handful of gay men in Los Angeles. Soon after, several news outlets, starting with the *Los Angeles Times*, briefly noted those findings.

Another month passed before the *New York Times* mentioned the unknown illness that had now killed forty-one gay men. AIDS exposed social and cultural fault lines that made coverage more complicated than workaday reporting. Over the next few years, the paper, reflecting the quandary of newsrooms nationwide, grappled with reporting on the mysterious contagion, and its reporters encountered obstacles during their investigations. Iphigene Ochs Sulzberger, the daughter, wife, mother, and grandmother of four *New York Times* publishers, was not involved in the paper's daily decision-making, but she made it known that homosexuals should not receive prominent coverage.[71] Moreover, many staffers considered Abe Rosenthal—executive editor of the *Times* when the AIDS crisis began—a homophobe. Thus, despite serving the city with the largest gay community and the highest number of reported AIDS cases in the nation, the paper's early coverage was spotty. And since the *Times* was the industry's standard-bearer, its reticence provided cover for other newsrooms to ignore the growing problem.

Consequently, despite the rapid spread of the disease, few news outlets were providing ongoing accounts. A mix of homophobia, disinterest, and squeamishness kept much of the press at bay but not all. Some outlets, including the San Francisco papers, the *Philadelphia Inquirer*, and *Long Island Newsday*, reported regularly on the new disease. But the desultory coverage characterizing most of the mainstream AIDS reporting during the first eighteen months of the epidemic ended when the contagion entered its second year. Although physicians were unsure how the disease spread, a growing consensus agreed that blood was a carrier and that even "casual contact" could lead to infection.

AIDS was no longer just a gay plague, as the media had initially dubbed it. Using words that stoked alarm among the *general population*, the catch-all term that news outlets used for all heterosexual Americans, a National Public Radio story reported in January 1983 that AIDS was "incurable," spreading rapidly, and "often fatal." That same month, after nine cases were reported among hemophiliacs, the National Hemophiliac Foundation recommended that people in high-risk categories—predominantly homosexuals but also drug users and Haitians—no longer donate blood. In response, gay leaders warned that such restrictions "would lead to discrimination, persecution and hysteria."[72] NPR's framing of the story gave listeners a choice between gay civil rights and public safety.

The NPR piece raised themes that would resurface throughout the year: panic as the disease struck the "general population," fear about contaminated blood, and questions of blame and responsibility. Was AIDS a homosexual disease, and, if so, how did that affect press coverage and public response? Representatives from the National Gay and Lesbian Task Force argued that calling AIDS a homosexual disease had "hidden it from view of the world and limited funding."[73] Subsequent reports explained that the nature of the epidemic had made it easy to hide. Stories linking "bad" behaviors to a high risk of contracting the disease marginalized AIDS for heterosexual Americans and stigmatized it for religious conservatives.

Gay activists worried that the taint of "bad blood" would increase that stigmatization. National Gay and Lesbian Task Force director Virginia Apuzzo told NPR, "I don't have to tell you if you're in the media what gay blood/bad blood could mean to a group of people who have historically been discriminated against."[74] Although neither Apuzzo nor the reporter explained what *bad blood* signified, listeners with a passing knowledge of Western civilization understood the reference. Jews and Christians deemed blood a life force as well as a sacrificial medium for atonement. Blood was not just a physical substance; it also was symbolic of life and death and, in some religions, purity and impurity. Jews conducted blood sacrifices of animals in their ancient temple, and Christians spiritualized the practice of sacrificial atonement through the bread and wine of the Eucharist. In the Middle Ages, *blood libel* referred to the Christian accusation that Jews were "Christ-killers" who kidnapped and killed Christian children to use their blood for making Passover matzoth.

Intimating that gays had "bad blood" raised myriad allusions, ranging from death and pollution to sacrifice and reconciliation. While the news media did not address these subtexts, journalists nevertheless fueled moral anxieties with their sourcing and sound bites, structure and narratives. Contaminated blood became a common news trope in the early months of 1983. Its medical ramifications were obvious, and the moral and religious implications significant, especially since the number of new AIDS patients was on the rise. Six new cases were being diagnosed each day, further proof that AIDS might soon "strike beyond" the homosexual population.

On March 8, the same day that Reagan denounced the "Evil Empire" in Orlando, news outlets reported the development of a new test for HIV detection. The eleven-paragraph story by the *Los Angeles Times*' medical reporter appeared inside the paper's second section; the *New York Times* carried a four-paragraph wire service story even deeper inside its pages. By this time, AIDS—a disease whose origin, pathology, and cure were unknown—had killed at least 400 people and infected more than 1,100 others in the United States.[75] But despite being more deadly than two other recent outbreaks—Legionnaires' disease and toxic shock syndrome—AIDS received less coverage. Many news outlets had only recently discovered the gay community as a source for human-interest stories, and reporters who covered gay rights parades and dance clubs did not think that straight readers were interested in a devastating illness that seemed to target male homosexuals.

Putting a human face on the problem, *Time* magazine profiled an AIDS patient who possessed a memorable mix of traits. "Jack" was a midwestern minister's son who loved baseball and football. He stayed in "perfect trim," graduated from an Ivy League university, and was training for an operatic career. He also was a "homosexual." Was *Time* complicating assumptions about AIDS patients, or was it providing a cautionary tale about the risks of high culture and elite education? Either way, Jack's case was exemplary: the operatic jock was now a desiccated wraith. Using the medical angle as a frame, *Time* laid out the bad news: a growing epidemic, low survival rates, and no end in sight. Moreover, the "most feared route into the general population" was through blood transfusions. Even worse, hemophiliacs were not the only ones at risk. At least eight cases had been diagnosed after routine procedures, including open-heart surgery and hysterectomies. Some blood centers were asking members of at-risk groups to refrain from making donations; others were instituting procedures to screen out donors who could be medically compromised.[76]

In April 1983, *Newsweek* highlighted the medical mystery in its first cover story on the health issue. "The AIDS Epidemic: The Search for a Cure" presented one of the most comprehensive mainstream news accounts to date on the disease's genesis and prognosis. Also included were frank facts about transmission: gays who had the most sexual partners were more likely to be infected, as were drug users who shared needles. The story began and ended on histrionic notes. Vivid locutions, including "gay plague," "ravages the body," "frustrating and depressing situation," and "likely to die," peppered the first paragraph. At the article's end, similarly evocative words—"anguish," "afflicted," "despairing," "killer," and "victims"—reminded readers that AIDS was as much of a morality tale as it was a medical story.[77]

From the perspective of religious conservatives, the fact that disease seemed to target homosexuals indicated divine retribution, and their spokesmen made the claim explicit. The frame proved popular. Magazine articles linked gays' health predicament to their behavior, and newspapers adopted a similar narrative, reporting the story using a moral/medical axis. Coverage and placement also changed, from briefs and articles buried in back pages to front-page news. Medical updates increased the story's relevance, spurring editors to assign articles addressing the human toll of AIDS. One *New York Times* piece described the disease's "emotional anguish. According to Stuart E. Nichols Jr., a gay psychiatrist who had treated patients since the epidemic began, even the best-adjusted gays "experience[d] a feeling of being punished" if they contracted the disease. By the same token, the Reverend William Sloane Coffin, a well-known liberal minister, noted that some "AIDS victims" whom he had counseled "felt that this was in some way God's punishment." Coffin assured them that "being gay was not a sin."[78]

Another *New York Times* news feature explored the "pain and fear among ill and healthy alike." Reporter Dudley Clendinen profiled patients to demonstrate how "AIDS is torturing not only its victims but also challenging the ethic of 'the gay life style,' which, roughly translated, meant the freedom to live openly and to seek sex as one wished." Unlike medical stories, this piece probed the devastation triggered by personal suffering and what many gays perceived as public indifference to their plight. Clendinen described how AIDS patients had been thrown out of their family homes, shunned by hospital staffs, and refused burial by funeral directors. He also detailed the harsh response of some religious conservatives. A New Orleans physician said if AIDS was God's punishment, "it ain't enough." Pastors in Houston demanded the closure of gay bars, and Dallas lawyers lobbied for a bill to outlaw homosexual conduct. Ron Goodwin, a spokesman for the Moral Majority, said the government should spend money "to protect the general public from the gay plague" instead of supporting research that enabled "diseased homosexuals to go back to their perverted practices without any standards of accountability."[79]

Clendinen's piece exemplified the shift in coverage from a predominantly medical frame to a medical/moral axis. Much of the daily reporting still focused on the disease's transmission and spread, but stories also

14 THE NEW YORK TIMES **Style** MONDAY, MAY 30, 1983

Relationships

Friendship By Letter: A Lasting Tie

Charles Waller

THEY are a dwindling band, an anachronism, those people who nurture friends through the mail with regular, descriptive, contemplative letters. But they say they are rewarded by relationships imbued with special qualities when, avoiding the easy communication of the telephone, they put their thoughts on paper.

"A phone conversation simply evaporates — a letter is palpable in your hand," said Kathryn Joyce Hohlwein, professor of English at California State University, Sacramento.

Today the letters Professor Hohlwein and Patricia Frazer Lamb exchanged, starting after their student days, are in many hands. A selection of ones they wrote over more than a decade, when they believed they had made some peace with their feelings about subjugation by their husbands — both are now divorced — was recently published by Harper & Row. The volume is entitled "Touchstones: Letters Between Two Women, 1953-1964."

The letters let each of them into the other's life, often from distant locales. They wrote of routine events and philosophical dilemmas; of men they considered marrying, those they did marry, others they wished they could have married; of pursuits repressed

Facing the Emotional Anguish of AIDS

By GLENN COLLINS

The tragic medical consequences of Acquired Immune Deficiency Syndrome, known as AIDS, have been measured in the 558 known deaths caused by the disease. But for the living victims, AIDS has profound psychological consequences that are only beginning to be understood.

"It just hangs over your head," said Philip Lanzaratta, a 41-year-old AIDS patient in Manhattan who has been struggling with the [illegible] overriding uncertainty that on any day you'll come down with something new that your suppressed immune system can't repel."

New knowledge about the special emotional difficulties of AIDS victims is emerging as mental-health professionals develop strategies for treating these patients who live with a mysterious, often fatal contagious disorder that has no known causes or cures.

Last week the Government's chief health official said that investigating the illness was "the No. 1 priority" of the United States Public Health Service. Half the 1,450 cases reported nationally have occurred in New York, and social workers, psychiatrists and psychologists here have been treating AIDS victims for several years.

'There Were No Guidelines'

"We felt as if we were in uncharted waters," said Dr. Stuart E. Nichols Jr., a psychiatrist at Beth Israel Medical Center who began treating AIDS patients 18 months ago. "There were no guidelines and not much in the psychiatric literature for coping with anxiety about such a mysterious disease."

Subsequently, Dr. Nichols has interviewed and studied more than 100 AIDS patients, including Mr. Lanzaratta, who attended the doctor's first support group, started in April 1982. "One of the special problems for patients is the lack of hard medical data," Dr. Nichols said. "We don't know what causes AIDS, or how long the incubation period is. Such a situation can be a fertile ground for misinformation, superstitiousness and magical thinking."

"Some of the therapeutic issues are the same as with other chronically ill patients," said Noreen Russell, a social worker at New York University Medical Center who has been working with terminally ill patients for seven years now. "But the intensity of anxiety can be greater because we're dealing with a very great unknown."

Miss Russell, along with a co-worker, Virginia Lehman, started a therapy group for AIDS victims in December 1981 and began another group last June. "What's unique," said Miss Russell, "is that, in the presence of such sophisticated medical technology, we seem to be so powerless. AIDS reminds people of cancer, yet it has the sense of contagion about it. In a sense AIDS is like herpes — but herpes doesn't kill."

One of the victims' greatest fears is that they may spread AIDS to family, friends or [illegible] ed," said Dr. Kenneth S. Wein, clinical director of Gay Men's Health Crisis Inc., a nonprofit social-service agency that has treated more than 150 AIDS patients in support and therapy groups. "Some really do feel like lepers, even though it appears that AIDS is not transmitted by simple social contact."

AIDS is believed to be transmitted through sexual or intimate contact. Most cases have involved male homosexuals, intravenous drug users and people from Haiti. However, other patients have included hemophiliacs who have received blood products, recipients of blood transfusions, and women who had sexual contact with AIDS victims.

A focal point for AIDS treatment in the city has been the Gay Men's Health Crisis office in Manhattan, which, in addition to its support and therapy groups for AIDS patients — including Haitians and intravenous drug users — runs groups for patients' parents and partners. Among its other programs, the agency sends crisis counselors and home attendants to visit AIDS victims and runs an AIDS hotline number, 212-685-4952.

The initial shock after AIDS is first diagnosed can be considerable, said Dr. Nichols, but reactions vary greatly from patient to patient. "One of the responses to any serious health insult is 'Why me?'" said Dr. Nichols, president of the Caucus of Gay, Lesbian and Bisexual Members of the American Psychiatric Association. "In the case of gays, it often seems that no matter how well they have come to terms with their gayness, when they learn they have AIDS they experience a feeling of being punished for being gay."

"For some the experience is a sort of second 'coming out,'" said Miss Russell. "They [illegible] over again."

The Rev. William Sloane Coffin, senior minister of Riverside Church in Manhattan, has counseled a number of AIDS victims. "Some felt that this was in some way God's punishment," he said. "I reassured them that they have no right in the world to feel in any way that this is God's will. Being gay is not a sin. But once they get sick, it's as if when their immune system breaks down, their psychological immune system breaks down, too."

After patients' initial shock, said Dr. Nichols, many experience considerable anger. "They become angry at God, at society, at government, at government research funding levels and at doctors. We are medical people, and we're supposed to have answers. But essentially, there aren't any answers."

"Some of them believe that society is only interested in AIDS now that straight people may be at risk," said Dr. John B. Montana, an attending physician at Cabrini Medical Center who has treated many AIDS patients and counseled them at St. Marks Clinic in Greenwich Village.

Some of the patients have used their experience to examine the role that sex plays in their lives. Dr. Nichols said, "Some patients are learning to do loving things together that are totally nonsexual, and redefining the meaning of intimacy."

One of the important tasks of therapy with AIDS victims is to get them to reconnect with their families, where possible. For some homosexuals this has been difficult. "Many are not 'out' to their families, or are in a different city by choice and find it awfully hard to ask for support," said Dr. Nichols.

One AIDS patient got up the courage and [illegible] his mother replied, 'Thank God you told us you're gay. We thought you didn't know. We figured we had to tell you, and we just didn't know how.'"

Miss Russell said that many of her patients were quite pleasantly surprised by family members who provided generous assistance unexpectedly. However, this has not always been the reaction.

'Some Real Horror Stories'

"There have been some real horror stories," said Dr. Montana. "The family of one AIDS patient who died refused to accept the body. "They didn't know their son was gay, and they wouldn't accept it."

He said that patients' friends and families often rally round, but not always: "I've seen some people die in utter loneliness. I was with one patient in the hospital when he died. He was 22, and he was everybody's best friend — people loved him. He died alone. I said to him, 'Close your eyes now and go to sleep.' And then he died."

For the living, anxiety must constantly be coped with. "Having the fear, that's the worst thing," said a 45-year-old illustrator in Manhattan who has Kaposi's sarcoma, a cancer often seen in AIDS patients, and who asked that his name not be used. "I woke up with a temperature this morning, and I'm very worried right now. It could mean that I'll have to be hospitalized again."

The emotional toll of treating AIDS patients can be a problem for professionals as well. "I've wept," said Dr. Montana. "There are times when I feel like pounding my head against the wall. It's always hard on a hospital staff losing a young patient. These patients are often young and recently healthy."

"But the work can be extraordinarily rewarding, too," said Miss Russell. "I am moved again and again by my patients' great courage in the face of life-threatening disease." Mr. Lanzaratta said, "The struggle has been difficult, but it has given me a sense of strength and a certain dignity." ■

'I've seen some people die in utter loneliness,' abandoned by friends.

FIGURE 17. The medical/moral axis, which in 1983 became increasingly common for AIDS reporting, is evidenced in this *New York Times* article.

explored the human aspect of AIDS, invoking questions such as Why am I suffering? and What does this mean? In developing stories that explored morality and mortality, reporters turned to familiar sources for comment, and by early summer, religious conservatives were ready. Falwell had a sound bite that castigated not only gays but also anyone who accepted them: "AIDS is not just God's punishment for homosexuals, it is God's punishment for the society that tolerates homosexuals."[80]

FRAMING GOD'S JUDGMENT

Falwell's ascendancy in the national spotlight was closely tied to Reagan's presidency, though at first glance their association seemed unlikely. Reagan radiated Hollywood glamour; Falwell was small-town, plainspoken, and southern. Reagan socialized with Jews, gays, and atheists; Falwell would have tried to convert them. The two had distinct political agendas, and they did not always agree on social issues. In the late 1970s, for example, the former governor had opposed the Briggs Initiative, a California state ballot measure that sought to ban gays and lesbians from teaching in public schools. Reagan knew many homosexuals from his Hollywood days, and he had a libertarian, live-and-let-live approach to their sexual orientation. Though he would never publicly support gay rights, he did not go out of his way to attack gays, either.

Falwell disapproved of the former governor's stance, but he still came through for the Republican presidential candidate in the 1980 election. Reagan was a better choice than incumbent Jimmy Carter, who did not share Falwell's conservative Christian values and seemed oblivious to the communist menace. Falwell knew that if the Soviets conquered the United States, his social agenda would never be realized, which is why Reagan's hawkish views on military spending and opposing the Soviets held great appeal. Before the election, Falwell's Moral Majority aided voter education and registration. He also sermonized on Reagan's behalf and organized a National Day of Prayer before the vote. Soon after his election, Reagan cemented an alliance with the religious Right when he invited its leaders, including Falwell, to a meeting at the White House.

During his first term, Reagan focused on the fixing the economy and neutralizing the Soviet threat. He supported the religious Right's issues, but he didn't aggressively pursue them. He encouraged conservative Christians to lobby for their causes and did not object when they used his name to promote them. But his lackluster accomplishments concerning school prayer and abortion were among the reasons his advisors worried about his reelection. They are also among the explanations for why he did not speak out on AIDS until 1985, when his friend, actor Rock Hudson, died of the disease. Reagan's advisors had warned him that anything he said about AIDS or the gay community could be used against him.

Reagan's silence may have empowered Falwell to speak out about the epidemic. Although he did not represent the president, his association with Reagan was well known. Journalists sought him out because the pastor had the president's ear. Therefore, when Falwell emerged as the go-to source for religious responses to the AIDS crisis, some may have assumed he was a surrogate for the administration. Reagan was allied with the religious Right, and one of the religious Right's most outspoken leaders held strong opinions about gays and AIDS. It seemed likely that Reagan shared some of those ideas, especially since he never publicly disavowed them.

Coinciding with the 1983 Fourth of July celebrations, Falwell rolled out the I Love America campaign to publicize a new Moral Majority report on AIDS. The televangelist was just several weeks shy of his fiftieth birthday and an important source for political as well as religion reporters. To some members of the secular media, Falwell seemed an ideal spokesman, perhaps because they lacked firsthand experience with evangelical religion. In their 1986 study *The Media Elite*, S. Robert Lichter, Stanley Rothman, and Linda S. Lichter reported that 86 percent of journalists at seven elite news outlets in New York and Washington, DC, seldom or never attended religious services, and 50 percent said their religion was "none."[81] These

FIGURE 18. President Ronald Reagan and Rev. Jerry Falwell at the White House, March 15, 1983. Courtesy Ronald Reagan Presidential Library and Museum.

results were cited as proof that the secular media was inclined to ignore religion, but they also may explain why media elites—reporters at the *New York Times*, *Washington Post*, *Newsweek*, *Time*, and NPR—were drawn to Falwell. He embodied the clichés and stereotypes that many held about religion. And at the same time, he was all too happy to be represented as the presumed authority on religious orthodoxy.

During a July Fourth rally in Cincinnati, Falwell pulled out all the stops, declaring that AIDS was a "gay plague" and "God's way of 'spanking' us." He also challenged the president, whom he had worked hard to elect: "If the Reagan administration does not put its full weight against this, what is now a gay plague in this country, I feel that a year from now, President Ronald Reagan personally will be blamed for allowing this awful disease to break out among the innocent American people." The minister called AIDS and sexually transmitted diseases "a definite form of the judgment of God upon a society." Even if most Americans were "innocent," heterosexuals who countenanced homosexuality were rebelling against God.[82]

Invoking the same cosmic framework that Reagan had used in the "Evil Empire" speech, Falwell reminded listeners that divine blessings had a cost: sexual morality was the righteous path, and when people veered away from it, they suffered. He added that he did not hate homosexuals, only "their perverted lifestyle."[83] Although he stated that AIDS was a religious issue, Falwell had civic concerns too. As a religious leader speaking in the public square, he called for policy solutions to advance Americans' safety. Emphasizing that his sole aim was preventing the spread of the disease, he advocated screening blood donors, closing gay bathhouses, and providing guidelines for professionals who worked with people who had or could soon have AIDS.

Several days later in Washington, DC, Falwell accused the government of inaction, charging that "officials fear the political potency of the gay community." This time, instead of rebuking the president, he blamed Congress for not closing bathhouses and monitoring the blood supply. But his harshest words were directed at those who contracted the disease. "AIDS is God's way of punishing those who 'break the laws of nature and the laws of moral decency,'" he declared, and he paraphrased Galatians 6:8—"The Scripture is clear: 'We do reap it in our flesh when we violate the laws of God.'"[84]

In fact, Falwell's beliefs may have fared poorly among the American public in comparison with the perspectives of gay activists who said, "Blaming AIDS on homosexuals is like blaming polio on kids."[85] Yet the news outlets needed balance, and Falwell was not just quotable but also newsworthy. Moreover, his stance reflected the opinions of many conservative readers

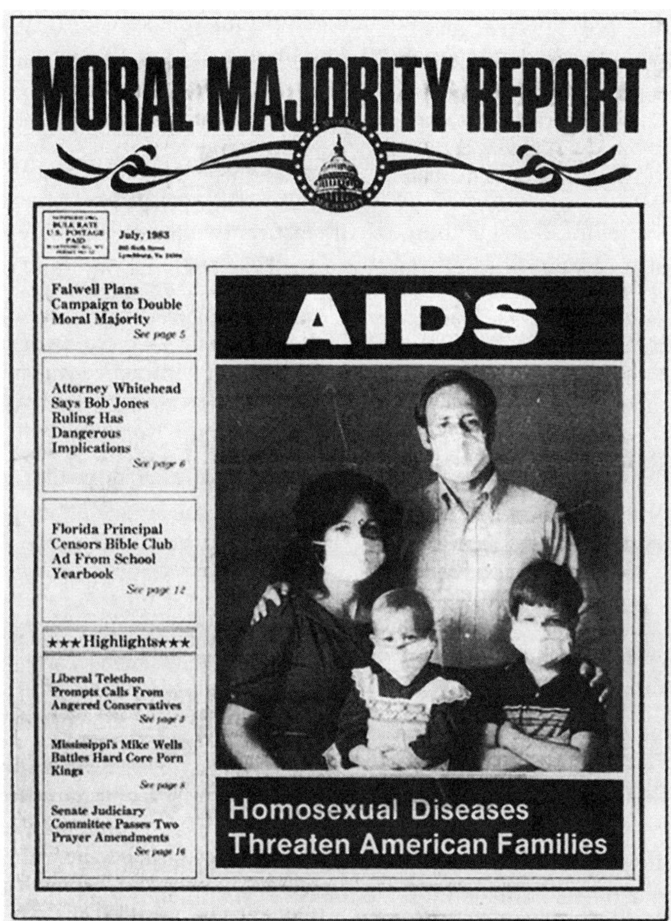

MORAL MAJORITY REPORT

BULK RATE
U.S. POSTAGE
PAID

July, 1983

Falwell Plans Campaign to Double Moral Majority
See page 5

Attorney Whitehead Says Bob Jones Ruling Has Dangerous Implications
See page 6

Florida Principal Censors Bible Club Ad From School Yearbook
See page 12

★★★Highlights★★★

Liberal Telethon Prompts Calls From Angered Conservatives
See page 3

Mississippi's Mike Wells Battles Hard Core Porn Kings
See page 8

Senate Judiciary Committee Passes Two Prayer Amendments
See page 16

AIDS

Homosexual Diseases Threaten American Families

FIGURE 19. In July 1983, Rev. Jerry Falwell rolled out a campaign targeting homosexuals as spreaders of AIDS. The cover of the July issue of the *Moral Majority Report* newsletter featured a photograph of a traditional family threatened by the disease. Courtesy of Liberty University.

and listeners. The *Post* described the Lynchburg pastor as "influential," and NPR devoted substantial airtime to his opinions on public health policy.

In particular, NPR featured Falwell's call to close down gay bathhouses, long a flashpoint in the AIDS crisis. Staples in American cities before the advent of indoor plumbing, bathhouses emerged as popular meeting places for gay men in the 1950s, and by the 1970s they had become synonymous with casual sex. After medical researchers discovered that AIDS could be transmitted by sexual contact, public health officials conjectured that bathhouse culture perpetuated conditions that spread the disease. But many gays had stopped visiting bathhouses before Falwell called for their closure. In May of 1983 Randy Shilts, who pioneered the AIDS beat for the *San Francisco Chronicle*, reported that business at local bathhouses was down 50 percent.[86] Still, it was one thing for gays to choose not to frequent the baths; it was another thing for a fundamentalist minister to call the establishments sinful and urge their closure. When asked whether bathhouses were a public safety risk, Apuzzo of the National Gay and Lesbian Task Force rebutted the charge.[87] But Falwell had succeeded in framing media coverage and setting the agenda.

Even when he was not being quoted, Falwell's influence was present in the underlying, if not explicit, framing of AIDS as a moral issue. On August 8, *Newsweek* ran a second cover story on the epidemic. Instead of focusing on the medical angle, as the newsmagazine had done that spring, "Gay America" examined the impact of AIDS on the afflicted community. The new article, like the earlier one, was the product of lobbying efforts by a reporter whose brother was HIV positive.[88] The story was written in the same perfervid prose characterizing much of the AIDS coverage, and the inside teaser promised "shattered taboos," "a new sobriety," "deadly affliction," "human tragedy," a "troubled past," and "doubt, anger and anxiety."[89] The promise was more than kept in the first paragraph of the piece. Starting with a description of the Hothouse, a "legendary" San Francisco "pleasure palace" for "kinky sex" that had recently closed its doors, the writers explored how AIDS ended "a decade of carefree sexual adventure, a headlong gambol on the far side of the human libido."[90]

The article's subheadings included "Punishment," "Hostility," and "Backlash"—all Falwellian themes. Its text noted that after 743 deaths and 1,922 "victims," some gay activists were questioning the movement's valorization of sexual freedom. One even seemed to echo Falwell by saying, "Maybe we *are* wrong—maybe this is a punishment."[91] Appearing to affirm that perspective, the piece implied a difference between the "bad" sexual behavior that led to the epidemic and the "good" ethos of restraint.

This message was communicated through language, sourcing, and structure. For example, the article contrasted the "Mardi Gras flamboyance" (30) of gays who are "conspicuously and distressingly hedonistic" and participate in "pansexual excess" (33) with "homosexuals" who have made "tremendous strides towards dignity" (30) and who display a "sober unity of purpose" (33). Quotes and sourcing reinforced the dichotomy between good and bad behavior, albeit a nonexistent distinction to religious leaders like Falwell.

But even though Falwell's beliefs were far from universal among faith leaders, his opinion became authoritative, even normative, since no other religious figure was quoted as frequently as he was across all mainstream news outlets. The *Newsweek* article noted that "many straights" believe that AIDS is a divine punishment, and a quote by Falwell confirmed their judgment. "'A man reaps what he sows,' the Rev. Jerry Falwell declaimed in a recent San Francisco television show. 'If he sows seed in the lower field of his nature, he will reap from it a harvest of corruption.'" In addressing the etiology of homosexuality, the article again turned to Falwell for an expert opinion: "Falwell believes homosexuality is a choice and a perversion, a blasphemy against the laws of God" (33).

Most gay leaders quoted in the article reflected on the "new maturity" engendered by the crisis. According to Toby Marotta, a gay social scientist, "This is the most profound, maturing incident for the gay community in its history" (33). For Bill Jones, the owner of a San Francisco bathhouse, "Many gays are beginning to see the party is over. You find more people interested in monogamy and their homes and their health." An older activist who favored "recreational sex" over monogamy was described as a "pioneer" of the gay movement whose opinions were not shared by many in the rising generation. The goal was not free sex, countered a "younger" man, but rather "the freedom to be yourself" (36).

In the context of culture war conflicts over family and gender, *Newsweek* presented both sides of the debate about family values and sexual behavior. Yet the orientation and organization of "Gay America in Transition"—what was mentioned and what was left unsaid as well as how opposing positions were sourced and described—presumed that monogamy was preferable to "excess" (33), "sobriety"[92] to "flamboyance,"[93] and middle-class values to hedonism. The piece stigmatized "recreational sex" (36) through disparaging language and critical sources. It implicitly argued that gays should embrace traditional economic and social values. According to San Francisco's mayor, many already had. "'The great bulk of the gay population . . . goes to work in the morning and comes home at night, like everybody else,' says Mayor Dianne Feinstein. 'It runs the political gamut as far as ideology is concerned, and I suspect that, in the majority, it is probably conservative" (34). Next to Falwell's rhetoric of sin, perversion, and punishment, the new sobriety of middle-class, monogamous homosexuality must have seemed a reasonable option to many readers.

Subsequent media coverage of the AIDS crisis, owing to Falwell's political stature and colorful quotes, continued to support the minister's framing of the disease. Even if individual reporters disagreed with him, their desire to have a "balanced" narrative required his perspective: AIDS raised moral issues that demanded a religious response. And if you needed a religious voice, who better than a Bible-quoting televangelist who was close to the president and had millions of followers? Falwell's view may not have resonated with many journalists, but it had become the news media's de facto religious frame: AIDS was a judgment, not just against them (gays), but also against "us," heterosexuals who countenance their behavior. *Newsweek* did suggest that normative commitments to work and family could dissolve the differences between us and them. "Good" gays, like straights, accepted monogamy and capitalism, while "bad" gays had casual sex and reaped the fatal consequences. AIDS coverage policed the possible, and both Falwell and Feinstein called for their own version of middle-class respectability. Falwell wanted a "traditional" nuclear family; Feinstein was fine with family, straight or gay. The success of either would be a win for the forces of conservatism, since the midpoint of American political life would shift to the right regardless.

Just as Reagan's "Evil Empire" speech reminded audiences of America's divine covenant and its responsibility to promote freedom worldwide, so his religious surrogates, Falwell and other Christian leaders on the right, used the AIDS crisis to exemplify domestic evil and the consequence of flouting God-given norms of personal responsibility and appropriate sexuality. The Reagan-era religious imaginary needed clear distinctions between good and evil, and these two stories—AIDS and the communist threat—helped delineate them. Thus did the imaginary enter the national conversation.

CHAPTER FIVE

The "New Patriotism"

The Mission in Grenada

Here's my strategy for the Cold War: We win, they lose.

PRESIDENT RONALD REAGAN, Moscow Summit, June 1988

Days after the 1980 Democratic National Convention portrayed Ronald Reagan as "a combination of Ebenezer Scrooge and the mad bomber," the Republican presidential candidate addressed the Veterans of Foreign Wars Convention in Chicago.[1] Repeating a pledge he had made during the primary season, Reagan stated, "Let us tell those who fought in that [Vietnam] war that we will never again ask young men to fight and possibly die in a war our government is afraid to let us win."[2] VFW members, whose endorsement of Reagan ended eighty years of their organization's nonpartisanship, roared their approval.[3]

Reagan and his handlers were walking a fine line. His conservative base approved of his call for a strong military and peace through strength. But other voters feared what Democrats alleged to be his reckless warmongering, A backlash against the Vietnam War had made many Americans wary of overseas entanglements. Reagan, seeking middle ground, urged voters to learn from the past but not be limited by it. In his opinion, the public's aversion to protracted foreign wars was misguided: "For too long we have lived with the 'Vietnam Syndrome.' It is time we recognized that ours was, in truth, a noble cause."[4]

According to Reagan, the Vietnam syndrome had weakened the United States. He viewed the Soviet Union as an existential threat, which demanded opposition. Once elected, he increased military spending, kick-starting a "renaissance in Defense Department technology."[5] He also provided a justification for foreign wars: it was America's divine duty to crush the evil communist empire. Reagan conjured that rationale in October 1983, when he deployed US troops to the island nation of Grenada. Concerned that a Cuban- and Soviet-backed coup threatened not only Americans on the island but also the entire region, he went on the attack. Neither he nor America's Caribbean allies wanted more armed communists in the region. The four-day blitz toppled the Grenadian government and dealt a crushing blow to the Vietnam syndrome. But the incursion also had a secondary effect: it served notice on the press, which the administration viewed as critical of, if not hostile to, its policies.[6] Military leaders barred journalists from accompanying the operation and banned them from going to Grenada on their own. The result was an unprecedented absence of third-party, on-the-ground war coverage, a staple of American news since the 1846 Mexican War.[7]

Even after journalists were permitted on the island, military-imposed delays slowed their ability to investigate what had occurred. When reporters finally had access to information, their stories did little to change the government's narrative. The initial absence of independent reporting and the success of White House spin led to several wins for the president: Grenada strengthened the conservative tide and helped catalyze what pundits called a new patriotism. Many said the mission restored America's self-confidence and role as an international leader. Reagan's popularity soared: less than two weeks after the attack, 63 percent of participants in a *Washington Post*–ABC News poll approved "his handling of the presidency," and 71 percent supported "the invasion of Grenada."[8]

The swell of support reflects a political truism: in times of crisis, citizens rally behind their leaders. But it also suggests that many accepted Reagan's explanation of events. News stories about AIDS and the nuclear freeze demonstrated that the president and many Americans wanted clear-cut criteria for good and evil. Grenada became another battleground in this cosmic struggle. Reagan's religious imaginary, which held individual freedom as sacrosanct and democracy as its political expression, circulated in media tropes that excoriated communism and celebrated freedom. These tropes previously had played out in news stories about the downing of a Korean Air Lines jet in September 1983 and the bombing of Marine barracks in Lebanon that October. Now they reached a crescendo in Grenada, in part because the mainstream press was excluded during the early days of the invasion and could not offer a different narrative. As this chapter will explain, Reagan's control of the story reinforced his religious imaginary, and the US troops' victory, according to the news media, helped dispel Vietnam syndrome and reawaken the country's sense of righteous patriotism.

GRENADA: THE BACKSTORY AND THE INVASION

In 1974, Britain granted independence to the 220-square-mile island of Grenada, and Eric Gairy became its first prime minister. Gairy enjoyed good relations with the United States, but his standing at home was marred by his mix of authoritarianism, idiosyncrasy (he was obsessed with UFOs), and indifference to financial realities. While Gairy was in New York discussing extraterrestrials, Maurice Bishop, the Marxist leader of the leftist New Jewel (Joint Endeavor for Welfare, Education and Liberation of the People) Movement,[9] was in Grenada advocating for reform. Bishop, whose political career had been inspired by the American civil rights movement, was a London-trained lawyer who promised to help Grenada's poor. Seeing his calls resonate with his countrymen, he declared himself prime minister of the People's Revolutionary Government in March 1979.[10]

The Carter administration considered intervening, but the Senate Intelligence Committee blocked the plan. Other international developments loomed larger. In January Reza Pahlavi, the shah of Iran, had fled his country due to widespread discontent with his regime. Concurrently, an Islamic Republic was forming under the leadership of Ayatollah Ruhollah Khomeini, who after decades of exile in France was poised to return to Tehran. The Iranian Revolution ended almost four decades of a key US alliance at a moment when the administration faced a slew of international and domestic setbacks. Military ties with Nicaragua had been severed, Muslim extremists had assassinated the US ambassador to Afghanistan, and a nuclear meltdown had rocked the Three Mile Island nuclear power plant in Pennsylvania. Rather than act against Bishop—who headed a very small nation of just under one hundred thousand people—US leaders distanced themselves from his regime. The gap widened under the Reagan administration. Bishop's growing dependence on Soviet-backed Cuba, compounded by his disparaging remarks about Reagan and the United States, nettled the president and his advisors. When Congress rebuffed another plan to destabilize Grenada's Marxist government, the administration used diplomacy to halt the flow of international loans to the country. Since Grenada's economy was already precarious, this additional pressure made life even harder for the islanders, and communist support became vital to the regime. In the summer of 1981, the United States intensified its opposition by staging naval maneuvers that simulated the invasion of a hostage-holding "enemy in the Eastern Caribbean."[11]

Grenada may have been a small, impoverished island, but its strategic symbolism propelled Washington's interest in its fate. Historically, US leaders viewed their primary sphere of influence, intrinsic to the national interest, as extending from the continental United States (later including Alaska and Hawaii) to the Caribbean and Latin America.[12] The Cuban Revolution, which ended in 1959, imperiled US hemispheric hegemony, and subsequent Marxist activities in the region were viewed as a threat. Emboldened by the US stalemate in Vietnam, the Soviets, according to some US foreign policy experts, had increased their activities around the globe, fomenting communist insurgencies in Africa, the Middle East, and Latin America. As *Time* magazine noted, "U.S. timidity in recent years has encouraged Soviet mischief in diverse parts of the world. Particularly in the Caribbean, the U.S. has felt it has a responsibility to stand up against hostile influences and ensure that there are no more Cubas."[13]

Added to these foreign policy calculations were Reagan's beliefs in America's mission to spread freedom and his deep-seated anticommunism. The eponymous Reagan Doctrine took a proactive view of opposing communism wherever possible and supporting "freedom fighters," including Afghani *mujahideen*, Nicaraguan *contras*, and Poland's Solidarity movement. Detractors called him a cowboy, but Reagan believed that neither polite diplomacy nor economic sanctions would stem the Soviet tide. Congress thwarted his plans to fight in Nicaragua, but he secretly harbored hopes for active engagement.[14] Thus, when the opportunity arose to make a public stand in Grenada, the president moved swiftly.

American policy makers knew that Bishop had a warm relationship with Cuban leader Fidel Castro, whose country was supplying Grenada with military hardware as well as personnel for construction projects. By the early 1980s, Grenada also was receiving military assistance from the Soviet Union and North Korea.[15] Reagan officials saw these circumstances as cause for worry, and throughout 1982 and 1983, the president's speeches telegraphed the threat. Announcing the Caribbean Basin Initiative, which did not include Grenada, Reagan criticized "states that 'have turned from their American neighbors' to serve as agents of 'a new colonialism' that 'threatens our independence.'"[16]

In early 1982, the American president noted "the tightening grip of the totalitarian left" in the region. Later that year, he denounced Grenada's "Soviet and Cuban trademark" and expressed concern for US national security. In March 1983, when Reagan announced his Strategic Defense Initiative, he cast Grenada as an instigator. The president "unveiled aerial reconnaissance photographs of Cuba, Nicaragua, and Grenada, presenting these as evidence of the buildup of a 'red triangle.' Proof of the rapid growth of a Soviet-Cuban military presence in the Caribbean, he argued, was the construction of an international airport with a '10,000-foot runway'"[17] at Port Salines in Grenada. Reagan maintained that the airport was for military purposes, even though Grenada and several European countries that helped fund the construction insisted it was to improve tourism.

Seeking to defuse tensions, Maurice Bishop visited Washington in the spring of 1983. He had come to power promising to alleviate poverty, but his pledge to fix the economy, like his commitment to a constitutional government, faltered after he assumed control.[18] When Reagan refused to meet with him, Bishop unsuccessfully appealed to administration officials. Back in Grenada, his hold on power was deteriorating: He faced internal rivals as well as external threats. Deputy Prime Minister Bernard Coard, exploiting widespread unrest spurred by a weak economy, accused Bishop of insufficient revolutionary ardor. After rallying most of the New Jewel Movement's leadership, Coard deposed and imprisoned Bishop on October 13. Six days later, Bishop and five members of his inner circle were executed. Closely monitoring events from Washington, the Reagan administration worried about escalating violence by a regime that promised to be even more militant than Bishop's. As a result, the Joint Chiefs of Staff began discussing evacuation plans for one thousand Americans on the island, including medical students, tourists, and others in residence.[19] The State Department opined "that the entire island had to be secured in order to 'save American lives and serve broader goals.'"[20]

After Bishop was killed, the prime minister of Barbados asked the United States to restore order in Grenada. Around the same time, Reagan rerouted a ten-ship Marine fleet headed to the Middle East to the Caribbean. The president decamped to Georgia on a golfing trip, but his vacation ended abruptly when his advisors, fielding requests for assistance from the Organization of East Caribbean States (OECS), called to discuss options. Fearing a reprise of events in Iran four years earlier, when student revolutionaries held fifty-two American hostages for 444 days, the president and his team opted for decisive action. They planned an invasion, and by the following day US troopships were under way. Cuba, aware of the escalating crisis, informed Washington that no Americans had been harmed in Grenada and asked that its own citizens, working peacefully on the island, remain safe too.

Even as plans for Reagan's "rescue mission" unfolded, terrible news came from the other side of the world. On Sunday, October 23, a truck armed with twelve thousand pounds of dynamite exploded at the US Marine barracks near the Beirut airport. The suicide bombing killed 241 US military personnel and wounded 60 more. Minutes later, a similar strike hit a French base, killing 58 soldiers.[21] Islamic Jihad claimed responsibility for the attacks, which were prompted by grievances against the multinational forces stationed there. Although international troops were deployed as neutral UN peacekeepers, some Muslims believed their real purpose was to prop up a weak, Western-backed, Christian government that was aligned with Israel, which had invaded Lebanon in 1982.

Reagan denounced the attacks and pledged to keep US forces in the small Middle Eastern nation. He did not retaliate, even though the United States had sustained the highest number of one-day casualties since World War II. In a solemn address to the American people, Reagan said that now, more than ever, the United States had a vital role in Lebanon. But the *New York Times*, among other newspapers, questioned that purpose, calling the fallen Marines "victims of a murky diplomatic cause that the President feels bound to reaffirm but still cannot fully define."[22] Touring the bombed-out site, Vice President George H. W. Bush pledged that "terrorists" would not dictate foreign policy. But Marines would soon be stationed offshore, and four months later, all were redeployed.

The unsigned *Times* editorial opined that "merely proving American mettle to the Russians is a poor reason for persisting" in Lebanon. Yet at the very moment that the nation was mourning the slain Marines, Reagan was preparing another salvo against the Soviets. He was determined to invade Grenada. His thinking, according to *Time* magazine, was, "We cannot let an act of terrorism determine whether we aid or assist our allies in the region. If we do that, who will ever trust us again?" The next day—Monday, October 24—Reagan authorized Operation Urgent Fury, the code name for the Grenada mission, and on Tuesday morning US and OECS troops landed on the island. The campaign was major news, as *Time* noted: "For the first time since the end of the Viet Nam War, the U.S. had committed its troops to a combat attack."[23]

That morning, Reagan held a press conference to explain his decision. When asked why it was necessary to invade Grenada, Prime Minister Eugenia Charles of Dominica, standing by the president's side, said it was both a "rescue mission" aimed at Americans on the island and a response to Grenada's neighbors' appeal for help. Other than Barbados, Grenada was the only OECS member to have an army. As a result, regional leaders worried about their ability to protect against external and internal threats from Grenada's radical new regime. Their request, which dovetailed with the administration's plans, offered grounds for the mission and justification under international law.[24]

Over the next two days, US officials repeated these reasons to Congress and the news media. In the meantime, seven thousand US and Caribbean troops engaged in sporadically heavy fighting against the Cuban and Grenadian soldiers. Some victories came easily: the Pearls Airport was captured early on, and the American students were rescued from one of two campuses. But US Rangers were met with antiaircraft fire as their helicopters approached the Point Salines airstrip,[25] where construction was under way to improve the facilities. US troops were prepared to fight, but they were surprised by the strength and size of the defense. Several hours later, American fighters secured the airport and captured many combatants, but skirmishing around the island continued as Americans tried to rescue the remaining students and to recapture St. George, Grenada's capital. By Wednesday night, much of the island was under American control, but resistance continued for the next few days. By week's end, eleven US servicemen were dead, seven missing, and sixty-seven seriously wounded.[26]

On October 27, Reagan went on television to explain why US troops were in Lebanon and Grenada. Both situations had unsettled the American public: the terrorist attack in Beirut was shocking, and the Grenada invasion was a mystery. A clutch of Democratic congressmen criticized the latter, as had several foreign leaders, most notably Prime Minister Margaret Thatcher of Great Britain. Americans knew very little about the incursion, since the military had precluded independent press coverage. In fact, the first news reports were from the Department of Defense, affirming that the Rangers "had quickly achieved their initial goals and suffered 'minimal' losses"[27]—an account that later proved to be less than the full truth. With news limited to governmental sources, print and broadcast outlets supplemented official statements with stories filed Stateside: analyses of "previous debacles" that caused the administration to fear "another Iran,"[28] articles on why Congress "split sharply over the wisdom of the policy,"[29] updates on local protests against the invasion, and coverage of the first evacuees.

These images—angry demonstrators, arguing congressional representatives, and the long shadows of Iran and Vietnam—vied with government communiques and photos as the predominant representations of the invasion. Occurring only forty-eight hours after the bombing in Lebanon, the Grenada mission struck some as a diversion. For Americans who had not tracked Carter's and Reagan's concern with Cuban influence on the small island, the military action seemed a misplaced show of might. On October 26, a CBS poll found that a slim majority, 53.8 percent of the public, supported Reagan's decision to invade. The same percentage felt favorably about stationing troops in Lebanon, despite the recent casualties.[30] The numbers may have suggested a reflexive "rallying 'round the flag," but they were soft in the context of an upcoming reelection campaign.

THE GREAT COMMUNICATOR

Every president, by virtue of his position, sets the news agenda, but few can use that position to shift the nation's sense of mission, identity, and purpose. Reagan was a master at this, and the successful invasion of Grenada helped. In a January 1981 poll, only 27 percent of respondents felt that the country was on the right track; in December 1983, shortly after Grenada and amid an economic revival, that number had risen to 60 percent. Another survey that month asked interviewees whether things looked better or worse for 1984 than the past year. The proportion that expected a better year was the highest since the poll was first taken in 1971.[31]

The upsurge benefited from the president's likability. Even people who disliked Reagan's policies liked the man. The Great Communicator, as he was called, told simple stories that revivified America's sense of mission and restored its central myths. His themes—"America's greatness, its commitment to freedom, the heroism of the American people, the moral imperatives of work, the priority of economic advancement, the domestic evil of taxes and government regulation, and the necessity of maintaining military strength"—highlighted the country's mission to spread freedom and personal liberty. To a nation adrift, Reagan's stories also offered meaning and moral direction. By focusing on ends rather than means, he turned opposition to his arguments into a matter of principle rather than policy.[32] Describing this tack and the leverage it provided him, Reagan said his oratory was channeled from a higher source. "I never thought it was my style or the words I used that made a difference: It was the content. I wasn't a great communicator, but I communicated great things, and they didn't spring full bloom from my brow, they came from the heart of a great nation—from our experience, our wisdom, and our belief in principles that have guided us for two centuries."[33]

Of course, not all listeners, either then or afterward, agreed that Reagan was a great communicator or channeling great things. Opponents said the former actor was simply adept at reading lines and following cues. Some in his administration concurred. Donald Regan, initially Reagan's secretary of the Treasury and later White House chief of staff, noted, "Every moment of every public appearance was scheduled, every word was scripted, every place Reagan was expected to stand was chalked with toe marks."[34] The bottom line, for the president and his men, was providing journalists with images and sound bites that advanced the administration's goals.

For example, Reagan's stories provided frames for listeners to map onto their own perception of meaning. Communications scholars use the term *schema* to refer to the processes that human beings use to make sense of the world. Schema enable people to synthesize new information by integrating it with their own assumptions. When Reagan referred to a "shining city on a hill," a frame evoking America's moral authority, listeners could connect it to schema about America's religious roots and its God-given destiny. Schema affect the opinions that people use to make judgments as well as the ways they act and interpret information.[35] Many of Reagan's most effective speeches used moralistic frames, such as the Soviet Union as an "evil empire," that meshed with schema entwining religion and nationalism. Thus, when he spoke about communism, as he did in the October 27, 1983, speech on the mission in Grenada, his listeners were primed to hear that their most cherished values were at stake.

The speech reiterated many of the themes Reagan had used in his March 8 "Evil Empire" address to the National Association of Evangelicals. He explained that America's guiding principles, such as freedom and personal liberty, were grounded in the nation's religious commitment—specifically, its willingness to seek and accept God's blessings. He implied that Americans obeyed God by opposing the expansion of communism in the Middle East and the Caribbean. Implicit in his words, but clear to evangelical ears, was another religious priority: Israel, a nation that the president identified as a force for democracy in the Middle East as well as a strong American ally, was at risk. Israel also was important to those evangelical Christians who believed that the founding of the Jewish state heralded Jesus' Second Coming. Even those who did not share this apocalyptic view but believed in America's mission as a beacon to the nations found in Reagan's argument a pragmatic rationale for action: doing the right thing for America made the world better for all.

Just as the Israel argument appealed to some religious constituents, so, too, Reagan's second justification for the Grenada mission made sense to many secular listeners. Echoing Wilsonian foreign policy, the president claimed that the United States, the world's best hope for freedom and democracy, was obligated to act internationally. He appealed explicitly for American exceptionalism, the notion that "the United States is both destined and entitled to play a distinct and positive role on the world stage."[36]

Mounting his argument with clear and vivid language, Reagan's words highlighted his administration's central narrative—the cosmic showdown between the United States and the Soviet Union. His opening remarks set the frame by referring to the recent tragedy that he ascribed to Russian disregard for human life, the September 1 attack on KAL 007. On October 27, when Reagan addressed the nation, the Soviets' malfeasance in the Korean tragedy was fresh in the public's mind. As a result, the president's initial sentences, seemingly unconnected to the rest of the speech, set up an equivalency among the downing of KAL 007, the attack on the US Marines in Lebanon, and the Marxist threat in Grenada. The passengers on the doomed jet, the casualties in Lebanon, and the people of Grenada were all victims of the same evil empire. The president was implying that in less than two months, the Soviet will to dominate, regardless of the consequences, had resulted in three tragedies.

Reagan's simple descriptions made events real. He conjured sixteen hundred Marines in south Beirut "just a mile or so" from the Italian contingent and "not far from" French and British troops. He colored in details that collapsed time and distance into a familiar early morning cityscape: "This past Sunday, at 22 minutes after 6 Beirut time, with dawn just breaking, a truck, looking like a lot of other vehicles in the city, approached the airport on a busy, main road." But this truck was different, Reagan said, because "at the wheel was a young man on a suicide mission." The young man, ignoring guards who tried to stop him, drove the truck through barbed-wire barriers and a chain-link fence before he "smashed through the doors of the headquarters building." The truck exploded on impact, with the blast from the explosion killing "more than 200 of the sleeping men."[37]

Just as carefully as he portrayed the particulars of the attack, Reagan repeated the plaintive questions he had heard from bereaved family members and the nation at large: "Why should our young men be dying in Lebanon? Why is Lebanon important to us?"[38] His answers reiterated his administration's key principles: Lebanon was important to America's economic well-being and the future of its democracy as well as to world peace and the security of Israel. Israel, said Reagan, was America's closest ally in the Middle East, and the nation had a "moral obligation" to protect it.

Syria, the Soviet Union's proxy, endangered Israel, Lebanon, and, by extension, the United States. Backed by "7,000 Soviet advisers and technicians who man a massive amount of Soviet weaponry," Syria not only threatened Lebanon's autonomy but also targeted Soviet missiles on "vital areas of Israel." US support ensured democracy in Lebanon, peace in the Middle East, and the future of the Jewish state. It also enabled oil to flow to the United States and her allies. The Marine presence in Beirut, Reagan said, "is vital to our national security and economic well-being."[39]

The president also implied that a preemptive desire to protect Americans from "terrorist" attacks determined the mission in Grenada. (Reagan did not use the word *invasion* and chastised reporters who did.)[40] He repeated earlier explanations for Operation Urgent Fury: several Caribbean states had asked the United States to restore order, and American citizens were in danger. Stressing parallels between the Syrian presence in Lebanon and the threat posed by the Cubans on the Caribbean island, he noted, "The events in Lebanon and Grenada, though oceans apart, are closely related. Not only has Moscow assisted and encouraged the violence in both countries, but it provides direct support through a network of surrogates and terrorists."[41] (According to the *New York Times*, a senior administration official later said that the president was not trying to blame Moscow for the Beirut bombing, but the speech was more equivocal.)[42]

Driving home his point, Reagan said that US troops "discovered a complete base with weapons and communications equipment" that proved Cuba was preparing to take over Grenada. US servicemen also found a warehouse with "weapons and ammunition stacked almost to the ceiling, enough to supply thousands of terrorists." Asserting "we got there just in time," the president praised American forces for preventing the establishment of a "Soviet-Cuban colony" that would "export terror and undermine democracy."[43]

Reagan's repeated use of the words *terrorist* and *terrorism*—he invoked them five times in the first three pages of the six-page address and once again toward the end—as well as his mention of "hostages" resonated with his audience. The spectacle of American captives in Iran, a fourteen-month ordeal that dominated daily television news just four years earlier, was still fresh in their memory. There was no universally accepted definition of *terrorism*, but it was generally understood to be "premeditated, politically motivated violence perpetrated against noncombatant targets by subnational groups or clandestine agents."[44] For many Americans, terrorism and hostage-taking were two sides of the same coin: terrorism the creed and hostage-taking the deed.

The hostages in Iran had been American embassy personnel, some with CIA connections, but the president and the news media presented them as private citizens who were victims of terrorism.[45] That their captors were fomenters of Islamic revolution reinforced long-standing anti-Muslim sentiment as well as new outrage. During the 1970s, a faction of the Palestinian Liberation Organization had mounted terrorist attacks against Israeli citizens, including the 1972 massacre of Israeli Olympians in Munich; the 1974 massacre in Ma'alot, Israel, which entailed hostage-taking and the killing of twenty-two Israeli children; and several attempted hijackings, including the 1976 diversion of an Air France flight that ended with the counterterrorist raid on Entebbe Airport in Uganda. The fact that the PLO was a secular organization with Christian as well as Muslim members was lost on many Americans, who conflated an ethnic Arab identity with Islam.

The Marines stationed in Beirut were serving as peacekeepers, which is not the same as being noncombatants. They were servicemen defending a contested political status quo, and they symbolized US military power. But Reagan, glossing over the mandate that had brought the fighters to Lebanon, referred to them as "sleeping men," "young men," and "victims." By turning troops into civilians, he recast the Marines as fathers, husbands, and sons. Moreover, he linked the "terrorists" who killed the "sleeping men" to potential hostage takers in Grenada: both were communist proxies who threatened America's citizens, national security, and economic well-being. Reagan's rhetorical strategy transferred Islamic characteristics onto the Cubans and Grenadians who fought the US "rescue mission" so that the enemy's otherness encompassed racial and religious difference. Similar to the "Muslim terrorists," they were dark skinned and, as communists, dark souled.

Given his bully pulpit and oratorical skill, Reagan's explanation of events promoted his political position. His words were newsworthy, and the press's job was to convey them to the public. A follow-up story might present alternate perspectives, and op-ed writers and editorialists might challenge the president's claims, but he established the narrative. The first account of an event shapes public perception, making it hard to dislodge, and Reagan's October 27 speech had this effect.

REPORTING THE CONFLICT

While Reagan worked his magic as the Great Communicator, journalists scrambled to cover the war. The US government waited several hours before announcing that its forces had landed in Grenada. Reporters immediately clamored to be let onto the island. But James Baker, Donald Regan's predecessor as White House chief of staff, announced that the military had vetoed onsite news coverage, and the White House had agreed. When pressed, officials cited the need for secrecy. Equally important, according to government sources, was that troops engaged in battle could not guarantee the press's safety.

The military's rationale for excluding reporters coincided with the Reagan administration's desire to control the news. Aligning public opinion behind the Grenada mission was crucial, and neither the president nor his generals felt they could count on journalists to cover the story in a favorable light. Vietnam had shown that the American public had little appetite for battle gore when the victims or perpetrators were the nation's young. For the first two days of fighting, official communiques reported that casualties were low, but the administration did not release the numbers of dead and injured troops. In like manner, the Americans' shelling and destruction of a hospital for the mentally ill went unreported for almost a week.[46]

Assessing the invasion after the fact, Michael Deaver, deputy chief of staff at the White House, told Mark Hertsgaard, an investigative journalist, "It was obvious to me it had a very good chance of being successful and it would be a good story."[47] But to be a good story, it had to be vetted and monitored. Thus, the first news of the troops' landing was delivered in a statement by the president, who explained that the mission's goals were to rescue Americans, protect regional governments, and restore law and order. Second-day communiques emphasized early successes and minimal casualties. According to the *New York Times*, the administration had placed "extraordinary restrictions on news coverage."[48] But even as the heads of major news organizations bombarded the White House with appeals to lift the restrictions, their staffs did not turn the blackout into a major story.

More than three hundred journalists waited on Barbados for entry onto Grenada. On Thursday, October 27, two full days after the mission began, fifteen were invited to join the reporters' pool, a representative group expected to share its interviews, photos, and films with the rest. Among the lucky ones were journalists from the three major television networks and the three major press services.[49] None, however, were from a daily newspaper, and newsmagazines were included only after negotiations. For several hours, the military escorted pool reporters around the island before

FIGURE 20. Reporters at an airport in Barbados awaiting a flight to Grenada. Mark Scheerer.

whisking them back to Barbados to update the others. Their stories, along with the president's televised address the same day, guaranteed positive coverage on the front pages of most morning newspapers and at the top of radio and television news broadcasts.

Two more days had passed before the press was given full access to the island. But when news outlets noted their exclusion from the action, few called it censorship or even a blackout. Instead, they emphasized the challenge of reporting under government restrictions. An October 26 *New York Times* story noted that the US military's decision "to maintain secrecy" and reduce "logistical problems"[50] left journalists dependent on government accounts, diplomatic and intelligence sources, Grenadian radio, and telephone calls to the island's residents to cover the invasion. The articles implied that these conditions made coverage difficult, but they did not publicly remonstrate against the government's decision. (Private correspondence from news chiefs to the administration was more forthright in expressing frustration, and some columnists and senior journalists publicly decried the ban.)

Coverage had been limited even before the invasion. Grenadian leaders expelled most reporters after the coup that deposed Maurice Bishop. News stories were reported Stateside or from Barbados, and most were placed deep inside newspapers. But American involvement changed everything. Reports that Marines and battleships bound for Lebanon had been diverted to Grenada made the front page of the October 22 edition of the *Los Angeles Times* and many other papers. The change of course was "to assure the safety of American citizens,"[51] and official sources said there were no plans to send troops ashore. By this time, the American public had become aware of the problem: several hundred Americans were medical students at St. George's University, near Grenada's capital, and the local government was in turmoil. NPR aired an interview with a student there, notable more for what was not said than what was. After admitting, "I have to watch what I say on the phone because I don't want to cause any problems,"[52] Paul Dubrich said the situation was "pretty hairy." But he also said there was no immediate danger and that "supposedly" there was an evacuation plan. Grenadian and Cuban officials had told the Reagan administration that the students were in no danger, and foreigners were leaving the island up until the day before the US forces landed.

Once the invasion was launched, news outlets had only the government's story to report. The following day, the *Washington Post* dedicated most of its front page to invasion updates from official sources. Further back in the *New York Times*, reporters quoted government sources stating that invading forces had "quickly achieved their initial goals,"[53] with very few losses. NPR located American ham radio operators on the island, but, pinned down by the attack, their knowledge of events was limited.

The absence of details made it difficult for Americans to grasp what was happening. Members of Congress, knowing little more than the public, responded along party lines. Republicans supported Reagan's decisiveness, while Democrats wondered whether their trigger-happy president had behaved rashly. In its defense, the administration evoked Iran. During a press briefing on the first day of the mission, Secretary of State George Shultz wondered what would have happened if the government had not acted decisively and if Americans were taken hostage or killed.

Shultz added another reason for the mission: the need to stop Cuban and Soviet expansion in the region. As the week progressed, this would emerge as an overriding concern. Reagan and his surrogates hinted at caches of secret weapons as well as documents showing that a "major Cuban military buildup had been discovered 'in the knick [*sic*] of time.'"[54] Without hard news to report, reporters used the "nick of time" story and the return of the American medical students as their central narratives. Before the students' rescue, news outlets reported that the university's chancellor, as well as some parents, doubted whether the students' lives were endangered. But when they deplaned, the students profusely thanked the president for bringing them home. Some even kissed the ground.[55]

FIGURE 21. An American student evacuated from the St. George's University School of Medicine in Grenada, upon arriving in the United States. Courtesy US National Archives and Records Administration.

Thereafter, the tone of the story switched from tentative to triumphant. The students' reaction seemed to prove there was a problem, and judging from the apparent presence of Cuban military personnel on the island, the president had ended a communist threat there.

Both story lines—the Beirut bombing and the invasion of Grenada—dominated the news on October 28, the day after Reagan's speech to the nation. That very morning, five of the seven front-page *New York Times* stories were about Grenada, and the remaining two were on Lebanon. Under a banner headline reporting that "Cuba Aimed to Take Grenada, Bastion Reported to Fall; Battle Goes On," one of three lead stories focused on mounting congressional criticism of the invasion. But the newspaper—like the legislators who "muted"[56] criticism of the president while waiting to see how the mission fared—focused on positive angles. Stories updated American victories on the island, quoted the president's warning that a "Soviet-Cuban colony" was blocked "just in time,"[57] and described the rescued students' "gratitude" and "praise" for the administration.[58]

A week after the invasion, the government-fed news still focused on the "just in time" trope of the failed communist takeover. According to officials, US troops, after rescuing the students and securing the capital city and countryside, uncovered Cuba's takeover plans. When news outlets asked for evidence of communist infiltration,[59] government spokesmen cited "a potential terrorist training base," "secret treaties between Grenada, the Soviet Union, Cuba and North Korea," and stockpiles of weapons.[60] But when reporters examined the documents and viewed the stockpiles, a different story emerged. The *New York Times* reported that the US government had "disseminated much inaccurate information and many unproven assertions." The paper said that some of the errors occurred during combat and its attendant confusion. But others were the result of "selective and incomplete reporting" that put the government in the best light possible, and still others were "deliberate distortions and knowingly false statements of fact."[61]

The administration's aim, surmised the *Times* and other news outlets, was to justify the invasion. The first step was to claim that Americans on the island were in greater danger than they were, and the second was to find evidence of a planned Cuban occupation. The paper reported that in both cases, government officials either misled the press or exaggerated the threat. Likewise, officials were slow to admit their own "mishaps that cost the lives of Grenadian civilians and American servicemen," including at least seventeen fatalities when a civilian mental hospital was mistakenly bombed.[62]

Similarly disturbing were the government's shifting reports about the

"All the News That's Fit to Print"

The New York Times

Late Edition

VOL. CXXXIII . . No. 45,845 — NEW YORK, FRIDAY, OCTOBER 28, 1983 — 30 CENTS

REAGAN SAYS CUBA AIMED TO TAKE GRENADA; BASTION REPORTED TO FALL; BATTLE GOES ON

MOVE IN CONGRESS

House Panel, 32-2, Votes to Apply Law Limiting Right to Wage War

By STEVEN V. ROBERTS

3D DAY OF COMBAT

Army Chief Said to Hold Out South of Capital — Prison Overrun

REPORT TO NATION

President Says Invasion Was 'Just in Time' to Avert Occupation

By HEDRICK SMITH

MARINES RELEASE DIAGRAM ON BLAST

But Questions on Security at Beirut Compound Remain

By THOMAS L. FRIEDMAN

Nations in Lebanon Peace Force Are Reported to Discuss Reprisals

By JOHN VINOCUR

Havana Agrees to Mediation On Return of Cuban Captives

By JO THOMAS

From Rescued Students, Gratitude and Praise

By ROBERT D. McFADDEN

INSIDE

Divisions in Glenn Camp

Hope for Sterile Women

79 Feared Lost Off China

FIGURE 22. On October 28, 1983, the *New York Times* devoted five of seven front-page stories to Grenada. The other two reported on the bombing of the US Marines barracks in Lebanon.

number of Cubans on the island. Over the week, their numbers rose from a low of 400 to a high of 1,100. Information on the Cubans' status was equally inconsistent. Initial reports called them construction workers, whereas later dispatches said they were well-trained soldiers masquerading as construction workers. The final number was 784 Cubans on Grenada, among whom were approximately 100 combatants and more than 600 workers. Similarly, warehouses that were said to contain enough ammunition to sustain "thousands of terrorists" were found to be only half full of outdated weaponry. Released documents showed no evidence of a terrorist training base or Cuban plans to take over the island. Rather, the papers described Grenada's weak military, dismal economy, and faltering government. "What the documents suggest," said an NPR reporter, "is that Grenada posed less of a threat to its neighbors in the Caribbean than to itself."[63]

Even as news outlets began debunking the official government story, Congress, including members who were initially skeptical of the invasion, declared its value. The change of heart was due to positive public opinion about the mission. Two delegations, one a bipartisan commission and the other a group of conservative Republicans concerned about the official commission's impartiality, came to the same conclusion. As Rep. Tom Foley, House Majority Whip and head of the official committee, told NPR, "The majority, and I would say the very large majority, of the delegation, feels that, under the circumstances, the President acted correctly to protect American lives."[64]

The two delegations also agreed that US troops should come home and that the US government should provide economic aid to Grenada. But they differed on lessons learned. Foley's group said its support for the Grenada mission should not be construed as backing for the president's Latin American policy. The Republican delegation said there was ample evidence of Soviet designs on the island and that similar circumstances could provoke similar responses elsewhere in the hemisphere. "If you have a thief in the night stealing in through the back door, you have to do something about it," said Rep. Don Ritter, a Republican congressman from Pennsylvania.[65]

In the following weeks, the press's criticism of its exclusion from the mission grew more strident. *Time* described the administration's press ban as "an abuse of power"[66] and noted that during World War II and the Korean War, generals had briefed reporters on surprise attacks so that press coverage would be well informed. The information was embargoed, but both sides trusted the other, since the nation's welfare was paramount. But mutual trust was another casualty of the war in Vietnam. Some generals, convinced that Vietnam had been lost in the American press rather than on the battlefield, had vowed that reporters would never again have full access to ongoing warfare. Noting that the military's hostility to the press was "one of the sadder aspects of the Grenada invasion," *Time* concluded that "the U.S. got off to a wrong start by trying to shut off the facts. If we are lucky, perhaps this is one post-Viet Nam lesson we have now learned."[67]

NEWS AND PUBLIC OPINION

The wrangling for control over the narrative of the US mission in Grenada occurred because both the press and the Reagan administration sought to influence public opinion, especially in the critical first days of the war. Public opinion is a difficult concept to pin down. Scholars have described it as whatever the majority believes—that is, an externally projected social norm; the outcome of subtle manipulation by special interests; the elite's perspective adopted by the masses; and a convenient fiction deployed by politicians, policy makers, and the news media to project ideas or opinions that are useful to their own ends.[68] Yet if the creation and meaning of public opinion are contested, its outcome as prevailing sentiment is clear. It seals a feedback loop that constrains what the president or the press says about a given topic.

That's because public opinion, once set, is slow to change, as members of the news media discovered when their stories questioned the official Grenada narrative. Despite reporting information that disputed the president's scenario of a Cuban takeover, journalists could not shake the public's belief that the mission was both justified and successful. And congressional representatives who initially opposed the invasion, after appraising their constituents' support for it, realized there was no value in criticizing it. Reagan's October 27 speech was the turning point in galvanizing public opinion. The next day, support for the invasion rose 22 percentage points among those who heard it, compared to 3 points among those who did not. Those who listened also showed greater agreement with the statements that "the new government in Grenada threatened its neighbors" (from 65.4 to 75.7 percent) and "the new government put Americans in Grenada in danger" (from 59.6 to 75.9 percent). After the address, support for US troops in Lebanon also rose, from 53.8 to 66.8 percent of the public.[69] According to the *Washington Post*, "Almost all movement in support of Reagan came from people who had . . . seen, heard or read about the President's speech."[70]

The speech itself was not the sole reason for the uptick. The data showed that increased support correlated with how the president managed information and what the public knew independent of the speech. If the president is the sole source of information, then the public accepts his expertise. If the public has independent information, then the president is less influential.[71] In other words, the military's effort to influence public opinion by restricting press coverage of the invasion was successful.

Several years after the invasion, independent journalist Mark Hertsgaard argued that the corporate press actually helped squelch an accurate account of events because of its "tendency to accept the basic truth of what its government told it."[72] But journalists who had been denied press access by the military were angry that they were prevented from doing their job. According to Walter Cronkite, who had recently retired as anchor of CBS's evening news show, "These are our marines, our Rangers down there. This is our foreign policy and we have a right to know precisely what is happening, and there can be no excuse in denying the people that right."[73] Both Cronkite, the grand old man of American journalism, and Hertsgaard, a gadfly investigative reporter, acknowledged the importance of agency: journalists should be free to do their jobs. Yet given the systemic constraints under which they operate, journalists have less autonomy than they would like to think.

There is little agreement among the press, the public, and the academy on how news is defined and the extent of journalists' ability to pursue it. News consumers, as well as some journalists, credit reporters' news judgment as the ultimate criterion for newsworthiness. In this paradigm, reporters use professional standards to decide what to report and how to present their findings. Critics of the press use this journalist-centered model to explain biases in news coverage. At best, reporters assume that their own ideological leanings are normative. At worst, the press is out to brainwash the country.

Since the late 1960s, conservatives have complained that the "liberal press" skews news coverage. But from the Progressive Era up through the New Deal, press critics cited the opposite problem: advertisers controlled the news pages, and as a result reporting favored business concerns and the conservative status quo. Writing in 1911, William Irwin—who had spent a decade as a reporter—called the system "dishonest to its marrow," noting the hypocrisy of publishers who controlled the news to suit their own economic interests.[74] Reporters were complicit; before the Great Depression, for example, many downplayed the stock market's instability and the banks' looming problems. After the 1929 crash, journalists rarely wrote about the depth and extent of the nation's financial crisis, including massive unemployment. Their choices may have been in line with publishers' positions, but they also reflected their own self-interest, since "many Wall Street reporters were on the payrolls of stock market representatives, securities firms and banking interests."[75]

Newspaper publishers, like many business magnates, disliked Roosevelt and his New Deal. According to *Time* magazine, as many as 80 percent of the nation's news outlets opposed the president's reelection in 1936.[76] Yet Roosevelt won decisively, carrying forty-six of the forty-eight states and all but eight votes in the electoral college. Following his success, press reformers urged greater professionalization as an antidote to the collusion between business leaders and journalists as well as to charges that publishers pursued profits ahead of civic duty. But little changed, which is why in 1943 Henry Luce financed the Hutchins Commission to make recommendations for improving the profession. As discussed in the first chapter, the commission's recommendations were widely denounced, and even Luce was disappointed. Yet the vision of a responsible press committed to the public welfare and, by extension, democracy slowly spread from the margins to the center of the profession.

The shift was apparent in 1971 when the *New York Times* published the Pentagon Papers, exposing truths about the Vietnam War that the government had hidden from the public. That same impulse inspired the *Washington Post*'s investigation of a failed 1972 break-in at the Watergate apartment complex, a story culminating two years later with the resignation of President Richard M. Nixon. In both instances, journalists demonstrated allegiance to democratic ideals rather than to corporate masters or elected leaders.

Yet the exhilaration that many reporters felt in the decade after Vietnam and Watergate, a sense of purpose that came with safeguarding democracy, was not always shared by the public. Reporters swore by the public's right to know, but the public did not always want to know and, once it did, was not always happy with what the news told them.

For example, reporting on Vietnam turned public opinion against the government's policy and helped end the war. But when the war was over, many Americans felt less a sense of empowerment than one of loss—the loss of lives, military stature, international prestige, and national mission. In the same way, the Watergate crisis demonstrated the importance of a free press in a democratic society, but it also demoralized citizens who had believed in the integrity of the presidency. While the press was not responsible for the debacle in Vietnam or the shame of Watergate, its role in bringing national failures to light left a sour taste, and many blamed the messenger: the liberal press was responsible for America's sorry state.

Journalists, however, might disagree with the theory that reporters and their ideologies drive coverage. An alternate perspective, event-centered journalism, places less onus on journalists' agency and more on their mission to reflect the world around them. In this paradigm, journalists aim for objectivity, the reporting of facts that eschew a journalist's personal bias. But objectivity is more aspirational than actual. The very act of choosing sources and organizing information requires judgments about what is important and what is not. Journalists frequently say that their professionalism enables them to dispassionately make such judgments, but variations in coverage belie their presumption. Reagan's October 27 speech was covered in multiple ways. In the *Wall Street Journal*'s front-page story, the second paragraph informed readers that the death toll in Grenada had risen to eight.[77] The *New York Times* article did not mention that fact. (It was cited in another front-page story, but after the jump and on page 12.)[78] The *Times* made much of the "just in time" scenario, quoting the president's boast about the troops' timely arrival in the story's subhead, while the *Journal* never mentioned it. The *Los Angeles Times* ran the story on page A17. In the second paragraph, reporter Jack Nelson noted that Reagan had "emphasized" that the Cubans' presence on the island, as much as the welfare of American students, had prompted the mission. However, he did not cite the "just in time" quote. Instead, he focused on links between Grenada and Lebanon.[79]

In addition to journalist-centered and event-centered journalism, a third theory of news coverage is organization-centered. It holds that news is the product of social expectations, routines, and structures that operate independently of either journalists' predilections or daily events. The very ways that news is defined, gathered, and structured—who is a source, what is newsworthy, how reporting is organized, and where a story is placed on the page or in the newscast—align with organizational objectives such as maximizing corporate wealth, ensuring social stability, and maintaining the status quo.[80]

Reporters have agency and autonomy within the confines of the system, but they learn its limits through daily practice: Who are the go-to sources and who's beyond the pale? What stories lead the news and which are spiked? Which reporters cover the big political stories, and who is tapped to write obituaries? These delineations are object lessons that become normalized in the production routines and culture of newsrooms. Reporters experience them not as a form of social control but rather as background noise—it's the way things are. Many reporters don't agree with organization-centered theories of news, since they controvert journalists' belief in their own agency.

The overlap and slippage among different theories of news is apparent in the 1983 coverage of Grenada. Reporters complained they could not do their jobs because of government censorship. When stories did emerge that challenged the administration's version of events, they failed to gain traction, since public opinion was already fixed. The lack of alternate narratives to the mission and the president's October 27 speech to the nation closed the feedback loop.

From journalists' vantage point as autonomous actors responsible, especially in their eyes, for safeguarding democracy, the government's management of the Grenada story threatened not only the public's right to know but also their mission. Testifying before Congress in November, journalism's elite sought to uphold their professionalism while also defending their integrity as loyal citizens. Their job, they told the elected officials, was to inform the public. But they also said they would never violate national security or jeopardize a military operation.

When they finally were allowed on the island, many reporters filed stories that followed the government line. But in examining evidence for the "nick of time" scenario, some saw discrepancies between what they discovered and what the government had claimed. The "gotcha" pieces that followed—articles with facts that impugned faulty information—could be interpreted as proof that the military had been right to keep the mission secret for as long as possible. Yet critical articles had little impact; Reagan was more popular than ever. The military had ensured that its initial version of events would predominate, even after the press tried to set the record straight in the days and weeks that followed. Polls indicated that the public did not want to hear about the administration's exaggerations or outright fabrications. Many Americans felt positive about the troops' success, and Washington's version of events prevailed.

In addition to trying to set the record straight, news outlets jumped on the censorship issue once the fighting ended. Again, these stories did little to influence a public that seemed willing to accept press suppression in wartime. Commentators ranging from Daniel Schorr, NPR's in-house liberal, to William Safire, the *New York Times*' resident conservative, filed op-eds opposing restrictions on a free press. Schorr would be expected to condemn government bans, but Safire's censure[81] was striking: as a speechwriter in the Nixon White House, he had penned some of the administration's most colorful denunciations of the news media. (Safire wrote Vice President Spiro Agnew's 1970 denunciation of "nattering nabobs of negativism," a charge leveled at Democratic politicians but popularly remembered as a knock against journalists.)[82]

Public indifference to the news media's plight marked the midpoint of a thirty-year erosion of confidence in reporters and editors, fueled at least in part by a sustained attack on the news media begun by the Nixon White House. From the 1970s to the early 1980s, the number of Americans who considered the press a trustworthy institution steadily declined, although a majority still expressed more confidence in its integrity than in either the executive or the legislative branches of government.[83] But by 1983, public confidence in the news media had fallen to its lowest point in ten years, according to the annual General Social Survey. While there are economic, social, and cultural reasons that account for changing public opinion about journalism,[84] the invasion of Grenada also played a role. By accepting the decision of the executive branch to bar the press, the public countenanced the government's suspicion: reporters cared more for scoops than troops. The formulation assailed reporters' patriotism at the very moment when, in the face of a communist takeover in Grenada, freedom's future was at stake.

Reagan benefited from the military's dislike of the news media as well as the ongoing conservative project to depict journalists as liberals. He liked individual reporters, but he was wary of the press as an institution. Though not as blunt as Nixon in his bid to control the news, Reagan was, in the words of former *Washington Post* reporter Juan Williams, committed to "changing the framework of debate on issues."[85] He accomplished this, according to Hertsgaard and others, by staying on message; cultivating and rewarding reporters whose coverage was positive, especially those from smaller news outlets; and taking extreme stances (such as calling the Soviet Union an evil empire) that usually went unchallenged in initial stories, even if they were subsequently "balanced" in follow-up stories or disputed in editorials.

Reagan's easygoing personality also helped him; by most accounts, White House reporters liked the president. They also needed him, and those who toed the line were more likely to get interviews with him. Hertsgaard argues that the "palace court press" was unwilling and unprepared to do the hard-hitting, oppositional reporting that was its real responsibility, a charge that has been made against subsequent White House reporters.[86] From this perspective, the press's acquiescence to presidential authority combined with the structural limitations of organization-centered journalism made it difficult to sustain confrontational reporting.

Yet even as reporters were constrained by the need to stay in the administration's favor and within their organizations' definition of news, they faced accusations of liberal bias from conservatives. The charge, a hobbyhorse of William F. Buckley's *National Review* from its founding in 1955, gained momentum in the Nixon-Agnew years and grew stronger over the next decade. In 1982 S. Robert Lichter, Stanley Rothman, and Linda S. Lichter published "The Media Elite," an article describing the results of a survey of 238 American journalists. Interviewing reporters from the *New York Times*, the *Washington Post*, the *Wall Street Journal*, *Time*, *Newsweek*, *US News and World Report*, ABC, CBS, PBS, and NBC, the researchers found "few ideologues in major media newsrooms."[87] But they did discover that reporters' personal opinions were more liberal than those of business executives (the study's control group) and most of the public. They also found that these "leftist" attitudes colored the reporting and writing of news. Both reviewers and academics found fault with the study. Critics said that its methodology was flawed and that the biases of its authors shaped the results. But the findings bolstered a popular sentiment, and conservatives touted its argument as justification for their formerly anecdotal claims.

The most widely quoted media survey of the 1980s,[88] "The Media Elite" seemed to provide support for the view that journalists were atheist, cosmopolitan supporters of welfare, abortion, and homosexuality. But whether or not they were ideologically liberal, reporters also worked for profit-making companies in a business that sought to reach the widest possible audience. The goal was to make money by providing a product that consumers wanted and advertisers needed without disturbing the status quo. Accordingly, commercial considerations limited the ideological scope of what was reported in mainstream news by creating discursive spheres appropriate for coverage. These spheres, learned though social and cultural cues, act as internal guardrails in real life as well as in journalism. For example, it's fine to whisper softly in a movie theater. It's even acceptable to make some noise unwrapping a candy bar. But it's prohibited to stand up and yell "Fire!" if there is no emergency. Likewise, reporting on the bombing in Beirut was routine. Raising questions about what happened in Grenada was difficult but doable. But investigating why many Latin Americans had legitimate reasons to prefer Marxist leaders to US-backed, right-wing dictatorships would have been nearly impossible at corporately owned news outlets.[89]

In the immediate aftermath of Reagan's success in Grenada, many Americans incorporated events such as the rescue of the students and the stand against communism into a patriotic repertoire.[90] Critical stories faded, replaced by accounts of a "new patriotism." News outlets whose reporting questioned the "good news" narrative antagonized their audiences. When NPR reported on inconsistencies and inaccuracies in the government's story, letters from listeners called its coverage negative and biased. Testifying at a congressional hearing, NBC News' anchorman John Chancellor said that mail supporting the exclusion of the press (and against the network's criticism of it) ran ten to one.[91] Journalists could opine about the public's right to know and insist that access was a prerequisite for democracy, but many Americans believed that national security justified government secrecy and limits on the freedom of the press.

THE "NEW PATRIOTISM"

On December 18, a front-page story in the *Washington Post*'s Style section described a shift in the nation's mood. Examples included a rush on Uncle Sam posters, rising sales of GI Joe dolls, and an upswing in ROTC recruitment. Speculating that renewed interest in martial symbols and military experience betokened a "new patriotism," writer Art Harris contemplated "the end of an era of reflexive American hating, navel contemplation and ardent feminism."[92] Letters to the editor subsequently drubbed Harris's piece for its simplistic analysis and caustic tone. But the *Post*'s writer was just reporting a story: patriotism seemingly had rebounded.

The shift started when the economy improved, and Americans felt better about the nation's prospects and their own pocketbooks. It deepened and took on a more militaristic tone after Grenada. Although the examples Harris cited and the polls that he noted could be construed as representing a patriotic surge, the positive sentiment was far from universal. Other stories questioned the recovery's reach and the public's contentment. Yet negative poll numbers, skeptical op-eds, and critics of the administration (whether congressional leaders, "media elites," or everyday Americans) could not budge the patriotism-is-back narrative once it became a cultural meme. Nor did its enthusiasts question whether the new feeling represented the love of one's country (patriotism) or the belief in the superiority of one's country (nationalism).

Among *Time*'s headlines in the first half of 1983, "Bottom Lines Are Looking Up," "Beginning to Build Up Steam," and "Sunny Mood at Midsummer" trumpeted good news as the rise in employment and consequent buying power made Americans happy. According to a July poll, 57 percent judged things to be going "very well," as opposed to 45 percent who held that view in March and just 35 percent the previous December.[93] The ebullience even spilled into fashion. *Time* predicted big changes in 1984, when sober styles and a somber palette would give way to clothes that were "daring, distinctive and sometimes a bit naughty" in "brassy shades of red, blue and green."[94]

By November, the *New York Times* was calling the economic turnaround "a classic recovery." Noting that in the past year "the economy came roaring back," the reporter ticked off key indicators of economic health: a drop in unemployment, a rise in production, and an increase in consumer spending.[95] Viewed in relationship to the Grenada mission—on the same day as the recovery story appeared in the *Times*, another article detailed US efforts to rebuild the island nation[96]—reports of the economic turnaround could be read as more proof of American ascendancy.

The biggest win from the one-two triumphs accrued to the president. Reagan, whose popularity had dipped to 42 percent in January 1983, had a 63 percent approval rating following the invasion, according to a *Washington Post*–ABC News Poll.[97] *Time*, likewise, hailed his newfound political strength, noting how the public had rallied behind him.[98] A month later, the *New York Times* found the country still buoyant and backing Reagan's agenda. Describing a "selective patriotism," Adam Clymer reported that the citizenry "feels individuals should support wars they consider wrong and prefers, by a margin of 2 to 1, risking national destruction to tolerating Russian dominance." The same *Times* poll reported that the 47 percent of Americans who felt that the country was going in the "right direction" remained steady between June and November. Still, the *Times*, along with other news outlets, characterized the post-Grenada period as a time of rekindled patriotism, even though there was no actual shift in numbers. The paper also noted that those opining that the country was on the "wrong track" had dropped by only one point, from 44 to 43 percent, in the six-month period. Little was made of the fact that almost half those surveyed did not share in the positive assessment of the nation's direction, nor had their opinions changed despite the economic uptick and victory in Grenada.[99]

Polls are unreliable; the same questions phrased with different words can elicit opposite results. At best, polling data offer a fuzzy snapshot of reality and, at worst, distort what interviewees actually think. The 1983 year-end polls indicated that a majority of Americans felt good about the country and the president. However, whether the mood change was due to Grenada or was part of an ongoing shift related to the economic recovery is impossible to gauge. Polling results finding that Blacks and women were less enthusiastic than whites and men about the "new patriotism" and the country's direction were typically one-offs. Some reporters and opinion writers questioned the new patriotism—was it any different from the old kind, or just the newest example of knee-jerk jingoism—but many more wrote about the upsurge of national pride.

By spring 1984, the "new patriotism" had become a news staple. The *Baltimore Sun* and the *Christian Science Monitor* reported on the rise in flag sales, and the *Los Angeles Times* covered the ROTC's increased recruitment.[100] Even articles criticizing the trend—a *New York Times Magazine* story by R. W. Apple and a *Wall Street Journal* opinion piece by Hodding Carter III—affirmed its existence.[101] Events that occurred throughout the year, including the Los Angeles Olympics and the presidential election, were folded into the narrative. The success of the Los Angeles games as well as victories by many American athletes stoked Americans' esteem for their country. Inevitably, Reagan's reelection team foregrounded the new patriotism in his campaign narrative.

News reports also chronicled how the upbeat national mood spilled into popular culture. Madison Avenue was quick to see the possibilities for commercial tie-ins. During the 1984 Summer Olympics in Los Angeles, ABC broadcast thirty-seven separate commercials to promote *Call to Glory*, a new television series about a 1960s Air Force family. When the show finally aired, debuting right after the Olympics ended, the two-hour pilot was seen in 20.8 million homes, a whopping 44 percent of the television-viewing audience.[102] The story of a pilot and his family, *Call to Glory* opened with actual footage of President John F. Kennedy discussing the Cuban Missile Crisis during a news briefing. The plot interwove actual events with the lives of fictional servicemen, using real black-and-white news clips to create the mise en scène. As the *New York Times* review noted, "The leitmotif running all through this is patriotism and popular Americans."[103] *Call to Glory*'s mix of family drama and heroic flyboys made it an early hit.

Several reviewers speculated that the show sought to cash in on the patriotic surge. A "network insider" told *Time*, "The campaign to promote this program was all based on connecting the patriotism the network felt would be generated during the Olympics with that of this new series."[104] But the producers denied the charge, saying they wanted to explore a pivotal decade through the lens of a traditional family.[105] Intentionally or not, the program resonated with the administration's if not the public's ongoing concerns with family values, communist threats, and safeguarding the American way of life. Similar themes ran through *Red Dawn*, a critically panned but commercially successful movie that also premiered that summer and featured American teens vanquishing communist invaders. While nowhere near as successful as the year's blockbusters, such as *Beverly Hills Cop* or *Ghostbusters*, *Red Dawn* was among 1984's top twenty movie moneymakers, even surpassing cultural icons like *The Terminator* and the Oscar-winning *Places in the Heart*.

Red Dawn was more commercially successful and its brand more durable than *Call to Glory*. In fact, the 2003 mission to capture Saddam Hussein was named for the movie. *Call to Glory*, despite respectable reviews and a strong initial showing, petered out early in its first season and was canceled after the New Year. While it is impossible to fully know how the 1984 public interpreted and understood *Red Dawn* and *Call to Glory*, contemporaneous reviews and coverage illumine where and how they fit into the discursive worlds of the Reagan era. Both were commercial products conceived as moneymaking mass entertainment. But to succeed in the marketplace, they needed to resonate with their times. They did that by

FIGURE 23. Newspaper advertisement for the movie *Red Dawn*, 1984.

mirroring topical themes: love of country, fears about communism, and support for family values. Noting these correspondences, reviewers wondered whether producers were cynically exploiting the public's mood.

Debates about pure and exploitative representations of patriotism, as well as who could use or control commercial products, climaxed later that summer when conservative columnist George Will attended a Bruce Springsteen concert. Will, who was unofficially advising the Reagan campaign,[106] was invited to see Springsteen and his band by the drummer's wife. Will's subsequent *Washington Post* column went to great lengths to differentiate the pundit from the hoi polloi. Will wore a dress shirt and bow tie to the rock concert, stuffed cotton in his ears, and wondered whether that funny smell was marijuana. Stylistic differences aside, he identified "the Boss" as a fellow traveler and proclaimed his own solidarity with a crowd that embraced Springsteen's affirmation of traditional values, including hard work and love of country.

Five days later, at a speech in Hammonton, New Jersey, Ronald Reagan likewise praised the Garden State troubadour as an exemplar of Republican values: "America's future rests in a thousand dreams inside your hearts. It rests in the message of hope in songs of a man so many young Americans admire—New Jersey's own, Bruce Springsteen. And helping you make those dreams come true is what this job of mine is all about."[107] The quote, picked up by news outlets nationwide, suggested that Springsteen and his Born in the U.S.A. tour were another example of the new patriotism. Springsteen's progressive politics were at that time not fully formed, but the singer knew that Reaganism did not square with his own vision for the nation. As his tour continued that fall, he tried to make clear that his American dream had little in common with the president's.

However, for every fan who knew that "Born in the U.S.A." was an indictment of American militarism and free-market capitalism, many more heard only an upbeat anthem and a stirring chorus that the president himself had praised. Thus, throughout the summer and fall, the new patriotism, a media-driven trope that evolved into a cultural meme, wended through popular entertainments, assimilating meanings whether sympathetic (*Call to Glory*), exploitative (*Red Dawn*), or oppositional (*Born in the U.S.A.*). Moreover, the new patriotism had become the backdrop for the president's reelection campaign, and both the news and the entertainment media served as amplifiers for Reagan's message.

In truth, the new patriotism as defined by news accounts wasn't new. It was a feel-good, soft-focus, gauzy version of the old conservatism leavened by Reagan's reassuring smile and can-do attitude. Valorizing the nuclear family, the free-market economy, and the idea of one nation under God, the new patriotism reflected the Reagan-era religious imaginary and enabled the president to reach Americans beyond his evangelical audience. In an early summer story, the *New York Times* described how Reagan made these messages central to his presidency and offered them as the reason to reelect him. To that end, his inner circle pulled together the "Tuesday Team" (named for Election Day), an elite ad hoc group drawn from top advertising agencies nationwide. The team, intent on marketing the candidate just as they sold "pet food, Pepsi-Cola, soup and cigarettes," devised a $2 million "strategy of televised good feeling" for the campaign's pre–Memorial Day television spots.[108]

Basing their strategy on the "polished, joyous commercials for Pepsi-Cola," 1984's Mad Men shot scenes of "happy confident people,"[109] embodiments of optimism and patriotism, at work and at play. This was America as it wished to see itself. The actors in the commercials looked like wholesome, handsome denizens of Middle America, and their activities were familiar and reassuring. Reinforcing the message, a voiceover explained, "Life is better . . . America is back. . . . And people have a sense of pride they never thought they'd feel again."[110]

The commercials embodied Reagan's desire to stay positive rather than to attack his Democratic challenger, Senator Walter Mondale. Moreover, they used the past year's news narrative to sell a story about a revitalized American Dream. The narrative may not have been 100 percent accurate, since life was not better for many Americans. But the story rested, like the American Dream it represented, on a firm base of conservative social values, which the news media explicitly signaled in its focus on flags and military service, and implicitly in the growing coverage of culture wars and the religious Right. Similarly, entertainments like *Call to Glory* and *Red Dawn* exemplified these values in their depictions of hard work, self-sacrifice, familial bonds, and the willingness to fight for democracy. Secular emanations of religious and moral ideals, these values reflected what many Americans cherished in the conflation of personal and national identities. They were the Chosen People in God's Promised Land. Later that summer, Reagan's Tuesday Team delineated these identities in a television ad that intertwined America's economic recovery with its moral core and named Reagan as the nation's savior.

The actual title for "Morning in America," the fifty-nine-second commercial that encapsulated Reagan's message, was "Prouder, Stronger, Better." Focused on the electorate rather than on the candidate, the spot was a visualization of national purpose and identity. Though the commercial opened with two urban images—a water ferry framed by a downtown skyline and a businessman emerging from a taxicab—it quickly moved to more idyllic representations of American life: a farmer atop a tractor, a paperboy on a bicycle, a station wagon pulling up to a white picket fence, a young family moving into a new home, and Americans of all ages raising the flag. The narrator spoke soothingly about the signs of an economic upturn—more jobs, more home buying, and less inflation—while the white faces of Americans being portrayed looked earnest and radiant.

Religion and morality were integral to the new patriotism, but neither was explicitly referenced in "Morning in America." Rather, a church wedding stood in for both; the place and the activity witness to the vitality of young peoples' commitment to God. Unlike the commercial's rapid opening montage of Americans on the move, the wedding's images were rich with detail. The bride walks down the aisle; the couple stands before the priest; the newlyweds embrace; friends and family throng the beaming couple; and the bride runs into her grandmother's outstretched arms. Each shot is thick with religious symbols—liturgical candles, a priest in clerical collar and stole, and the bride's long-sleeved, high-necked gown—that telegraph sanctity. The commercial did not need to reference religion specifically, since its visuals telegraphed its importance.

What was left unsaid in the commercial was explicitly noted when Reagan spoke to groups such as the National Religious Broadcasters and the National Association of Evangelicals. In Dallas, the president told thousands gathered at an ecumenical prayer breakfast, "The truth is, politics and morality are inseparable. And as morality's foundation is religion, religion and politics are necessarily related. We need religion as a guide."[111] He also talked about religion and morality on the stump, making clear his affinity for conservative positions. Addressing a rally in Georgia, he said, "The time has come for Congress to give a majority of American families what they want for their children—a constitutional amendment making it unequivocally clear that children can hold voluntary prayer in their schools."[112] Several months later at a church fair in New Jersey, Reagan averred, "We are for life and against abortion. We are for prayer in the schools. We are for tuition tax credits. And in Central America, we're rather more inclined to listen to the testimony of His Holiness the Pope than the claims of Communist Sandinistas."[113]

The president did not need to win evangelical voters; he already had their support. But he did not back away from the election's most contested issues. Religion was key to Reagan's discursive universe, and America's exceptionalism began with its God-given freedom. That freedom, springing from the soil of religious liberty, blossomed into political democracy and a free-market economy. This was the revelation of the new patriotism, and its proof texts were America's economic recovery and its military victory in Grenada. Reagan brought these themes together in a national address the night before the vote. He proclaimed, "We can strengthen our economy, our security, and the values that bind us. . . . We can keep faith with the God who has made and blessed us as no other people have ever been blessed. . . . In speaking tonight of America's traditional values and philosophy of government, we must remember the most distinctive mark of all in the American experience: To a tired and disillusioned world, we've always been a New World and, yes, a shining city on a hill where all things are possible."[114]

Reagan's personal popularity translated into positive news stories, exemplified by *Time*'s gilded campaign coverage. The weekly newsmagazine, unlike most newspapers, encouraged writers to be colorful and conversational. The article "Yankee Doodle Candidate" noted, "The President rides high on feelings of patriotism and optimism," "chokes up on D-day," and "seems to glide from one glorious 'photo opportunity' to another." Whether signaling the start of a Daytona Beach stock car race or opening the Summer Olympics in Los Angeles, Reagan jauntily played to the crowd, causing the writer to note, "Such scenes could hardly do more to buttress Reagan's message that 'America is back' on top—and that he is the man who keeps it there." Even opponents were respectful. According to Rahm Emanuel, a young midwestern Democratic consultant, "Reagan is a ball game and a picnic on a weekend in July."[115]

Sprinkled throughout the article were phrases conjuring the president's political strength and personal charisma. He "takes the high road," he "stands tall," his "magic" is working, his leadership is "poised," and he "cuts a fine figure."[116]

Newspapers were neither as introspective nor as effusive. But it was difficult to ignore the president's popularity, and it was impossible not to quote his stump speech references to the new patriotism. Covering a pre-Games meeting between Reagan and America's Olympians, the *Washington Post* said the president's remarks were similar to a "campaign-style speech that linked patriotic themes to Olympic values."[117] Later in the year at a San Diego rally, a reporter from the *Los Angeles Times* used capital letters to convey the crowd's enthusiasm: "Reagan said Mondale believes 'every day is tax day. . . . We believe every day is independence day.' 'YEA!' the crowd said, waving hundreds of tiny American flags."[118]

Not everyone in the news media drank the Kool-Aid. Writing in *Harper's*, Lewis H. Lapham lambasted the new patriotism as a media construction. Noting "every three or four days another columnist or broadcaster makes the amazing discovery that ordinary Americans . . . love their country," Lapham maintained that "the current discovery of patriotism has less to do with the attitudes of the American people as a whole than with the pressures of the market in images." While Lapham poked at the press's jejune reporting and linguistic imprecision—he complained that they confused patriotism, nationalism, and jingoism—he did not deny that patriotism existed. Rather, he doubted that most Americans had ever stopped loving their country. "The new patriotism is the old patriotism, which has been there all along," he wrote. "Out of sight of the cameras the majority of Americans have been caring for the principles to which the nation was dedicated."[119]

Thanks to good luck, positive news, and the tactical management of the nation's press corps in a manner not seen in modern times, Grenada served as a turning point for the president and the nation. Its success spurred the "new patriotism" and boosted Reagan's bid for reelection. In the decades since the invasion, the import of the mission has been debated: Was it significant because it flummoxed the Soviets, stabilized the Caribbean, or ended Vietnam syndrome? Certainly, the American response to a perceived radical leftist coup sent a clear signal that the Reagan administration would not abide communist incursions in the hemisphere, further chilling relations between the United States and the Soviet Union.

In fact, the fight in Grenada was the final conflict of the Cold War.[120] It also was a key moment in the struggle between the president and the press to define and shape the news. That struggle began with the decision to ban independent coverage of Operation Urgent Fury and played out in editorials and opinion pieces questioning Reagan's motives and strategy. Overall, Reagan emerged the victor, effectively setting the agenda and focusing the national conversation on international strength and domestic economic recovery, two byproducts of his religious imaginary. But while many Americans basked in the nation's military and economic successes, millions more saw their hopes contract and their financial security upended—a reality we explore in the next chapter.

CHAPTER SIX

Scrooged

Moralizing Welfare and Racializing Poverty

> There are no easy answers, but there are simple answers. We must have the courage to do what we know is morally right.
>
> RONALD REAGAN, "A Time for Choosing," presidential election campaign, October 27, 1964

On December 8, 1983, presidential counselor Edwin Meese III met with reporters from Reuters, the Associated Press, and United Press International. Meese had worked at Reagan's side since his time as California's governor. As the two were close, Meese had the president's ear. Not only were they ideologically aligned, but they also shared the confidence of self-made men shaped by modest origins, religious convictions, and strong family ties. Neither believed that circumstance was destiny; their careers proved that self-discipline and hard work could propel a poor boy to the halls of power.

On that overcast Wednesday, a journalist asked Meese how he balanced the need for spending reductions with the plight of hungry children. "Well I don't know of any authoritative figures that there are hungry children," replied the presidential counselor. And, he continued, even if such "allegations" were true, why would there be hungry children when more federal money than ever was being directed to food assistance? The reporters, perhaps aware that Meese's words would sound callous during the Christmas season, asked for clarification. But Meese appeared oblivious to the impact his statements might have. He explained that the president's task force on food assistance would clear up the confusion about hunger in the United States, because "we have a system in this country that virtually everyone is taken care of by one program or another." In fact, Meese seemed more perturbed by freeloaders than by starving children. He opined, "I think some people are going to soup kitchens voluntarily. I know we've had information that people go to soup kitchens because the food is free and that's easier than paying for it."[1]

At another time of year, Meese's remarks might have gone unnoticed; but two weeks before Christmas on a slow-news Saturday, typically the least newsy day of the week, his words triggered headlines. The *Washington Post*, the *Los Angeles Times*, and the *Chicago Tribune* were just three of the national papers that placed the story on page 1. "Critics Growl over Meese Hunger Remarks," the *Tribune* punned in an above-the-fold banner headline. The *Post*, likewise, ran the story at the top of page 1, proclaiming "Meese: 'The Food Is Free and . . . That's Easier Than Paying for It.'" Among these large metropolitan newspapers, only the *New York Times*—struck by NATO's overtures to the Soviets, ongoing problems in Lebanon, and the novelty of home computers as Christmas gifts—relegated the Meese story to page 12.[2]

The *Chicago Tribune*'s story opened with the "outrage"[3] caused by the presidential advisor's remarks, and the *Los Angeles Times* cited a source who called them "ludicrous."[4] Similarly, the first paragraph of the *New York Times*' piece noted that "Democratic leaders and some experts on hunger called Meese's statement outrageous."[5] But the *Washington Post* had the quote that would haunt Meese throughout the holiday season. "'At Christmastime,' said House Speaker Thomas P. (Tip) O'Neill Jr. (D-Mass), 'there always appears to be a Scrooge on the scene.'"[6]

For the rest of year, Meese's statements ricocheted through the news. The story snowballed into features about hunger in America, soup kitchens and their clientele, fairness and politics, and the likelihood that the comments reflected a Meese and Reagan mind-meld. Underlying the coverage, and perfervidly addressed in op-eds and editorials, were questions about civic values. What is society's responsibility to the poor? Are some of the poor more deserving than others? What constitutes equality? How should people gauge fairness, the conviction that all Americans should be treated equally?

Such issues roiled reporters too. Most news stories, despite aiming for balance and objectivity, seemed slanted against Meese. Journalists did not openly call him heartless, but the structure, sourcing, and framing of their work suggested as much. Editorialists, on the other hand, had no compunctions about expressing their opinions. Sarcasm and outrage lashed not just the presidential counselor but also his boss. Three years' worth of frustration about budget cuts found a perfect foil in Meese's skepticism about the reality of hunger in America and his concern about soup kitchen freeloaders.

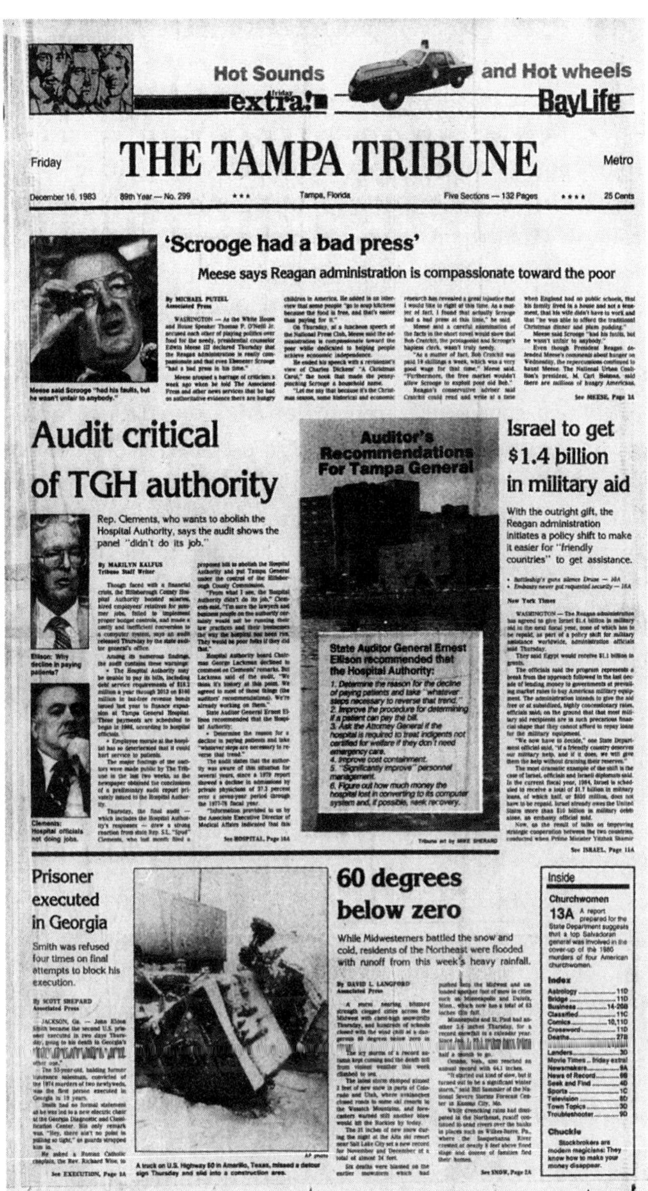

Hot Sounds

friday extra!

and Hot wheels

BayLife

Friday

THE TAMPA TRIBUNE

Metro

December 16, 1983 · 89th Year — No. 299 · Tampa, Florida · Five Sections — 132 Pages · 25 Cents

'Scrooge had a bad press'

Meese says Reagan administration is compassionate toward the poor

Meese said Scrooge "had his faults, but he wasn't unfair to anybody."

Audit critical of TGH authority

Rep. Clements, who wants to abolish the Hospital Authority, says the audit shows the panel "didn't do its job."

Ellison: Why decline in paying patients?

Clements: Hospital officials not doing jobs.

Auditor's Recommendations For Tampa General

State Auditor General Ernest Ellison recommended that the Hospital Authority:

1. Determine the reason for the decline of paying patients and take "whatever steps necessary to reverse that trend."
2. Improve the procedure for determining if a patient can pay the bill.
3. Ask the Attorney General if the hospital is required to treat indigents not certified for welfare if they don't need emergency care.
4. Improve cost containment.
5. "Significantly improve" personnel management.
6. Figure out how much money the hospital lost in converting to its computer system and, if possible, seek recovery.

Israel to get $1.4 billion in military aid

With the outright gift, the Reagan administration initiates a policy shift to make it easier for "friendly countries" to get assistance.

Prisoner executed in Georgia

Smith was refused four times on final attempts to block his execution.

A truck on U.S. Highway 60 in Amarillo, Texas, missed a detour sign Thursday and slid into a construction area.

60 degrees below zero

While Midwesterners battled the snow and cold, residents of the Northeast were flooded with runoff from this week's heavy rainfall.

Inside

Churchwomen

13A A report prepared for the State Department suggests that a top Salvadoran general was involved in the cover-up of the 1980 murders of four American churchwomen.

Index

Chuckle

Stockbrokers are modern magicians: They know how to make your money disappear.

FIGURE 24. After being dubbed Scrooge for doubting the reality of hungry children in the United States, presidential counselor Edwin Meese joked that the Dickens character suffered from "bad press." © The Tampa Tribune via ZUMA Press.

This chapter looks at coverage of Meese's statements on hunger as well as reporting on welfare and on fairness to explore the political, economic, and moral nexus of Reagan's religious imaginary and its depiction by the news media. News coverage contributed to changing notions about citizenship, responsibility, and Americans' moral obligation to collective well-being. Meese's remarks fit into an ongoing debate about poverty—specifically, whether the poor should be classified as deserving or undeserving of assistance. Examining how Reaganites framed poverty spills into a larger discourse about the economy, morality, race, and gender.

On a metalevel, the administration's stance on poverty played out in an ideological debate over how best to fulfill America's destiny. What configuration of politics, economics, and religion constituted the true expression of American exceptionalism? But in daily life, citizens framed the question more simply: Who was responsible for the poor? Reagan repeatedly said there was more to fixing the economy than ending unemployment and runaway inflation. Rather, the goal was to facilitate an economy that affirmed family, self-reliance, and the free market. In his December 3, 1983, radio address, he told listeners: "Families stand at the center of society, so building our future must begin by preserving family values. Tragically, too many in Washington have been asking us to swallow a whopper: namely, that bigger government is the greatest force for fairness and progress. But this so-called solution has given most of us a bad case of financial indigestion. How can families survive when big government's powers to tax, inflate, and regulate absorb their wealth, usurp their rights, and crush their spirit?"[7]

In connecting the economic recovery to the preservation of family values, Reagan found an audience, not just with voters but also with the media. When journalists reported on the president's ideas about families and self-reliance, they frequently picked sound bites critical of single-parent families, especially poor households headed by women of color. Following the axiom that conflict sells, journalists tend to pit ideas, individuals, and groups against one another. Therefore, many stories explored whether Reagan favored the rich over the poor and whether the country was worse off now than when he took office. Reporters could not directly criticize his policies, since their professional standards demanded objectivity. But framing stories around the administration's seeming insensitivity to poverty was a way to make their point.

However, the law of unintended consequences and the repetition of the Reaganites' talking points may have caused a different response from what some reporters expected. Repeating Reagan's message—normalizing his ideas about the undeserving poor, indolent welfare mothers, and a

Black underclass—softened public attitudes about fairness. Reagan and his surrogates also played on deep-rooted currents of racism and sexism as well as newer fears of economic displacement and cultural marginalization that many whites harbored. Their fears were not misplaced: between 1976 and 1984, the median inflation-adjusted income for white males fell 22 percent.[8] Thus, over time the president's perspective on family values, self-reliance, and the free market superseded allegiances to FDR's New Deal and LBJ's Great Society.

Studying welfare reform in the late twentieth century, social scientists identified a mutually constitutive relationship between morally framed discursive strategies and social policy.[9] In other words, a convincing ethical argument can influence policy making, and the subsequent policies tend to affirm the ethical stance. However, institutional strength and durability, along with inertia and the desire for continuity, enable social systems and their rationales usually to remain in place. But every so often, an interpretative challenge arises with the potential to change everything. To succeed, that challenge needs to "alter understandings,"[10] often through a transformative vision that shifts public opinion. Reagan built support for his vision by promising tax cuts. But his endgame was a restructuring of the welfare state that would change citizens' relationship to self, family, work, and government. The challenge he faced was framing the argument to emphasize the moral value of personal responsibility without seeming insensitive to those in need.

REFORMING WELFARE, 1630 TO THE 1970S

Edwin Meese's comments and Americans' reactions to them were part of a long and contentious history. For centuries, conversations about poverty oscillated between the poles of communitarian care and individual responsibility. When the Puritan leader John Winthrop described a model of Christian charity that would give rise to a "city upon a hill," he suggested that colonists be "willing to abridge ourselves of our superfluities, for the supply of others' necessities."[11] Just as God had covenanted to protect and sustain his saints, so the Puritans were bound to help one another. Even if Winthrop's words were not widely circulated among the colonials, as noted in chapter 1, his opinions were likely shared. He and his coreligionists believed that to deepen the bonds of fellowship, God created different types of people—wealthy and needy, tough and tender—and each was a boon to the other.

Still, some were more blessed than others. Financial success, according to the Puritans, was a measure of God's favor, but it could lead to worldliness and sin. The poor were saved from such temptations, but their sad circumstances were silent testimony to their inherent disorder. The Puritans distinguished between those who could not take care of themselves, such as orphans, widows, the sick, the elderly, and the disabled, and those of sound mind and body who chose not to work. Yet even if able-bodied paupers were considered undeserving by their coreligionists, they still received assistance through contributions to the community coffer. Over time, as the colonies grew and needs outstripped resources, some localities adopted British poor statutes, which distinguished between the deserving and the undeserving poor. The former received assistance in situ, but the latter were sent to workhouses.

This model of local charity could not be sustained as villages turned into towns, factories replaced homemade goods, and immigrants from small farms and distant lands turned tight-knit communities into faceless cities. Congregation-based or even locality-based philanthropy was no longer sufficient to meet the needs of a swelling underclass. Almshouses were one solution to the problem. These institutions were expected not just to house and feed the poor but also to teach them to be productive members of society. But when it became clear that their deplorable conditions and substandard care were compounding the problem, nineteenth-century reformers fought to return residents to local communities.

The plight of the poor remained an obdurate problem for successive generations. Tied to political and economic decisions about their fate was a theological conundrum: Were the poor part of the natural order, another testimony to God's great mystery? Or were they lost souls who needed salvation? Perhaps they were products of the social environment, and if society changed so would their situation. Or maybe they were the blighted victims of heredity and responsive only to coercive treatment. Yet whether poverty was ascribed to fatalism, morality, environment, or heredity, its solution, according to many nineteenth- and early twentieth-century policy makers, religious leaders, and reformers, depended on differentiating between the deserving and the undeserving poor. In fact, many of these self-avowed do-gooders seemed more concerned that excessive charity would create an idle underclass than in reducing privation.

Scientific charity, a development that preceded the Civil War but flourished in the decades after, offered what were modern solutions to the problem. Rather than provide indiscriminate aid to impostors, allowing sentimentality to foster indigence, a new breed of charity workers used scientific methods to distinguish cheats from the truly needy. Caseworkers received on-the-job training in taking client histories, keeping records, and providing targeted assistance to the deserving poor. They castigated "outdoor" relief—the breadlines, soup kitchens, and shelters that religious groups offered—preferring institutional options such as poorhouses, workhouses, and asylums if their own interventions did not lead to self-sufficiency.

From the decades after the Civil War to the Great Depression, public philanthropy was provided by practitioners of scientific charity, civic-minded elites, and religious groups. All faced compounded needs as immigration, urbanization, and industrialization exacerbated hardships. At the turn of the century, the Progressive movement alerted the nation to widespread problems of child welfare, public health, alcoholism, and homelessness, among other social ills. Progressive leaders called for government policies and programs as well as for a rigorous professionalization of social work to relieve suffering. By the 1920s, schools of social work had emerged at several universities. Members of the new profession, like the Progressives of an earlier era, tended to view poverty as a systemic problem rather than as proof of personal failings.

Such new ideas about poverty were instrumental to the success of Franklin D. Roosevelt's New Deal in the 1930s. The US government was unprepared for the economic catastrophe triggered by Wall Street's collapse and the onset of the Great Depression. Private charities and religious groups offered help but lacked the resources and infrastructure to supply food and shelter to millions in need. After his 1932 election, Roosevelt sought the passage of laws that created the Federal Emergency Relief Act, the Works Progress Administration, and the Civilian Conservation Corps, among other interventions. In the urgent crusade to provide jobs and deliver aid, there was no time to differentiate those who were worthy from those who were unworthy of assistance.

In addition to emergency relief, Roosevelt wanted ongoing buffers against indigence. Social Security—legislation guaranteeing financial support for the elderly and the disabled—and federal programs to assist the unemployed and to relieve childhood poverty represented a sea change in American policy. For the first time, the federal government was providing social insurance. Yet the price of admission was a job; Social Security benefits only accrued to the employed. Two job categories specifically excluded from benefits were farmworkers and domestics, both predominantly held by Blacks. The administration made this concession to win support from Dixie Democrats.

The government also established programs for unemployment and needy families, but similar to older forms of charity, these were means-tested assistance. In other words, aid was given only to those who could prove that they lacked the wherewithal to provide for themselves. Implicit to such testing was a judgment about an applicant's worthiness for aid.

Able-bodied men who failed the means test were, obviously, unwilling to work; thus, the religious and philosophical demarcation between the deserving and the undeserving poor was operationalized in Roosevelt's new economic order.

The programs and policies of the New Deal evolved into what critics called the welfare state. Dovetailing with America's postwar economic expansion, the system worked for almost thirty years. Welfare hardly seemed a problem in an era when a growing workforce enjoyed rising incomes. Some still complained: clergy, business leaders, and politicians who sniffed socialism in the New Deal still smelled it when millions sought governmental assistance during the postwar boom. Opposition to federal aid intensified, and Barry Goldwater's 1964 presidential campaign was one manifestation of these concerns. But the cultural winds still favored notions of a good and great nation that hallowed equality, opportunity, and compassion. All three came into play when Michael Harrington's 1962 book *The Other America: Poverty in the United States* awoke the nation to its needy, and a newly elected young president, aware of the problem, told Americans to ask not what their country could do for them but what they could do for their country. Many would answer his call.

After John F. Kennedy was assassinated, President Lyndon B. Johnson launched VISTA (Volunteers in Service to America) to honor the slain leader. The VISTA corps also would assist Johnson's plans to expand economic opportunities and support the burgeoning civil rights movement. Within two years, more than two thousand VISTA workers were stationed in urban slums, migrant camps, and rural Appalachia. Around the same time, the civil rights movement's campaigns to end segregation and to ensure voting rights were gaining strength. The Reverend Martin Luther King, among the most prominent figures in the struggle, also was committed to economic justice.

Johnson sought to help the poor and pass civil rights legislation through the most ambitious social welfare legislation since the New Deal. Declaring a War on Poverty, he promised a Great Society that would be achieved through job programs and vocational training, community-based aid, low-income housing, funding for low-income schools, food stamps, and medical assistance for the elderly and the poor.

At the same time that Johnson sought to lift up the nation's neediest citizens, many Americans were experiencing unprecedented prosperity. In early 1964, following up on Kennedy's pledge to lower taxes, the president introduced a bill that cut individual income tax rates by about 20 percent (the top bracket went from 91 to 70 percent) and lowered corporate tax rates from 52 to 48 percent. Within the year, unemployment fell while capital investments, consumer purchases, and tax receipts rose. At the very moment Johnson unveiled plans for his Great Society, many Americans, especially white Americans, seemed already to have achieved it.

However, many felt that the welfare system, rooted in the New Deal and expanded over the next four decades, needed reform.[12] Despite a growing number of government programs aimed at ending poverty, its effects—such as teen births, high school dropout rates, drug and alcohol abuse, hunger, homelessness, and crime—were on the rise. Critics on the left wondered whether the raft of government benefits missed the point or merely failed to reach enough people. Believing both to be true, two Columbia University sociologists proposed organizing all eligible poor people to apply for welfare and swamp the system. Richard Cloward and Frances Fox Piven hoped to replace piecemeal support with a guaranteed annual income to end poverty.[13] Seeking radical change, they played on class, racial, and ethnic divisions to disrupt what they saw as a failed welfare state.

A similar outcome tied to a more moderate strategy emerged from a 1969 presidential committee tasked with evaluating antipoverty programs. According to their findings, "The existing welfare system was founded on the untenable premise that good jobs at adequate wages were available to all."[14] Rather than providing help until circumstances improved, the authors said a guaranteed annual income would solve the problem of a labor market that would never provide full, much less universally gainful, employment. Poverty, stated the report, was not "some personal failing" but built into the current market system.

The committee advocated financial support regardless of personal circumstance. Aid should not depend on whether the recipient was deemed worthy because of age, disability, illness, or widowhood. Rather, all people who needed assistance should receive it because there weren't enough decent-paying jobs available for all. In 1970, a majority of the US Congress agreed with the committee's findings. That April, the House of Representatives, by a vote of 243 to 155, supported a bill for a guaranteed annual income. The bill subsequently languished in the Senate, and even President Nixon's support for aspects of the plan could not win its passage.

Many moderate policy makers and elected officials, Republicans and Democrats alike, felt that a guaranteed annual income would reach more citizens, offer more security, and end the stigma attached to receiving welfare. But conservatives held a different view. Rebutting the notion that welfare did too little, they claimed it did too much and at too high a price to society. At best, welfare created an underclass unwilling to work. At worst, it enabled scofflaws and cheaters to take advantage of a flawed system. Throughout the 1960s and 1970s, stories about welfare frauds became a journalistic trope, frequently cited by conservatives in business, government, and academia.[15] Among the most popular were narratives about unwed mothers who milked the system with fraudulent claims and then used AFDC (Aid to Families with Dependent Children) money for drugs and alcohol. These portrayals of mothers, typically urban African Americans, not only fueled racial stereotypes but also struck deep chords of religiously based sexism that depicted women as deceptive, promiscuous, and unreliable.

Reagan repeatedly told the story of one such "chiseler"[16] during his unsuccessful 1976 bid for the Republican presidential nomination. He recounted a tale, initially reported in the Chicago press, of a woman "who used 80 names, 30 addresses, [and] 15 telephone numbers to collect food stamps, Social Security, veterans' benefits for four non-existent deceased veteran husbands, as well as welfare. Her tax-free income alone has been running $150,000 a year."[17] Using the moniker popularized by the Chicago press, Reagan referred to the woman as a "welfare queen." The term became a cultural meme, and Reagan was often credited as its source. (The story has a tangled history. At the time, several news accounts claimed the fraud was not as serious as Reagan alleged. More recent reporting suggests that Linda Taylor, the woman in question, was an even worse criminal than he had realized.)[18] His description captured the public imagination, influencing perceptions about race, gender, and welfare for years to come.[19]

If Reagan's story about the "welfare queen" could become commonsensical, it was because many Americans were primed to believe the worst about the poor in general and African American welfare recipients in particular. This was a turnabout from public sentiment dominant in the early 1960s. Back then, flush from the 1950s economic boom and the shocking revelations of reports such as *The Other America*, Americans discussed how best to help those trapped in urban ghettoes and rural poverty. But the seeming failure of the Great Society, followed by the oil supply shock and then stagflation, caused many to worry more about their own well-being than that of their fellow citizens.

Moreover, Johnson's Great Society represented a significant shift from earlier social initiatives.[20] Roosevelt had either foreclosed or limited African Americans' access to New Deal programs. Moreover, many did not have the same opportunities as whites to find affordable housing and government-created jobs. The Great Society, on the other hand, was "an effort to eliminate the racial barriers of the New Deal and to integrate Blacks into the national political economy." Eager to make the system work for all people, welfare rights activists campaigned to register African American single mothers for benefits. Their efforts were successful, and "by 1967, a welfare caseload that had once been eighty-six percent white had become forty-six percent nonwhite."[21] In hard numbers, this meant that by 1969, the welfare caseload had risen to six million from four million earlier in the decade.[22] Both the increase in recipients and the rising percentage of Blacks in the mix resulted in public clamor for reform. While white people still constituted a majority of people receiving welfare benefits, many white Americans worried that Blacks were taking advantage.

But ultimately, it was the War on Poverty's linkage with the civil rights movement that doomed it. Many whites did not want to end the economic exploitation and political marginalization of Blacks. Even if racism did not materially benefit whites, it guaranteed their social and cultural dominance. Soon after Nixon was elected, he began dismantling Johnson's programs. Some he stopped altogether, others were cut back, and still others, as a result of GOP policy and conservative punditry, were stigmatized along race and gender lines. AFDC, in particular, was increasingly criticized as a government giveaway that supported shiftless, single Black mothers or, worse, cheats and welfare queens.

The push for welfare reform that had begun under Nixon, when the economy was strong, intensified during the economic downturn that marked the Jimmy Carter era. As the recession spread, welfare rolls unsurprisingly spiked. By the mid-1970s, the number of recipients had grown from six million to eleven million, while those receiving food stamps had risen from one million (in 1969) to nineteen million.[23] President Carter's plan, Program for Better Jobs and Income, featured a negative income tax, given to those whose income fell below a certain level. It also mandated the creation of minimum wage and public service jobs for welfare recipients who could not find work. Everyone on welfare, except for single mothers with children under age seven, was expected to find a job and would be penalized if they did not. Aspects of the program had appeal: liberals liked the negative income tax, which was similar to a guaranteed annual income, and conservatives applauded the work requirement. But the legislation was doomed, because it would have increased welfare spending instead of reducing it. The system remained unchanged, and its critics grew in number and in urgency.

REAGAN'S CRITIQUE

One of those critics was 1980 Republican presidential candidate Ronald Reagan. By 1980, many Americans had experienced financial hardships for almost a decade. Most understood there were many reasons for their predicament. Some of the problem stemmed from the nation's oil dependency and concomitant rising prices, caused by spiking oil costs, for goods and services. Another factor was government spending, a bill footed by taxpayers. In 1979, government spending totaled $504 billion. Of that, 29 percent was for defense, 23 percent for pensions, and another 24 percent for health, education, and welfare (the remainder was for "other").[24] Some voters felt that the defense budget was too high, but others chafed at domestic spending, especially the 8 percent earmarked for welfare.

Reagan addressed these concerns when he asked voters whether they were better off now than they were when Carter was elected president. Financially, most were not. The recent Iranian Revolution and the subsequent Iran-Iraq War had spurred a new inflationary cycle in the United States. The decrease in oil production and rise in prices led to stagflation.[25] Often referred to as the worst of both worlds, *stagflation*—a term first used in Britain during the 1960s—described a stagnant economy also hit by inflation and high unemployment. Reagan believed that stagflation was caused by the high taxes required to fund welfare payments, a problem compounded by the fact that welfare recipients paid no taxes at all.[26] He proposed lowering taxes, not just to provide financial relief, but also because the subsequent drop in revenue would force the government to reduce spending, especially for welfare programs.

Reagan viewed welfare as more than just an economic issue. He considered it a moral scourge, weakening families and fostering a culture of dependency.[27] He made his stance clear when, as governor of California, he fought to reform the state's welfare system. Calling it a "costly and tragic failure," he declared welfare to be the nation's number-one problem.[28] In California, AFDC payments had quadrupled between 1963 and 1970.[29] Troubled by the drain on the state's coffers as well as on recipients' sense of responsibility, Reagan proposed the 1971 California Welfare Reform Act. The new law not only made it harder to receive benefits, weeding out what the governor believed were widespread fraud and cheating, but also mandated workfare for all able-bodied recipients who were not parents of young children.[30]

In Reagan's view, high taxes and welfare were conjoined problems. The two enabled government bloat and, worse, were obstacles to America's God-given destiny as a nation of free citizens with free souls participating in a free-market society. Moving toward this goal required moral guidance wrapped in economic policies that restructured the nation's social compact. By invoking a rhetorical strategy echoing the Puritan covenantal tradition and intimating the importance of an "economy of grace,"[31] Reagan sought to convince voters that spiritual and economic renewal went hand in hand and that the free-market system was critical to both.

In his 1980 presidential campaign, Reagan rolled out a platform similar to the one that had won him California's top spot. His team bet that voters, disgruntled by the economic crisis, were unhappy with the status quo. Many wanted new options, and the oldest-ever presidential candidate had plenty. But instead of offering proposals teeming with details, a strategy that had not helped Jimmy Carter, Reagan kept things simple. During the primaries, he promised tax cuts. During the campaign, he promoted welfare reform. Long on vision but short on specifics, Reagan played up his track record. As governor of California, he had overhauled the state's welfare system. Now he proposed a similar shake-up for the nation. In his view, welfare and taxes were twin evils that fostered an overweening federal bureaucracy, financially burdened citizens, and, worst of all, sapped the poor of their dignity and autonomy.

Cutting taxes would put money into voters' pockets and nurture the free market. It also would reduce tax revenues and force cutbacks to targeted federal programs like welfare. (Reagan proposed cuts in health, education, and welfare spending but not in defense, a budget he increased significantly.) Equally important, cutting welfare would force the able-bodied poor to take responsibility for themselves, find jobs, and support their families. The result would be less government waste, more capital investment, increased consumer spending, and a productive citizenry in place of a federally funded underclass. Inflation would fall and employment would rise. His plan played well in an election year when inflation was considered the nation's top problem.[32] And since Americans tend to vote their pocketbooks, they supported the candidate who pledged economic growth.[33]

Soon after winning the White House, Reagan set his budget proposal in motion. At this point, "the prime interest was still above 20 percent, inflation was 12.4 percent, and unemployment was 7.4 percent."[34] According to his Plan for Economic Recovery, announced to Congress on February 18, a key goal was reducing the high levels of federal spending that fueled inflation. As Reagan noted in his inaugural speech, "Government is not the solution to our problem; government is the problem."[35] Several months later, he proposed legislation to solve that problem—the Omnibus Budget Reconciliation Act of 1981 (OBRA 1981) and the Economic Recovery Tax Act of 1981 (ERTA 1981, or the Kemp-Roth Tax Cut). OBRA increased the defense budget, cut nondefense spending, and mandated lower tax rates for individuals and corporations, which were spelled out in ERTA 1981.

This last effort drew on strategies suggested by economist Arthur Laffer and congressman Jack Kemp. Though their rationales differed, the two agreed that lower taxes would not only benefit individuals and improve the economy but also, because of those outcomes, increase federal revenue.

ERTA's centerpiece was a reduction in personal income tax rates phased over three years. Top taxpayers' rates would drop from 70 to 50 percent, and those in the lower brackets would see their rate fall from 14 to 11 percent. The bill also decreased taxes on inheritances and windfall profits, increased the limits on contributions to individual retirement accounts, and offered tax breaks for businesses.

OBRA, which detailed many of the administration's cost-cutting measures, proposed $30 billion in savings. Unlike ERTA, which affected almost every taxpayer, OBRA's effects hit the nation's neediest. (OBRA cut benefits for other groups, but the amounts were smaller and hardships less visible than to the poor.) The legislation tightened eligibility for AFDC and penalized the working poor, with 408,000 families losing eligibility and another 299,000 seeing their benefits reduced.[36] Specifically, AFDC was reduced by 14.3 percent, food stamps by 13.8 percent, and Medicaid by 2.8 percent.[37]

Reagan was not interested in simply reducing the government's outlay for welfare. He also wanted to end entitlements, which he believed were a disincentive to finding employment and maintaining stable, two-parent households. OBRA cut back payments to the working poor and encouraged states to develop workfare programs. The administration intended these strictures to decrease the welfare rolls, but results were mixed.[38] Some recipients did leave the program, others left but came back, and still others had no choice but to stay on the dole since jobs were hard to find.

Unemployment remained a problem. In January 1983, almost eighteen months after OBRA and ERTA became law, the national unemployment rate was 10.4 percent,[39] and most Americans were dissatisfied with Reagan's progress on the issue. According to a *New York Times*–CBS poll, approval for his job performance hit a low of 41 percent, and just 35 percent thought he was "in control of his administration." For many, the key issues were the president's inability to improve job numbers and to help the unemployed. Americans also were unhappy with the growing federal deficit, and 60 percent were ready for a cut in military spending and to forego further tax relief if it would make a difference. The poll held an additional surprise. Even though many would give up a tax break to bring down the deficit, 61 percent were prepared for an increase in the deficit rather than further reductions in social programs. Likewise, 75 percent were willing to incur greater debt if it enabled the creation of new jobs.[40]

Reagan had a different opinion, and his 1984 budget, which was presented to Congress just days after the January 1983 poll, included further cutbacks in social programs. The president specifically asked for reductions in food assistance for needy children, food stamp eligibility, and health insurance and medical assistance for the elderly.[41] At the same time, he made clear that he had no intention of rolling back intended tax cuts. (The cuts were scheduled over three years, with the last occurring in 1983.) His economic plan was working, he said, and he refused to "sabotage recovery." Visiting a Chrysler plant in Missouri, Reagan told autoworkers that "the shoots of an economic recovery were beginning to push up." Not everyone in the audience agreed. One listener told a *New York Times* reporter, "Ninety percent of the people are mad at him. . . . They hate Reaganomics."[42] This posed a problem for the president. He needed the support of workers, like those at the Chrysler plant, if he wanted to win reelection in 1984.

To secure those voters, the president needed to defend Reaganomics, the popular portmanteau for his economic policies, and he did so in many speeches as well as in his weekly Saturday radio addresses. Noting that the word was "used as a term for something that's supposed to have failed," Reagan sought to set the record straight. He had inherited a bad situation—"everything has been a mess for three years or more"[43]—but economic figures showed an upturn. When a *Washington Post* reporter annotated the speech, however, neither facts nor figures were quite what Reagan had claimed.[44] His achievements were less impressive than advertised, and his plan had more shortcomings. Nevertheless, the "shoots" Reagan mentioned in Missouri had been spotted by others.

In late February, *Time* magazine glimpsed "tentative auguries of economic revival" akin to the "first fragile buds of spring." Both production and new orders were up, as were "demands for durable consumer goods." Home sales and construction were rising even as mortgage rates and wholesale prices dropped. Unemployment remained a concern, but Congress was working on a bipartisan jobs bill. *Time* observed that it contained "less than first meets the eye"[45] but that its success would look good for both parties.

Even if the recovery had begun—economists subsequently dated its start to November 1982[46]—Reagan's fiscal plan encountered obstacles. In March, the House passed a budget that threatened to subvert many of the president's aims: it increased spending for social welfare programs, decreased defense outlays, and raised taxes. Reagan said it "would bring joy to the Kremlin," and the *Los Angeles Times* called it "the biggest setback the President has suffered on an economy measure since he entered the White House."[47]

Aware of popular discontent, some House Republicans even switched sides to vote with the Democrats. They told the *Times* that Reagan's military budget was "unrealistic," and cuts to social programs had gone deep enough.[48] Their concern was borne out the following month when a report from the Department of Health and Human Services found that AFDC rolls had added 159,000 people during the preceding summer, and by fall 1982, the total number of recipients exceeded 10 million. Moreover, the number of beneficiaries was predicted to increase another 4 percent in 1983. Poverty's rising tide renewed the debate over Reagan's decision to cut welfare benefits for the working poor. The president had ended support to those with part-time jobs, maintaining they should find full-time work rather than pad their earnings with federal funds. Not all experts agreed. Some said there were not enough well-paying jobs. Others predicted that welfare recipients, especially single mothers, would quit part-time positions so they could take care of their families and keep their benefits.[49]

The news did not improve over the summer. In August, the Congressional Budget Office reported that cuts in social programs, which would save $110 billion between fiscal 1982 and 1985, fell hardest on families with yearly incomes under $20,000. The numbers were harsh: spending for education was down 17 percent; for student loans it fell 27 percent; for job training and public employment it dropped 60 percent; and for child nutrition it decreased by 28 percent. During the same period, defense spending increased by $90 billion, rising from "25.7 % of the budget in fiscal 1982 to almost 30% in fiscal 1985."[50] Poor families were not alone in their economic distress. A study by the AFL-CIO Public Employees Department found that federal tax cuts resulted in higher state and local taxes, federal gasoline taxes, and Social Security payroll withholdings for "average-income Americans."[51] Despite federal tax cuts, many Americans were paying more in taxes. The study confirmed conclusions from an earlier report by the Tax Foundation: middle- and working-class Americans were suffering. A middle-class family in Ohio with an annual income of $25,000 would save $550 as a result of federal tax cuts. But rising state taxes, local taxes, property taxes, sales taxes, and income tax surcharges, along with bracket creep, would raise their taxes by almost $200.[52]

Reagan's critics flaunted the numbers. Columnist Michael Kinsley posed the question that had won Reagan support in the 1980 campaign: "Are you better off than you were four years ago?" Kinsley told his readers that they were not.[53] Other publications enumerated Reagan's failings. Average workers' weekly earnings were down 3 percent, the gross national product was barely higher than in 1981, and tax cuts had increased the federal deficit and enriched the upper classes but accomplished little else.[54] The nation's economic base was changing from heavy industry to service and technology, but the administration seemed oblivious. Millions of superfluous workers, mostly men over the age of fifty who had worked in factories, had lost jobs to automation and foreign competition. They were

FIGURE 25. Demonstration against Reagan's policies, April 6, 1983. AP Photo/ George Widman, File.

unable to find work at their previous salaries, if at all. Even if they were eligible for job retraining programs, many doubted they could compete against younger applicants.[55] When the *Washington Post* reported that Reagan's "ambitious domestic agenda" was "being put on hold" as the White House prepared for the 1984 presidential run, few were surprised. A former Reagan economic advisor said that with an election looming, "the administration's economic policy is to do nothing and pray the recovery continues."[56]

By fall, those prayers seemed to have been answered. The shoots and buds that some spied in the spring had blossomed. Even the Midwest, the nation's ailing industrial center that was especially hard hit by the recession, was bouncing back. "Everything is not rosy by any means," a University of Chicago economist told the *New York Times*. "But we're having a strong economic recovery in the region."[57] Increased automobile sales helped the local economy, as did an upswing in construction and the government's grain subsidy program. Yet even as people went back to work, the long shadow of the recession, along with the inequities of Reagan's recovery plan, darkened the landscape for small farmers and unionized workers. Rising costs for land and equipment strained family farms; many factories, including those operated by the major automakers, pressed unions for givebacks or moved operations to right-to-work states or low-wage countries. Formerly middle-class farmers and unionized workers had to make do with less, accepting low-paying jobs in sales and service.

When Reagan addressed the International Monetary Fund that fall, he gave no quarter to critics of his policies. Rather, he reiterated his vision of a political system that trusts in the market to promote human freedom. He offered thinly veiled criticism of communism and its subjugation of the individual, and he questioned the wisdom of previous presidents who seemed to place their trust in the US government rather than in the nation's citizens. (The juxtaposition of these remarks seemed to imply that previous leaders had leaned too far left.) Rejecting the misguided policies of the 1970s, which "permitted our governments to overspend, overtax and overregulate us toward soaring inflation and record interest rates," he said his administration placed its faith in "the magic of the market place" and the "human spirit."[58] Recent economic gains confirmed his faith, and there would be no tax increases to undermine the recovery. The growing federal deficit, he said, would come down because of tax cuts, and it would be shortsighted to change course now.

Not long after, members of Congress returned to their districts for the Columbus Day recess. Many found their constituents less sanguine about the nation's economic recovery than the president was. Across the country, citizens worried that the ballooning federal deficit, which was averaging nearly $150 billion annually under Reagan but had been less than $50 billion under Carter,[59] would lead to inflation and rising unemployment. Yet these very anxieties reflected a measure of relief. Many could worry about the federal deficit because their own troubles—job furloughs and layoffs, high interest rates, diminished purchasing power—had eased. "When people start worrying about deficits, you know things are turning up," Rep. Lynn Martin, a Republican from Illinois, told a reporter.[60]

Main Street fretted about the deficit, but Wall Street had moved on. When third quarter profits were announced, a front-page *Wall Street Journal* story reported that the "economic boom" had resulted in "the sharpest year-to-year gain in 4 1/2 years." Some industries posted triple-digit profits: building materials producers were up 133 percent and drug and variety stores 181 percent. The airlines, rubber companies, and textiles concerns similarly showed strong gains, but the biggest winners were the automakers. The third quarter of 1982 for the Big Three (Chrysler, Ford, and General Motors) revealed a combined loss of $186.6 million. But in 1983, they were up $1.17 billion.[61] Such successes would extend beyond corporate America, according to Reagan. The trickle-down economic theory he espoused claimed that corporate returns spurred capital spending, which led to the increase in jobs and salaries that fueled consumer spending, which alleviated the federal deficit.

Three months after Reagan used his radio address to defend Reaganomics, a *Los Angeles Times* poll found that a majority of Americans believed that his economic plan was working. Sixty-three percent called it a success, and 52 percent said they were better off than when he took office. The president's job approval rating had soared to 61 percent, a strong comeback from numbers earlier in the year. The poll also revealed an interesting inconsistency. Support for the president's efforts was up, but backing for his programs was down. Americans did not want further cutbacks to social programs or more reductions in governmental regulations. Even support for expanded military spending had dropped from 77 percent in April to 51 percent. Reagan's approval ratings were tied to the success of his policies, not to their merits. "By a ratio of almost 2 to 1, the poll shows that those who support Reagan's economic ideas do so because his ideas seem to be working—not because they believe the ideas are right."[62]

That pragmatism was based on results: productivity, retail sales, and investments were up, and the stock market was bullish. However, not all signs were strong. The federal deficit remained a problem, as did high unemployment and job dislocations caused by a national shift from "heavy industry to high technology." There were other worries too, reported the *New York Times*: "As ever, young blacks accounted for a disproportionate part of the unemployed. Their continuing distress stood in dismaying contrast to the year's symbols of black achievement: a black astronaut, a black Miss America, a black Mayor of Chicago and a black contender for President."[63] In an otherwise typical *New York Times* article, uncluttered by adjectives and modifying phrases, these two sentences stood out. While they were factually correct, their construction was striking, reinforcing the very problem that they addressed. "As ever," "distress," and "dismaying" implied that young Blacks were an ongoing problem. Even at a moment when some African Americans had shown they could do anything—run for president, win beauty pageants, or conquer the stars—many still did not have jobs. Their unemployment in the face of others' success created a "dismaying contrast," because their "distress," one could infer, might be self-inflicted.

RACE AND FAIRNESS

Even if the *Times* insidiously blamed poor Blacks for their situation, readers might not have noticed. The casual racism that underlay the article's descriptions likely seemed commonsensical; the *Times*' readers and critics alike agreed that the paper was liberal. Unsurprisingly, then, its reporters paid close attention to the fairness issue when it became a factor in the 1982 midterm election. Between January 1982 and December 1983, four major newspapers—the *New York Times*, the *Washington Post*, the *Los Angeles Times*, and the *Chicago Tribune*—ran more than 120 stories on that issue, with peaks in coverage before the 1982 midterm elections, during the summer of 1983, and in December of 1983 (coinciding with Meese's remarks on hunger).[64] Since most stories began with the charges that the tax cuts were unfair and only then presented the other side of the argument, much of the coverage could be seen as biased against the president's policies.

At the start of 1983, Reagan's advisors had begun efforts to defuse and mute this line of attack. They wanted to improve the president's standing among women and Blacks as well as to bolster support among white working- and middle-class men. Their strategy "was to Platonize the problem, describing it as a matter of perception separate from reality."[65] Throughout the year, Reagan and his team did just that, arguing that the budget cuts were anything but unfair. Poverty? The Democrats created the problem, but Reagan was fixing it. Hunger? More people than ever received assistance, and there were programs for all who needed them. Unemployment? This again was the Democrats' fault, but the economic recovery would spur new jobs. Still, the fairness issue did not go away.

It first emerged when the public grasped the ramifications of the tax cuts on social welfare programs. Reducing funds for hungry children and single mothers seemed wrong, especially when the savings would be a windfall for the rich. The president and his advisors were so unsettled by accusations that he was insensitive to the poor that they launched a "fairness-to-poor" offensive in March 1982. At every public appearance, Reagan assured listeners that he was not only compassionate but also deeply upset by accusations to the contrary. The president said that he favored helping truly needy people who could not help themselves, and his tax cuts would result in jobs for "average citizens."[66] But the issue's import increased when Democrats realized its impact on working- and middle-class voters. Appropriating the term for the 1982 campaign, Democrats made fairness a trope that telegraphed Reagan's tilt toward the rich at the expense of the average Joe. Pollsters predicted that fairness would be a central factor in the midterm elections.

Democrats initially sought support from liberals and minorities by emphasizing the inequity of Reagan's budget cuts, another example of the president's preference for the wealthy. Since moving to the White House, the Reagans lived sumptuously and were surrounded by affluent friends.

Nancy Reagan had spent $25,000 on clothes for the inauguration and soon after paid $200,000 to update the White House china.[67] (Mrs. Reagan explained that the purchases had been made with private funds.) Reagan repeatedly told voters that he was born poor—"I was raised in poverty and I remember very well what poverty is"[68]—and that he cared about the needy. But his free time was spent playing golf and riding horses.

Eager to show that Reaganomics targeted Middle America, Democrats' messaging played on class antagonisms to gain ground with white working- and middle-class voters who didn't approve of reductions in programs that helped them, such as student loans, mass transit, and services for the elderly.[69] The strategy worked: on Election Day, the GOP suffered one of its biggest losses in decades. Twenty-six Republican representatives were replaced by twenty-six Democrats. The Democrats' edge in the House went from 243–192 to 269–166, and although they were a 47–53 minority in the Senate, their ranks had grown by 1. Many observers ascribed the Republicans' loss not just to the weak economy but also to the fairness issue.[70]

When the Democrats' strategy succeeded, Reagan's handlers realized they needed to reframe the debate. Throughout 1983, they made class, race, and gender central to fairness, and much of the subsequent media coverage intimated that those most hurt by tax cuts were undeserving poor, Black single mothers. Reagan and his team used a variety of strategies, alternately drawing on numbers, history, and stereotyping to show that the president's programs were fair and that the Democrats were the real culprits.

Reagan also invoked the past, especially what he saw as the mistakes of his predecessors, to defend his policies. The president launched a vigorous attack on Lyndon B. Johnson's Great Society initiative that sought to end poverty and racial discrimination. But the buildup of government programs had the opposite effect, Reagan maintained. It had "contributed to family breakups, welfare dependency, and a large increase of births out of wedlock." LBJ's initiatives "had destroyed the economy and made Americans poorer than they were 15 years ago." The root of the problem, concluded the current president, was the Democrats' belief that "'government and bureaucracy' were 'the primary vehicle for social change.'"[71]

Throughout the year, Reagan and his supporters blamed the Great Society not just for destroying the economy but also for causing the disintegration of poor families and the enrichment of government bureaucrats. But dead presidents were not their only targets. Reagan also blamed the nation's economic plight on both the current crop of politicians who supported big government programs and the chiselers and cheats who exploited those initiatives. In a July radio address, he blasted the "big spenders" (that is, Democratic leaders), whose notion of fairness "revolves around government spending programs" and whose "deliberate government economic planning" led to inflation. He also called out the "nonneedy," who siphoned off "2 out of every 5 dollars in benefits."[72] And, as he routinely did, Reagan chastised the press, inveighing against "the drum beat of doom and gloom from the misery merchants in some of the media."[73] The economy was improving, "contrary to the propaganda blasts you hear," and his administration was "committed to fairness."[74]

Reagan and his allies played with numbers, berated Democrats, and complained about press coverage to bolster their claims, but the real turning point came when they gave welfare a human face. Democrats had tried to make fairness an issue that cut across racial, gender, and class lines. The tax cuts were equally unfair to white steelworkers, Black women on welfare, and middle-class students who lost their college loans. But when the US Census Bureau released figures on poverty showing a rapidly increasing number of women and children in need, the administration, according to the *Washington Post*, embraced "a new defense of the domestic spending cuts that have embroiled the president in the 'fairness issue.'"[75] The new defense was asserting that poverty, especially in the Black community, resulted from the prevalence of female-headed households. The breakdown of Black families, according to this theory, was beyond the government's control. If anything, government programs had made the problem worse.

This was not a new strategy. Reagan had previously used stereotypes to deprecate Blacks and to question their dependence on welfare. During his unsuccessful 1976 presidential campaign, he had derided "the welfare queen" as well as "the strapping young buck" (a pejorative southern term for a Black man) who used food stamps to buy steaks. After his election, Reagan was more circumspect, blaming Great Society programs for hurting poor families. Rather than raise stereotypes about frauds and cheaters, he said that Blacks had fallen into a culture of dependency that was destroying not just individuals' moral fiber but also the well-being of their community and, by extension, the nation.

Republicans seemed resigned to conceding women and minorities to the Democrats, but they could not give up on men. Taking advantage of long-standing race, gender, and class anxieties, the administration gave fairness a face, and it was not the one that white men saw in their mirrors. By identifying poverty with single African American mothers, Reagan and his team transformed the fairness issue from a concern affecting all but the very wealthy to a problem of an undeserving underclass.

The 1982 United States Census Report provided cover for racist and sexist stereotyping. According to its most recent survey, 15 percent of Americans lived in poverty—the highest number since 1965, when the Great Society programs began. The fastest-growing segment of the impoverished population were female-headed households, which represented 46 percent of poor families. (In 1960, women headed 24 percent of families living below the poverty line.) While it was not unusual to see the poverty rate rise during a severe recession, government officials as well as independent researchers said that the typical bounce back might not help women on welfare, who often lacked job skills and, if they had young children, could not work full-time. According to Bruce Chapman, a White House staff member and former head of the Census Bureau, "Fatherless families represent 'an underclass [that] an expanding economy won't reach.'"[76]

Echoing Chapman, other Reagan appointees told the *Washington Post* that female-headed households were a serious problem and could result in a "permanent underclass." Overall, women headed one in seven American families, but among Blacks, the ratio rose to almost one in two. According to the president, the best solution for such families was to end programs "that increase dependency and break up families."[77] A year earlier, Reagan had told a gathering of Black Republicans "that blacks 'would be appreciably better off today' if the Great Society had never been inaugurated"; government programs had led to "a new kind of bondage" for those on welfare.[78] Others, however, said that the swelling numbers showed the need for more support, not less.[79]

The politics of fairness, by virtue of the media coverage that followed the lead of the president and other administration officials, increasingly focused on the plight of Black Americans, specifically the prevalence of poor, dysfunctional, female-headed households. Even when fairness was not mentioned per se, it hovered between the lines, prompting readers to wonder who was responsible: Were Reagan's programs unfair, or was Johnson the real culprit? Was it fair for Blacks to depend on government (that is, white taxpayers) for support? Was it justifiable for wealthy Americans to let the less fortunate languish in poverty?

Reagan's justification for tax cuts—a healthy economy would create jobs for the poor—was cited as a rationale for change, but the *Post* noted that the defense budget had grown, while middle-class programs such as Social Security and Medicare remained the same. The implication was that people with resources could protect their benefits. Several interviewees insisted that cuts were made not to hurt Blacks but rather because of the perception, common among Reagan's inner circle, that welfare did more harm than good and that the system was beset by "waste, fraud and abuse."[80] The bottom line was that government programs should focus on the truly needy. Voters cared about fairness, but they cared more about their own well-being. As one of Reagan's political managers noted, "If people have got jobs, can make their house payments and keep the kids in college, they're not going to worry about fairness."[81]

Almost two years later, a Democratic operative made a similar observation. "People are telling us, 'Please don't ask us to care for people down the street before we take care of our own family's economic security,' said George Burger, DNC [Democratic National Committee] political director."[82] Accordingly, despite doubts about the fairness of Reagan's tax cuts—56 percent of the public agreed "the elderly, the poor, and the handicapped have been especially hard hit, while the rich and big business have been much better off"[83]—Reagan was reelected by a whopping 58.8 percent majority. Apparently, American voters preferred an incumbent who lowered inflation and unemployment[84] to a challenger who promised fairness.

But voters were not just looking out for their own needs. Many had become skeptical, even cynical, about the plight of the able-bodied poor. They agreed that Reagan's cuts had been hardest on disadvantaged groups, but they did not feel moved to do anything about it. According to a 1985 DNC survey, the term *fairness* had developed a "negative connotation" and become a "code word" for "giveaways."[85] For many middle-class voters, fairness did not apply to them or the reductions in government programs that affected them. Rather, it referred to poor people who wanted something for nothing. Their attitudinal change reflected the shift from a collective willingness to support a welfare state to the belief that a free-market economy would benefit everyone. The mainstreaming of this perspective reflects the media's "potential to educate, raise consciousness, and shape public attitudes."[86] But those responsible for educating and shaping public attitudes did not always agree with the outcomes achieved by their content.

MEDIA MATTERS

For each of its stories, the news media provides a frame, the perspective from which a story is told and which then influences its interpretation.[87] Framing shapes news consumers' opinions about issues, such as poverty and society's relationship to the poor. Reporters decide on a frame by using sources such as speeches, interviews, and other information, including leaks, tweets, videos, memos, emails, and letters from top government, corporate, cultural, and religious leaders—as well as their own judgment. Among these sources, the American president commands pride of place; and in the 1980s, the Reagan administration's policies, speeches, and activities were central to framing the news agenda. Even if Americans disagreed with Reagan's budget cuts, they understood that the president's priorities affected their lives too.

As with any president, Reagan's messages and their meaning were delivered and understood within the cultural, political, and economic context of the current moment. Thus in the mid-1960s, during the Great Society initiative, some Americans may have worried that government programs would encourage indolence among able-bodied men and women. But in the context of the civil rights movement, a strong economy, and a new awareness of poverty in America, such suspicions would have had trouble gaining traction with many thought leaders and much of the public. But fifteen years later, Reagan framed the issue of poverty as a national problem, reflecting a moral and a spiritual crisis as much as an economic and a political one. He provided a new frame for thinking about welfare, which reflected a religious imaginary that hallowed individual freedom, and he legitimated a swath of popular opinion that had been out of favor when economic, cultural, and political conditions were different.

In addition to framing poverty as a moral and a spiritual issue best remedied by work, family, and self-sufficiency, Reaganites and the news media that covered them turned it into a problem of race and gender. Racial bigotry and sexism, mirrored in Reagan's comments about "young bucks" and "welfare queens," rendered African Americans the face of the undeserving poor. Poor Black men were "threatening and violent" while single Black mothers were "immoral and neglectful."[88] Blacks received a disproportionate amount of federal assistance, although they did not comprise the majority of America's poor. Yet "media images emphasizing the relationship between poverty and ethnicity clearly fuel[ed] the perception that most poor people are African American"[89] and "led directly to public misconceptions of the poor and a decrease in public support."[90]

By reframing the 1960s notion that poverty is a systemic problem requiring government intervention, Reagan cast it as an individual problem that required personal change. Solving the problem required an individual's commitment to strengthening his or her family and to achieving self-sufficiency.[91] Those who did not try to solve their own problems did not deserve sympathy, much less aid.

Media coverage reflected some of these prejudices. Highlighting the problems of Black Americans made for compelling stories that mined deep currents of misogyny and racism. Coverage also tapped middle-class ambivalence about the impact of Reagan's economic strategy on the poor. Regardless of which way the narrative tilted, most stories widened the gap between us and them. Citing rising divorce rates and single-parent households among Black Americans, the *Chicago Tribune* predicted that "the break-up of the black family threatens to undermine much of the progress blacks have made in education, health care, nutrition and politics. It almost certainly will affect crime rates, drug use, welfare and even the religious habits of black America." The front-page article drew on Census Bureau statistics to show that African American children in female-headed homes were economically disadvantaged. Describing a culture of poverty that destroyed children's sense of self-worth, the reporter outlined how poverty led to crime, drug use, unemployment, and the loss of a religious compass. Moreover, Blacks who found a way out and joined the middle class would, as likely as not, turn their backs on those less fortunate.[92]

The *New York Times* went to Los Angeles for its story on the misfortunes of Black families. The feature piece introduced the McNeeses, a family of two parents, ten children, and two grandchildren living together in South Central (today often known as South Los Angeles), one of the city's poorest areas. The McNeeses, living at the edge of poverty, were "adopted" by local Black professionals willing to be role models as well as to dispense advice to the less fortunate. Yet the reporter noted that such modest efforts would not affect the growing number of single Black, female-headed families in the city, much less in the nation. In 1982, "55 percent of black infants were born to unwed mothers," and "47 percent of black households with children were headed by women." (The numbers of single white, female-headed households also rose, but to "just 15 percent" of all white families.)[93]

When the *Washington Post* produced its own series on Black families, it focused on "the leading edge of the fairness issue," the effect of spending cuts on the poor. Like the *Tribune*, the *Post* had lots of numbers: one in three Blacks lived below the poverty line, one in four were on Medicaid and food stamps, one in five collected AFDC, and one in seven lived in federally subsidized housing. Blacks also suffered from reductions in smaller government programs, including student aid, child nutrition, and job training. The takeaway? "Blacks are much more reliant on federal aid than is generally realized," which is why budget cuts "had a far greater impact on black than white Americans."[94]

The entertainment industry reinforced the perception of the undeserving poor, especially those who were Black.[95] Starting in the 1970s, researchers studied this effect on white and Black audiences, measuring how and why portrayals by entertainment media fed racist attitudes.[96] According to their findings, this media, similar to news media, had the power to establish agendas, inform public opinion, and confirm ingrained perspectives. Yet notwithstanding these conclusions, little changed in television and film during the early to mid-1980s. If anything, some critics and commentators felt that Blacks had better roles and more opportunities in Hollywood during the 1970s than they did a decade later. In other words, entertainment media of the 1980s did not challenge the news media's racial depictions. Instead, television and film appeared to affirm them.

Other than scattered roles as regulars and one-shot appearances as criminals and lowlifes, Blacks had a limited presence on televised drama series. These had few Black regulars, with *Hill Street Blues* (1981–87) and *St. Elsewhere* (1982–88) being notable exceptions. When a Black was cast as a dramatic lead, he (it usually was a male character) took second billing to a white colleague, as in the relationship between *Miami Vice*'s (1984–89) Ricardo Tubbs (Philip Michael Thomas) and Sonny Crockett (Don Johnson). Black leads also had quirks that simultaneously played on and defused stereotypes. The breakout star of *The A-Team* (1983–87) was Mr. T as B. A. Baracus, a big, angry Black man. (*B. A.* stood for both Bosco Albert and Bad Attitude.) A standout among his square-jawed, stylish white colleagues, Baracus sported a Mohawk, gold chains, and leopard-print shirts. He was the brawniest team member with the badass one-liners.

Blacks were featured more frequently on television comedies, a genre that finds humor in caricature and stereotype. Sitcoms such as *Sanford and Son* (1972–77), *Good Times* (1974–79), and *The Jeffersons* (1975–85) repeated familiar formulas. Most Black television families were working class, if not poor. George Jefferson, an exception who, as the show's theme song said, had moved "on up to the East Side," was funny because of his faux pas and bourgeois pretensions. His wife, Louise, spent much of her time smoothing over George's mistakes. When *The Cosby Show* (1984–92) debuted, critics hailed it as a game changer. A sitcom about an upper-middle-class Black family in Brooklyn, *The Cosby Show* eschewed Black stereotypes and white paternalism. It was an endearing family comedy whose upper-class characters could just as easily have been Caucasian. The show was a hit and reenergized the family sitcom, but it did not spawn new programming about successful Black families. Thus, despite the popularity of *The Cosby Show*, in 1985 two sociologists could pessimistically describe the current state of television portrayals of Blacks as resembling the "stereotyped, demeaning minstrel-like roles"[97] of the early 1950s.

Movies were no better. In the early 1980s, two Black comedians, Richard Pryor and Eddie Murphy, had box office clout and starred in a dozen movies. Murphy became a familiar face on *Saturday Night Live*, where as the lone Black cast member (1980–84), he turned racist stereotypes into subversive humor. But in his first Hollywood film, *48 Hrs.* (1982), Murphy was pigeonholed as the Black sidekick, a precursor to the Black Best Friend trope.[98] He played a convict who helps a white detective catch a

FIGURE 26. The 1983 film *Trading Places* retold Mark Twain's 1881 novel *The Prince and the Pauper* through contemporary class and racial lenses. Trading Places © Paramount Pictures Corp. All Rights Reserved. Album / Alamy Stock Photo.

cop killer and makes quips that keep the audience laughing. The following year, Murphy again played to stereotype in *Trading Places*. This time, he portrayed a penniless grifter who, thanks to the machinations of two meddling millionaires, trades places with a wealthy commodities broker. Updating Mark Twain's novel *The Prince and The Pauper*, *Trading Places* both resisted and reveled in stereotypes. Blacks played almost all the low-status roles (servants, doormen, and waiters), while the white characters casually spewed racist taunts. Still, Murphy gets the best of every white he encounters. His triumph at the film's end implicitly acknowledges that the nature/nurture debate, which inspired the millionaire brothers' bet, is beside the point. Race is key to social and material success, and racism obscures Blacks' abilities.

Richard Pryor's *The Toy* (1982) lacked an equivalent wink at reality. A remake of a 1976 French film, *The Toy* was a comedy about a rich man who purchases a poor man as a plaything for his son. Pryor's character, Jack Brown, is an unemployed reporter working as a janitor at a department store. When the young son of the store's owner spots a funny Black man in the toy department, he tells his father that he wants to buy him. Offered a generous sum to play with the boy for a week, Brown demurs, "I'm not for sale; I thought we settled all this during the Civil War."[99] Yet, presented with an offer he can't refuse, he takes the job. In its spare 102-minute running time, the film makes sure that villains (including the Ku Klux Klan) are punished, families are strengthened, and goodness is rewarded (Brown lands a newspaper job). But the premise and casting remained problematic.

HUNGER IN AN ELECTION YEAR

Issues of fairness and hunger did not disappear after the New Year, but they did recede from the headlines. When the Presidential Commission on Food Assistance, popularly referred to as the Commission on Hunger, released its final-draft report on January 8, 1984, its findings echoed Edwin Meese's earlier remarks. According to the report, "Allegations of rampant hunger simply cannot be documented," although the authors conceded that "hunger does persist." The thirteen-member, mostly Republican panel also concluded that Reagan's budget cutbacks had not affected food relief for those living at or below the poverty line. (The administration previously announced that spending reductions had decreased food assistance for those living just above the poverty line.) With many public and private programs in place, there was "an effective safety net that offers access to food assistance to virtually all needy Americans." The report also distinguished between the persistence of hunger and the absence of malnutrition or starvation, noting that the latter was no longer a problem. The commission did not recommend "new spending initiatives or programs," although it made several suggestions, such as transferring programmatic oversight for food assistance from the federal government to states that sought it.[100]

The carefully worded report generated the expected range of reactions. Republicans were pleased, Democrats complained, and pundits reiterated many of the arguments that Meese had made a month earlier. Yet the heated coverage that followed Meese's earlier remarks was absent. Rather, hunger was a story that simmered throughout the year, briefly coming to a boil when related events occurred or when reporters found other reasons to revisit the issue. The *Chicago Tribune*, perhaps mindful of its location in the still-struggling Rust Belt, ran an ongoing series, "Hunger in America." Periodic articles reminded readers that hunger not only persisted but also had increased. According to the *Tribune*, many working-class white men, whose factory jobs had ended in the recession's early days, were still unemployed and needed food assistance for their families.[101] Other newspapers likewise kept the story local, focusing on the "new poor" whose plight was unknown by neighbors who hadn't seen their surreptitious trips to food pantries. In August, the Democrat-controlled House made "an election-year bow to the 'fairness issue' by voting to increase food stamp benefits,"[102] but the Republican-controlled Senate killed the bill.

Neither the prevalence of hunger in the United States nor the Reagan administration's denial of its existence appeared to have political implications. Instead, public opinion demonstrated a lack of concern either way. When the year began, some pundits had speculated that Democrats would make hunger the leading edge of the fairness issue, but the issue never jelled. As the Republicans had hoped, Reagan coasted on the success of the economic recovery. Democrats raised many related issues, including fairness and the escalating budget deficits, but they could not make a dent in Reagan's popularity. In late September, William Raspberry, one of the country's few African American columnists, wrote in the *Washington Post*, "Forget war and peace, forget fairness, forget the federal deficit. None of it matters for this election. The only thing that matters is whether individual voters think their personal finances are more likely to improve under a Mondale administration or a second Reagan term."[103]

Raspberry predicted the rise of "pocketbook selfishness" after seeing a *Washington Post*–ABC poll that revealed voters would put their own interests above those of the nation. A majority of respondents said that even though Democratic candidate Walter Mondale was more likely than Reagan to "reduce the threat of nuclear war" and "be fairer to all segments of the population," and that they shared Mondale's political views and felt that the "national economy was getting worse under Reagan," they still backed the incumbent. They explained their support by saying that Reagan would ensure they were "better off financially." Noting that voters typically explained their choice of candidates as a product of aligned views, Raspberry surmised, "Reagan has made greed an acceptable attitude."[104]

A *Washington Post* feature story put midwestern names and faces on the poll. Several suburban housewives, including Sue Daniels of Mequon, Wisconsin, explained why they were voting for the incumbent. "I'm going for Reagan because now I'm one of the haves and he's gonna take a little less from me and give a little less to some of the people who don't have.

Mondale's going to give my money to everybody, whether they're down and out because they're lazy or because they're not."[105]

Voters knew Mondale's policies were "fairer" than Reagan's, but many did not care. Among those who did care were public service workers whose income and benefits were affected by federal cutbacks and Blacks who knew that the president's policies penalized them. According to the *Post*'s reporters, "The strongest feelings on the fairness issue are heard in the black community on (Milwaukee's) Northside." Local statistics underscored why: test scores were low, soup kitchens were packed, and welfare rolls were swelling. Meanwhile, members of traditionally liberal white communities were questioning their responsibility to help. A wealthy and progressive-minded Democratic state legislator explained, "I'm beginning to wonder myself about government programs that suppress people's will to do better."[106]

Not long after Reagan's 1984 victory, Ellen Goodman, a syndicated columnist, penned a chilling postmortem. She wrote that in redefining the playing field in an "era of limits," Republicans gave new meaning to the terms *winners* and *losers* by justifying the former's success at the latter's expense. "If we are going to limit opportunities for those stuck in the Other America, it is much easier to think of these people as failures. If we are going to chip away at social programs for the have-nots, it is easier to name them losers."[107]

Goodman and Raspberry saw a problem and decried its impact, but neither of their columns described its full import. Both were at pains to note the innate goodness of the American people: Goodman said they were "not fundamentally ungenerous," and Raspberry expressed hope that when voters truly understood the difference between the candidates, they would favor Mondale. But racism, sexism, and classism were written into the Constitution, and the view that poverty was a moral shortcoming predated the founding of the nation. Reagan and his team updated these sentiments and added a religious gloss to white privilege and greed. For more than three centuries, Americans had judged the needy as either worthy or unworthy, and the resurgence of this perspective in the 1980s was just the most recent iteration of a familiar American theme.

Neither columnist probed the press's role in this shift. Yet by virtue of whom it covered and how it reported, the news media mainstreamed Reagan's religious imaginary, normalizing it and making it almost commonsensical. That Reaganomics materially benefited a sizable swath of white America only enhanced its ability to succeed. The sweep of fairness coverage over 1983 shows that in reporting the debate, journalists typically framed the story according to the administration's point of view, even when the story itself was sympathetic to those in need. Moreover, the repetition of certain tropes—broken families, entitlements, cheaters, and frauds—alongside deep-seated prejudices about Blacks and women eased the slide of public opinion into an us-versus-them mentality. And for those of "us" who were, in Goodman's terms, "not fundamentally ungenerous," the surge of articles, op-eds, and editorials bemoaning hunger and excoriating Meese may have provided a vicarious vent for guilt, embarrassment, and disquietude. But when the Christmas season ended, it was time to move on.

Implicit in the collective desire to move on was a growing conviction that America was on the right track. For many whites, that was the personally advantageous track, but most wanted to believe that it was also the ethical and spiritual track of an exceptional nation rebounding after more than a decade of decline. Americans had veered off course and the result was failure and loss, from Vietnam and a broken economy to women's lib and the implosion of the traditional family. Reagan had promised success and security, strength and respect. But his plan was more than a to-do list of material changes. Rather, it was a new covenant, a vision of citizenship based on religious and moral principles that could include Americans of any or even no religious affiliation. All they needed to believe in was America's national destiny, along with a lived religion of moral certitude, individual responsibility, and the primacy of individual freedom rooted in free-market values.

Under Ronald Reagan's leadership, the United States changed. Americans' views of themselves, their world, and their responsibilities shifted. Agreed-on notions of personal freedom, individual responsibility, limited government, and a free market supplanted belief in a communal good, a capacious government, and a regulated market. Freedom for religion and its role in the public polity supplanted freedom from religion and a secular civil society. Reagan's religious imaginary both shaped and reflected the spirit of the times, and it renewed many Americans' faith in the future. But the success of this vision was more than its affinity with the zeitgeist or its proclamation by the Great Communicator. The news media, the alleged bastion of liberal views, normalized and circulated Reagan's religiously inflected neoliberalism. Unable or unwilling to see their role as propagandists or to rethink their mission as truth tellers, America's journalists eased the way for subsequent decades of growing income inequality, militant unilateralism, and intergroup conflict.

Epilogue

The future doesn't belong to the fainthearted; it belongs to the brave.

PRESIDENT RONALD REAGAN, January 28, 1986

When I began research for this book in 2008, Barack Obama was president, and his backers, myself among them, believed that the United States had entered a progressive, post-racial era. It seemed an apt time to evaluate the almost three decades of conservative policies that the new president seemed poised to change. That transitional moment also struck me as the right juncture to interrogate the role of the media in social change and the ways in which cultural and social contexts shape events that, in turn, affect media narratives and inform public opinion. I also wanted to challenge the myth of the liberal news media and assert the role of religion in American life.

Obama, however, proved more moderate than many of his supporters expected, and Reagan's neoliberal framework remained in place. When Obama took office, the Great Recession had devastated economies worldwide, and although the new president prioritized bailout strategies to end the crisis, the economy was still recovering as his second term ended. Job creation lagged and economic growth was sluggish.[1] Many Americans wanted a change of party, and a billionaire businessman looked like a good bet, even if many dismissed him as a bully and a buffoon. But on November 8, 2016, to the shock and consternation of moderates and progressives, Donald Trump won Wall Street, Main Street, evangelicals, and whites who felt marginalized in a post-racial society.

The 2016 election complicated my project. Depending on one's point of view, Trump represented either the apotheosis or the nadir of the Reagan religious imaginary. New books flooded the market, all addressing a common question: How did we get here? My contribution to that literature puts the news media, infrequently examined in cultural histories, and religion, similarly unattended in social histories, front and center. I also posit that a compelling ideological vision—a religious imaginary—is a prerequisite for political, social, and economic change.

Whether Trump represented the fulfillment or the failure of Reagan's religious imaginary, he certainly plagiarized it. In 1980, when Ronald Reagan ran for president, he vowed, "For those who've abandoned hope, we'll restore hope, and we'll welcome them into a great national crusade to make America great again."[2] At the time, Trump was a thirty-three-year-old businessman. More than three decades later, when he himself ran for president, he was compared to Reagan. Encouraging the connection, Trump adopted the slogan "Make America Great Again," a clear homage to Reagan's successful campaign language.

Yet despite similarities between the two men's fiscal, political, and social conservatism, Trump neither embraced nor provided a compelling alternative to Reagan's religious imaginary. Even if he had, his ability to transform the nation would not have matched the Great Communicator's—the media landscape, which had fractured in the intervening years, no longer provided a unifying narrative. Nevertheless, Trump perceived the strategic import of a religious imaginary and exploited its images for targeted constituencies. Marching toward an Episcopal church during the 2020 racial protests, he held a book aloft and told reporters, "It's a Bible."[3]

Trump may have clung to the imaginary's symbols, but he was more concerned with his own destiny than the nation's, more mindful of his own freedom than his constituents', and more devoted to Mammon than to God. Drawing on a charged repertoire of racism, misogyny, class warfare, and xenophobia, Trump's imaginary circulated via social media, conservative talk shows, and evangelical pulpits. But it polarized rather than united, empowering right-wing and extremist groups that thrilled to its message of white supremacy, masculine rage, and jingoism.

By the time he ran for president, Trump had spent decades crafting his image as a successful real estate developer. Brash, confident, and ambitious, he was part of New York City's ruling class that Tom Wolfe skewered in his 1987 best seller, *Bonfire of the Vanities*. Trump was not a Wall Street trader, as Wolfe's "masters of the universe" were, but he shared their belief that money, masculinity, and a taken-for-granted sense of white privilege allowed him to say or do whatever he wanted. That sense of prerogative took root as Manhattan morphed from a dirty, crime-infested city to a playground for the rich and powerful.

Much of the city's shift stemmed from the impact of Reagan's optimism and economic policies on Wall Street. After the recession ended, the stock market soared and commercial real estate exploded. The "go-go '80s," as the decade was called, benefited from lower taxes, relaxed regulations, and the sense of possibility that Reagan stoked as he extolled America's greatness. But the spirit of neoliberalism, which looked to the market to solve social problems and economic inequities, also had a darker side, captured in Oliver Stone's 1987 film, *Wall Street*. Gordon Gekko, the avaricious corporate raider at the movie's center, is still remembered for his claim that "greed, for lack of a better word, is good." Less cited are the words of the wildly successful stock trader who had inspired Stone. Ivan Boesky, later convicted of insider trading, told the University of California–Berkeley's 1986 business school graduates, "I think greed is healthy. You can be greedy and still feel good about yourself."[4]

Donald Trump epitomized the spirit of the age. He expanded his family's real estate holdings, mostly middle-class apartment buildings in the outer boroughs, and erected luxury hotels and skyscrapers in Manhattan. He built a casino in Atlantic City, started a new football league, and launched the Trump Shuttle, which flew passengers between Boston, New York, and Washington, DC. The Trump name was everywhere. Talk show hosts interviewed the telegenic, self-proclaimed billionaire on everything, from his childhood to his future plans. In 1980, when Rona Barrett asked whether he wanted to be president, Trump gave a firm no. When Oprah Winfrey queried him about it seven years later, his answer was equivocal.[5]

Even then, Trump used marketing language to describe his persona. "I believe I'm portrayed in a rougher sense than the actual product," he told an interviewer. "I hope the actual product is a lot more mellow than the portrayal."[6] In referring to himself as a "product," Trump anticipated the transactional model that, in the coming decades, colored how Americans thought about themselves. College classes instructed students on building their brand, dating apps commodified sex and romance, and religious institutions marketed themselves online. Correspondingly, Trump intuited that carefully cultivated perceptions could eclipse reality, a significant insight since by 1990 he faced debts of $3.4 billion. According to a *New York Times* analysis, "It was decisions Mr. Trump made at the helm of his business empire during the 1980s that led to its nearly imploding."[7] With help from family and strategic bank loans, Trump tried to right his business empire. But since he withheld tax information during both the 2016 and the 2020 presidential campaigns, rumors about his indebtedness remained, and in October 2020 *Forbes* magazine reported that the then president was over $1 billion in debt.[8]

Donald Trump's surprising ascent owes much to Ronald Reagan, the right-wing evangelicals who supported both men, and the mainstream news media, which reported copiously on them. Like Reagan, Trump benefited from news outlets that acted as an echo chamber, normalizing his candidacy as it once did with Reagan's conservative worldview. But unlike Trump, Reagan's perspectives on individual freedom and civic responsibility were rooted in beliefs about the relationship between God and government. Trump, who has been a registered Democrat, Republican, and independent, appeared motivated by pragmatic self-interest rather than a religio-political ideology. Unlike Reagan, he showed little interest in fighting global antidemocratic forces, bolstering free markets, or expanding individual freedom. Nevertheless, the relationship that Ronald Reagan forged between evangelical voters and the GOP was key to Trump's success.

That relationship was not limited to shared religious convictions; it also entailed political and economic positions, including neoliberalism. Trump embodied neoliberalism, but he did not consistently advance a neoliberal agenda. He was no ideologue. As president, he charted his own course, one with hallmarks of fascism as well as neoliberalism.[9] Following a fascist model, he consolidated his base by promoting nationalism and racism.[10] After his 2020 loss to Joe Biden, he attempted to stay in power by disputing the election results and fostering an insurrection. Trump's neoliberalism surfaced in efforts to cut taxes, shrink government, end regulations, and encourage privatization. Moreover, his orientation to governing was economic rather than political, manifest in his CEO style of management. He hired and fired at will (sometimes over Twitter) and promoted Trump properties for governmental contracts that were paid for by federal tax dollars.[11] But his allegiance to neoliberalism was inconsistent. He opposed free trade, promoted unilateral, antiglobalist policies, and tried using federal power to intervene in states' decisions.

Trump replaced Reagan's religiously inflected neoliberalism with secular self-aggrandizement. His transactional strategies won voter support: He promised Wall Street that he would lower taxes, and he assured low-income Americans that he would sponsor federal infrastructure projects that provided jobs. He accomplished the former but not the latter, resulting in a soaring stock market and ballooning economic inequality during his tenure. He delivered on promises to conservative evangelicals that he would pack the Supreme Court with like-minded jurists and move the American embassy in Israel from Tel Aviv to Jerusalem. Seeing their goals achieved, a majority of white evangelicals chose to overlook Trump's history of bullying, lying, and sexual assault, voting for him with the same four-in-five majority they had reserved for more traditional Republican candidates such as George W. Bush and Mitt Romney.

Among recent presidents, Reagan and Trump were especially skilled at using the media. Their having worked as entertainers made them familiar faces worldwide and well practiced with cameras, microphones, and crowds. Reagan spent twenty-five years in Hollywood, achieving moderate success as a film and television actor, while Trump was host and star for eleven years of *The Apprentice*, a popular reality television show. Additionally, their positions as public figures—Reagan as California's governor and Trump as a billionaire businessman—gave them experience with the news media. During their presidential campaigns, each honed his image: Reagan as sunny and avuncular, Trump as cocksure and hot-tempered. When they ran for president, both men received more and better coverage than their Democratic opponents,[12] Jimmy Carter and Hillary Clinton, both of whom the media portrayed as dour and wonky.

But the 1980 news media was very different from that of 2016. As this book describes, print news was in flux when Reagan took office. Profits were hard won as costs for labor and materials rose, and shifts in reading habits led to the closure of many afternoon papers and the rise of neighborhood weeklies. Moreover, technological advances—including home computers and cable television—were poised to revolutionize the industry. Local owners were selling out to media conglomerates that streamlined operations to increase profit. At the same time, *USA Today* pioneered innovations in daily newspapers' style and substance. Cable News Network (CNN), which launched on June 1, 1980, made twenty-four-hour news a reality, threatening the tradition of daily newspapers and nightly broadcasts. Yet the guiding principles of the modern news media, established between the 1920s and the 1960s, held firm.

In those decades, mainstream news coverage, whether print or broadcast, was objective, conservative, and consensus driven. Reporters relied on "the view from nowhere,"[13] press critic Jay Rosen's description of journalistic objectivity that relativizes and equalizes all points of view. This made financial sense to news executives, who, eager for the largest possible audience, did not want reporters promoting a specific perspective, much less their own opinion. Instead, journalists strove for neutrality, likely unaware that their own subjectivities shaped their coverage—most were white men whose economic and professional status had risen steadily from the 1920s to the 1960s. For example, in the 1980 presidential race, reporters' perceptions of masculinity help account for why a confident cowboy-actor received better coverage than a modest peanut farmer and former governor. Reagan played into these tropes, making it known that his California ranch, where he could ride twelve miles of trails, split firewood, and clear brush, was his idea of heaven.[14] Carter, tone-deaf to gender norms and offending both liberals and conservatives, told *Playboy* magazine, "I've looked on a lot of women with lust. I've committed adultery in my heart many times."[15]

The 1980s emphasis on objectivity signified a resurgent conservativism, a reflection of the cultural moment. The Iranian hostage crisis along with other tribulations of the 1970s had sobered editors and publishers. As chains and conglomerates bought up local newspapers, new overlords pulled back on experimenting with style, challenging corporate America, or probing government policy. Their conservatism called for balanced coverage that, for the most part, upheld the status quo. This also made economic sense. Profit margins depended on advertising, which followed circulation, which meant reaching the widest and most affluent audience possible.

The mediaverse of the 1980s enabled consensus journalism because a limited number of producers turned out a (relatively) uniform product. Moreover, a small group of national newspapers, newsmagazines, and television broadcasts set the agenda. Elite reporters covering the same story might agree on the frame for their pieces.[16] While this tactic was most frequently used during instances of pack journalism (reporters gathered en masse to cover an event), it also shaped smaller outlets' daily coverage. Editors, reading the day's wires, assigned reporters to follow up on or localize stories from the national news. News consumers, whether reading the morning paper in Butte, Montana, or watching CBS national news in Jackson, Mississippi, found the same stories with a similar point of view.

Consensus on the selection and framing of news is why Benedict Anderson observed that reading the morning newspaper was the modern analogue to morning prayer: an orientation to reality that provided a common understanding of meaning, purpose, and identity among diverse and geographically dispersed citizens.[17] Other sources of information existed, reported and written from alternate viewpoints, but these media outlets tended to be marginal and their audiences small. By "consensus," I do not mean that all mainstream news outlets had the same perspective on politics and policy or that their editorial pages aligned. But most esteemed the Constitution, supported the two-party system, and strove to inform and educate citizen-consumers.

Reagan's religious imaginary flourished in this news environment. Recall that religious imaginaries provide a commonsense understanding of meaning, identity, and purpose by embedding "a particular chain of beliefs"[18]—that is, a theology or ideology—into ideas and images. In the guise of history and continuity, these beliefs establish and delimit notions of self and society. The belief that God chose America for a special destiny is the crux of the nation's most enduring religious imaginary, and it is one that Reagan employed and embroidered. He trusted that God chose America for a special mission and that he had a part to play in its success. Speaking with a reporter after becoming California's governor, Reagan admitted, "I'm not quite able to explain how my election happened or why I'm here, apart from believing it is part of God's plan for me."[19]

During speeches in the 1950s, Reagan often spoke about God's plan for the United States, and in the late 1960s he found an effective way to frame it. Linking his worldview to a usable past, he quoted the statement "We shall be as a city upon a hill, the eyes of all people are upon us" from John Winthrop's seventeenth-century text, *A Model of Christian Charity*. Many Americans think that Winthrop's text was a homily delivered to his Puritan coreligionists before they disembarked in the New World. Hence, they credit it as foundational for the Massachusetts Bay Colony. But according to recent scholarship, it's unlikely that Winthrop gave such a sermon or that his words were widely known among, much less significant to, early American settlers.[20] Not until twentieth-century historian Perry Miller began his groundbreaking research on the Puritans did the text reengage the public. Miller made it central to the Puritan experience, just as he made the Puritans foundational to the American narrative.[21] His work gave *A Model of Christian Charity* new life at a moment when the United States was becoming a world power, and the image of a city on a hill had resonance for the post–World War II generation.

By the mid-twentieth century, the image had begun appearing in political speeches, and Reagan adopted it in the late 1960s. Whereas Winthrop meant that the Puritan experiment would be judged by the witnessing world, Reagan's "shining city on a hill" conjured America's goodness and godliness as a model for other nations. That blessing, he believed, was manifest in the freedom that is every American's birthright. In this paradigm, freedom, grounded in personal responsibility, is the cornerstone of morality, democracy, and the free market. Rather than impose external restrictions, such as market regulations, federal law, or limits on the free exercise of religion in the public square, Reagan believed in individual accountability. His alignment with neoliberalism was summed up by his observation, offered at his 1981 inauguration, that "in this current crisis, government is not the solution to the problem; government is the problem."

Many evangelicals as well as libertarians, conservatives, and other opponents of the welfare state shared Reagan's perspective. They agreed that cuts in social services, reliance on the market, and a small central government best served individual freedom. By wrapping neoliberalism in religion and morality, Reagan's imaginary made hyperindividualism and consumer capitalism seem less like rampant greed and more like organic outgrowths of God-given freedom. For many Americans of both parties, this perspective became commonsensical, reflected in President Bill Clinton's cuts to welfare programs,[22] President George W. Bush's invasion of Iraq,[23] and presidential candidate Barack Obama's appeal to Black Americans to take responsibility for their lives.[24]

Reagan disseminated this powerful religious imaginary with the help of journalists, and many scholars and pundits agree that he was among the most media-savvy presidents of the twentieth century.[25] White House reporters either liked Reagan or acquiesced to his rules (he denied access to critical journalists), and the go-go zeitgeist accorded with his cheerful and reassuring outlook. He radiated strength, displayed a sense of humor, and almost always stayed on message, compelling reporters to focus on his concerns. Even when reporters and opinion writers criticized Reagan's policies, the public seemed disinclined to care or, more important, vote against him.

In 2016, when Trump ran for president, the media landscape was very different. The explosion of digital and social media ended the mainstream media's hegemony and revamped the playing field. Since the cost of setting up a website was low, an eclectic spectrum of bloggers as well as online news and opinion outlets blossomed. In December 2016, there were 1.7 billion websites in the world, almost double the number a year earlier. (Active websites were closer to 170 million.)[26] Social media also commanded staggering numbers. In 2016, Facebook had 1.8 billion users, while Instagram and Twitter had, respectively, 600 million and 325 million active monthly users.[27] Anyone and everyone could be a journalist or, in the new lingo, an influencer. Viewing options similarly grew as cable, satellite, and streaming services raised the number of choices to the thousands.

This new twenty-first-century mediaverse, increasingly accessed online, spelled the end of objectivity and consensus. The mainstream media, now online too, held on to balance and neutrality for as long as possible, but Trump's words and actions demanded new forms of response. Rather than holding press conferences or issuing news releases, Trump announced policy changes, diplomatic initiatives, and personnel updates on Twitter. His posts, often using inflammatory language and all-caps invectives, defied balanced reporting.[28] In 2019 the *Washington Post*, a pillar of mainstream coverage, conceded, "The president of the United States is a liar."[29]

Unlike previous presidents, who tried to hide their lies, Trump appeared to revel in disinformation. His falsehoods accomplished two key tasks. He undermined the trustworthiness of the mainstream media by repeating charges of "fake news," which then were spread by millions of his followers and echoed on Fox News and other conservative outlets. He also established a vital link with the public that was more dynamic than even FDR's or Reagan's radio "fireside chats." FDR made thirty broadcasts between 1933 and 1944, and when Reagan revived the custom in 1982, he recorded weekly radio shows. Trump took the practice of directly addressing the people even further. According to the Trump Twitter Archive,[30] he tweeted, on average, almost six times daily at the start of his presidency and almost thirty-five times daily at its conclusion.[31] On some days, he sent as many as two hundred messages.[32] At a time when many of his supporters had lost faith in the news media, Trump's unfiltered tweets were taken as factual.

The internet, by disrupting the power of the mainstream media, dealt a deathblow to consensus journalism. People could easily find news outlets that catered to their own viewpoints and watch commentators who reiterated their brand of partisan polemics, analogous to the highly partisan political media of the early republic. Conservative pundits on Fox News now had the same credibility—and more, according to some audiences—as veteran CBS or *New York Times* journalists. Americans no longer used the same sources for their daily orientation to the world and personal meaning-making. Thus, even if Trump had a religious imaginary, it could not have the same impact as Reagan's. News was too diffuse and consumers too skeptical to accept a common vision. Instead, the news media polarized Americans along conservative, moderate, and progressive lines. Each had its own religious imaginary, which provided spiritual and moral cover for attacking the others. Indeed, those motivated by QAnon and many who participated in the January 6, 2021, insurrection were influenced by a religious imaginary grafted from Reagan's vision of individual freedom and America's destiny.

The book of Proverbs tells us, "Without a vision, the people perish." But what if a vision causes the people to perish? After four decades of Reagan's vision, which animated greed and hyperindividualism in ways that he may not have foreseen, we are faced with debilitating climate change, increased economic insecurity, systemic racism, and a new class of global oligarchs beholden to no one. White supremacists and Christian nationalists have emerged from the shadows, and anti-Semitism, Islamophobia, and instances of other ethnic and religious prejudices are on the rise. In such circumstances, Americans need a new vision. Writing the history of that imaginary, with what will be a new and, it is hoped, redeeming interplay of religion and politics, will be a task for future researchers.

Acknowledgments

Many debts accrue when writing a book, and mine are myriad. I discussed ideas with friends and colleagues, presented chapters at academic and public gatherings, badgered archivists, and tried (not always successfully) to respond graciously when family members asked when the book would be done. As noted in the dedication, several beloved friends and family members passed away during these years; their memories, along with their contributions to this process, are a blessing.

I am especially grateful to those who read the entire manuscript and whose advice honed my arguments: Sharon Gillerman, Faye Ginsburg, Chris Bugbee, and two readers for the University of Chicago Press. Jana Reiss helped pull the manuscript into shape, and Sandra Hazel made certain that I dotted all the i's and crossed all the t's. I also am thankful for colleagues and friends who offered advice, suffered my complaints, answered questions, and kept me grounded: Leora Batnitzky, Tobin Belzer, Lisa Bitel, Kim Blanton, Ken Briggs, Hilary Brown, Anthea Butler, Lynn Schofield Clark, James Daniels, Larry Eskridge, Richard Flory, Michael Gilligan, Rosalind Hackett, Rebecca Isaacs, Sally Jacobs, Diane Krumrey, Mitchell Landsberg, Alan J. Lichtman, Brie Loskota, Mary MacVean, Peter Mancall, Anthony Petro, Ester and John Scheibel, Michael Schudson, Vanessa Schwartz, Terry Todd, and Lisa Webster. The editorial team at the University of Chicago Press has been patient and good-humored, and I am appreciative of the guidance offered by Kyle Wagner, Timothy Mennel, Dylan Montanari, and Kristin Rawlings.

A hearty thanks, too, to those who helped with research and provided editorial assistance: Brady Potts, Rebecca Sheehan, Nick Street, Ginger Mayerson, and Krys Baylor. Likewise, I am indebted to archivists at the Roman Catholic Diocese of Los Angeles, National Public Radio, *60 Minutes*, the Billy Graham Archives, the Ronald Reagan Presidential Library and Museum, and the Doheny Library at the University of Southern California, as well as USC librarians Richard Larabee, Melissa Miller, and Kelsey Vukic. Thanks to USC for a grant to work on the project. I was fortunate to present sections of the manuscript at New York University's Center for Media, Culture and History, the University of Tennessee, and the American Academy of Religion. My work also benefited from the many historians and sociologists whose recent books enriched my understanding of the religious Right, the confluence of conservative religion and American business, and American evangelicalism. I hope my work provides a generative intervention into how ideas circulate, why public opinion shifts, what role the media plays in paradigm swings, and what role religion plays in ideological constructions.

Finally, I am so grateful for the love and support of five strong and smart women whom I am fortunate to call family: Isabelle Winston, Erin Walters-Bugbee, Sara Heinz, Courtney Winston, and Suzanne Winston. A special shout-out to Chris Bugbee, who always has my back and proved it again with his help on this manuscript.

Notes

INTRODUCTION

1. Frank Newport, Jeffrey M. Jones, and Lydia Saad, "Ronald Reagan from the People's Perspective: A Gallup Poll Review," Gallup.com, June 7, 2004, http://www.gallup.com/poll/11887/ronald-reagan-from-peoples-perspective-gallup-poll-review.aspx.

2. "Economic Indicators," prepared for the Joint Economic Committee by the Council of Economic Advisers, January 1983, pp. 12, 1, https://fraser.stlouisfed.org/title/economic-indicators-1/january-1983-405.

3. John Greenwald, "Climbing Out of the Basement," *Time*, December 6, 1982, https://content.time.com/time/subscriber/article/0,33009,923103,00.html.

4. Peter Miller, "Mortgage Rates Chart: Historical and Current Rate Trends," the Mortgage Reports, August 22, 2022, https://themortgagereports.com/61853/30-year-mortgage-rates-chart.

5. Francis X. Clines, "Reagan Denies Administration Falters," *New York Times*, January 15, 1983.

6. Douglas Kellner, *Television and the Crisis of Democracy* (Oxfordshire: Routledge, 2019), 137.

7. Charles Taylor, *A Secular Age* (Cambridge, MA: Belknap Press of Harvard University Press, 2007), 23.

8. Daniel Robert McClure, *Winter in America: A Cultural History of Neoliberalism, from the Sixties to the Reagan Revolution* (Chapel Hill: University of North Carolina Press, 2021), 15–17.

9. K. Healon Gaston, *Imagining Judeo-Christian America: Religion, Secularism, and the Redefinition of Democracy* (Chicago: University of Chicago Press, 2019), 15–16.

10. Robert Orsi, "Everyday Miracles: The Study of Lived Religion," in *Lived Religion in America: Toward a History of Practice*, ed. David D. Hall (Princeton, NJ: Princeton University Press, 1997), 3–21.

11. John Winthrop, *A Model of Christian Charity*, accessed August 29, 2022, https://history.hanover.edu/texts/winthmod.html.

12. Daniel T. Rodgers, *As a City on a Hill: The Story of America's Most Famous Lay Sermon* (Princeton, NJ: Princeton University Press, 2018).

13. Perry Miller, *The New England Mind: From Colony to Province* (Cambridge,

MA: Belknap Press of Harvard University Press, 1983); Perry Miller, *Errand into the Wilderness* (Cambridge, MA: Belknap Press of Harvard University Press, 1956); Sacvan Bercovitch, *The Puritan Origins of the American Self: With a New Preface* (New Haven, CT: Yale University Press, 2011); Rodgers, *As a City on a Hill.*

14. Abram C. Van Engen, *City on a Hill: A History of American Exceptionalism* (New Haven, CT: Yale University Press, 2020), 1–16.

15. Rodgers, *As a City on a Hill*, 307.

16. Van Engen, *City on a Hill*; Rodgers, *As a City on a Hill*, 233.

17. Jimmy Carter, "Crisis of Confidence," transcript of a speech televised July 15, 1979, accessed August 16, 2022, http://www.pbs.org/wgbh/americanexperience/features/primary-resources/carter-crisis/.

18. Richard M. Fried, *The Man Everybody Knew: Bruce Barton and the Making of Modern America* (Chicago: Ivan R. Dee, 2005).

19. Robert M. Entman, *Projections of Power: Framing News, Public Opinion, and U.S. Foreign Policy* (Chicago: University of Chicago Press, 2004).

20. Mark Hertsgaard, *On Bended Knee: The Press and the Reagan Presidency* (New York: Farrar, Straus, and Giroux, 1988), 5.

21. Bernard Cohen, *The Press and Foreign Policy* (Princeton, NJ: Princeton University Press, 1963), 13.

22. Wayne Wanta, Guy Golan, and Cheolhan Lee, "Agenda Setting and International News: Media Influence on Public Perceptions of Foreign Nations," *Journalism and Mass Communication Quarterly* 81, no. 2 (June 2004): 364–77.

23. James Davison Hunter, *Culture Wars: The Struggle to Control the Family, Art, Education, Law, and Politics in America*, reprint ed. (New York: Basic Books, 1992).

24. Dan Berkowitz, ed., *Social Meanings of News: A Text Reader* (Thousand Oaks, CA: Sage, 1997); James Curran and Michael Gurevitch, eds., *Mass Media and Society*, 2nd ed. (London: Arnold, 1997); Howard Tumber, ed., *The News: A Reader* (New York: Oxford University Press, 1999).

25. Melani McAlister, *Epic Encounters: Culture, Media, and U.S. Interests in the Middle East, 1945–2000* (Berkeley: University of California Press, 2001), 6.

26. "How Americans View Government," Pew Research Center, March 10, 1998, http://www.people-press.org/1998/03/10/how-americans-view-government/.

CHAPTER ONE

1. Sheila Benson, "A World to Be Remade, a Life to Be Relinquished," *Los Angeles Times*, December 4, 1981.

2. Douglas Kellner, *Television and the Crisis of Democracy* (Oxfordshire: Routledge, 2019), 170.

3. Megan Brenan, "Americans Remain Distrustful of Mass Media," Gallup.com, September 30, 2020, https://news.gallup.com/poll/321116/americans-remain-distrustful-mass-media.aspx.

4. Megan Brenan, "Americans' Trust in Media Dips to Second Lowest on Record," Gallup.com, October 7, 2021, https://news.gallup.com/poll/355526/americans-trust-media-dips-second-lowest-record.aspx.

5. Norman P. Lewis, “The Myth of Spiro Agnew’s ‘Nattering Nabobs of Negativism,’” *American Journalism* 27, no. 1 (Winter 2010): 95, 90.

6. Lewis H. Lapham, “Journalists Are Only Storytellers,” *Washington Post*, December 31, 1983.

7. Mike Sager, “The Fabulist Who Changed Journalism,” *Columbia Journalism Review*, Spring 2016, https://www.cjr.org/the_feature/the_fabulist_who_changed_journalism.php.

8. S. Robert Lichter, Stanley Rothman, and Linda S. Lichter, *The Media Elite: America’s New Powerbrokers* (Bethesda, MD: Adler and Adler, 1986).

9. David Paul Nord, *Communities of Journalism: A History of American Newspapers and Their Readers* (Urbana: University of Illinois Press, 2001), 31–64.

10. Nord, 88.

11. Paul E. Johnson and Sean Wilentz, *The Kingdom of Matthias: A Story of Sex and Salvation in 19th-Century America* (New York: Oxford University Press, 1994).

12. Judith M. Buddenbaum, “The Religion Journalism of James Gordon Bennett,” paper presented at the annual meeting of the Association for Education and Mass Journalism, Norman, OK, August 3–6, 1986, http://www.eric.ed.gov/?=id270803.

13. Judith M. Buddenbaum, “‘Judge . . . What Their Acts Will Justify’: The Religion Journalism of James Gordon Bennett,” *Journalism History* 14, no. 2 (Summer 1987): 54–67.

14. Michael Schudson, *Discovering the News: A Social History of American Newspapers* (New York: Basic Books, 1978), 26.

15. Diane Winston, *Red Hot and Righteous: The Urban Religion of the Salvation Army* (Cambridge, MA: Harvard University Press, 1999); Richard Wightman Fox, *Trials of Intimacy: Love and Loss in the Beecher-Tilton Scandal* (Chicago: University of Chicago Press, 1999).

16. Ronald D. Rodgers, *The Struggle for the Soul of Journalism: The Pulpit versus the Press, 1833–1923* (Columbia: University of Missouri Press, 2018).

17. Richard W. Flory, “Promoting a Secular Standard: Secularization and Modern Journalism, 1870–1930,” in *The Secular Revolution: Power, Interests and Conflicts in the Secularization of American Public Life*, ed. Christian Smith (Berkeley: University of California Press, 2003), 398.

18. Flory, 406.

19. Hornell Hart, “Changing Social Attitudes and Interests,” in *Recent Trends in the United States: Report of the President’s Research Committee on Social Trends* (New York: McGraw-Hill, 1933), 390.

20. James D. Startt, “The Media and National Crises, 1917–1945,” in *The Media in America: A History*, ed. William David Sloan and James D. Startt (Northport, AL: Vision Press, 1999), 324.

21. Donald G. Godfrey, “Radio Comes of Age, 1900–1945,” in Sloan and Startt, *The Media in America*, 343.

22. Margaret A. Blanchard, “Press Criticism and National Reform Movements: The Progressive Era and the New Deal,” *Journalism History* 5, no. 2 (Summer 1978): 36.

23. Richard L. Rubin, *Press, Parties and Presidency* (New York: W. W. Norton, 1981), 124.

24. Betty Houchin Winfield, *FDR and the News Media* (Urbana: University of Illinois Press, 1990), 127, 128.

25. "United States Presidential Election of 1940," *Encyclopaedia Britannica Online*, accessed August 25, 2022, https://www.britannica.com/event/United-States-presidential-election-of-1940.

26. "Robert M. Hutchins, Long a Leader In Educational Change, Dies at 78," *New York Times*, May 16, 1977, https://www.nytimes.com/1977/05/16/archives/robert-m-hutchins-long-a-leader-in-educational-change-dies-at-78.html.

27. Jana L. Hyde, "The Entertainment Media, 1900–Present," in Sloan and Startt, *The Media in America*, 381.

28. David R. Davies, *The Postwar Decline of American Newspapers, 1945–1965* (Westport, CT: Prager, 2006), 114.

29. Charles Storch, "Aging Newspapers Searching for Cure for Circulation Woes," *Chicago Tribune*, November 15, 1981.

30. Davies, *Postwar Decline of American Newspapers*, 114.

31. Paulette D. Kilmer, "The Press and Government," in *American Journalism: History, Principles, Practices*, ed. W. David Sloan and Lisa Mullikin Parcell (Jefferson, NC: McFarland, 2002), 29.

32. Michael Coakley, "Dying Newspapers—a National Epidemic," *Chicago Tribune*, November 21, 1982.

33. Coakley, "Dying Newspapers."

34. Ben H. Bagdikian, *The Media Monopoly*, 3rd ed. (Boston: Beacon Press, 1990), 13.

35. Edward Herman and Noam Chomsky, *Manufacturing Consent: The Political Economy of Mass Media* (New York: Pantheon Books, 2002), 10.

36. Bagdikian, *The Media Monopoly*, 4.

37. Davies, *Postwar Decline of American Newspapers*, 118.

38. "John F. Kennedy and the Press," John F. Kennedy Presidential Library and Museum, accessed August 25, 2022, https://www.jfklibrary.org/learn/about-jfk/jfk-in-history/john-f-kennedy-and-the-press.

39. For further background on Kennedy's relations with the press, see Davies, *Postwar Decline of American Newspapers*, 103–10.

40. Jon Herskovitz, "How the JFK Assassination Transformed Media Coverage," Reuters, November 21, 2013, https://www.reuters.com/article/us-usa-jfk-media/how-the-jfk-assassination-transformed-media-coverage-idUSBRE9AK11N20131121.

41. Darrell M. West, *The Rise and Fall of the Media Establishment* (Boston: Palgrave Macmillan, 2001), 58.

42. Schudson, *Discovering the News*, 176–83.

43. Todd Gitlin, "The Whole World Is Watching," in *The News: A Reader*, ed. Howard Tumber (New York: Oxford University Press, 1999), 271.

44. Daniel Hallin, *The "Uncensored War": The Media and Vietnam* (Berkeley: University of California Press, 1989).

45. Ben H. Bagdikian, *The New Media Monopoly: A Completely Revised and Updated Edition with Seven New Chapters* (Boston: Beacon Press, 2004), 156.

46. Mark Hertsgaard, *On Bended Knee: The Press and the Reagan Presidency* (New York: Farrar, Straus, and Giroux, 1988), 85.

47. Edward Herman, *The Myth of the Liberal Media: An Edward Herman Reader* (New York: Peter Land, 1999), 73.

48. Robert W. McChesney, *Rich Media, Poor Democracy: Communication Politics in Dubious Times* (Urbana: University of Illinois Press, 1999), 49.

49. Thomas C. Leonard, *News for All: America's Coming of Age with the Press* (New York: Oxford University Press, 1995), 188–89.

50. Davies, *Postwar Decline of American Newspapers*, 2–4.

51. Davies, 6.

52. Davies, 114–15.

53. Davies, 133.

54. Michael D. Murray, "The Contemporary Media, 1974–Present," in Sloan and Startt, *The Media in America*, 465.

55. For more on the decisions to go public, see Christopher B. Daly, *Covering America: A Narrative History of a Nation's Journalism* (Amherst: University of Massachusetts Press, 2012), 335–38.

56. Daniel C. Hallin, "Commercialism and Professionalism in the News Media," in *Mass Media and Society*, ed. James Curran and Michael Gurevtich (London: Arnold, 1997), 248.

57. Bagdikian, *The Media Monopoly*, 3rd ed., 109–17; Leonard, *News for All*, 177–79.

58. New York Times Company, "History," accessed August 19, 2022, http://www.nytco.com/who-we-are/culture/our-history.

59. Leonard, *News for All*, 184.

60. Charles Layton and Mary Walton, "Continuation of Missing the Story at the Statehouse," *AJR*, July/August 1998, https://ajrarchive.org/article.asp?id=3280&id=3280.

61. William L. Bird Jr., *Better Living: Advertising, Media and the New Vocabulary of Business Leadership, 1935–1955* (Evanston, IL: Northwestern University Press, 1999), 202.

62. Bagdikian, *The New Media Monopoly*, rev. and updated ed., 162.

63. Robert L. Kerr, *Rights of Corporate Speech: Mobil Oil and the Legal Development of the Voice of Big Business* (El Paso, TX: LFB Scholarly Publishing, 2005), 1; emphasis in the original.

64. Douglas Kellner, "The Media and the Crisis of Democracy in the Age of Bush-2," *Communication and Critical/Cultural Studies* 1, no. 1 (2004): 6.

65. Bagdikian, *The New Media Monopoly*, 18.

66. Carly Hallman, "Who Owns Your News? The Top 100 Digital News Outlets and Their Ownership," *TitleMax*, accessed August 19, 2022, https://www.titlemax.com/discovery-center/lifestyle/who-owns-your-news-the-top-100-digital-news-outlets-and-their-ownership/.

67. Joseph Winski, "What's Black and White and Edgy?," *Chicago Tribune*, March 30, 1980.

68. David Shaw, "*USA Today*: New Paper to Try Wings," *Los Angeles Times*, September 14, 1982.

69. Storch, "Aging Newspapers."

70. Donald Lowery, "The Increase in Newspaper Stock Prices: Comparing Newspaper Stocks and the NYSE Composite Index," *Boston Globe*, May 29, 1981.

71. Lowery, "Increase in Newspaper Stock Prices."

72. Charles Storch, "Analysts Attracted to Prospects of Newspaper Firms," *Chicago Tribune*, May 19, 1981.

73. Bill Sing, "Papers Are Becoming Part of the Gloomy News They Report: But Belt-Tightening Has Kept Some Healthy," *Los Angeles Times*, August 15, 1982.

74. Coakley, "Dying Newspapers."

75. Knight News Service, "Bright Future Seen for Newspapers despite Demise of Some," *Baltimore Sun*, January 9, 1983.

76. Thomas B. Rosenstiel, "In Newspaper Industry, News Is Getting Better after a Year of Gloom," *Los Angeles Times*, August 7, 1983.

77. Debra Whitefield, "Opinion Leaders Given a Peek at *USA Today*," *Los Angeles Times*, July 1, 1981.

78. Whitefield, "Opinion Leaders Given a Peek."

79. William H. Jones, "Gannett Board May Approve National Paper," *Washington Post*, December 15, 1981.

80. Neuharth told the *Washington Post* that 100 million Americans had moved during the past ten years and that every day 1,730,000 people stay in a hotel or motel. Daniel Machalaba, "Gannett Has Big Hopes for National Paper, but Some Are Skeptical about Its Chances," *Washington Post*, May 21, 1982.

81. Machalaba, "Gannett Has Big Hopes."

82. Staff reporters, "Gannett Sets September 15 to Launch *USA Today*," *Wall Street Journal*, April 20, 1982.

83. Weather map, *Washington Post*, September 15, 1982.

84. To see the original map, see Mario R. García, "*USA Today* Turns 30, Part 3: A Weather Map That Created a Global Tsunami," *Mario Blog*, September 12, 2012, http://www.garciamedia.com/blog/usa_today_turns_30-part_3-a_weather_map_that_created_a_global_tsunami.

85. Shaw, "*USA Today*."

86. Shaw, "*USA Today*." Shaw reported that financial analysts speculated Gannett would lay out $20 million to $25 million in the paper's first year and $30 million to $35 million during its second.

87. Jonathan Yardley, "The Newspaper of the Future(?)," *Boston Globe*, September 25, 1982.

88. Yardley, "Newspaper of the Future(?)."

89. Jonathan Friendly, "Questions Remain after *USA Today*'s First Year," *New York Times*, September 16, 1983.

90. "*USA Today* Gains Commercially but Is Criticized by Many Editors," News Roundup, *Wall Street Journal*, January 28, 1983.

91. Thomas B. Rosenstiel, "*USA Today* 1 Year Old and the Jury's Still Out," *Los Angeles Times*, September 14, 1983.

92. Alex Jones, "Circulation Audit Puts USA Today in 3rd Place," *New York Times*, June 26, 1984.

93. Mark Potts, "Gannett Says *USA Today* Ad Linage Up," *Washington Post*, September 15, 1984.

94. David Shaw, "Newspapers Going for a New Look," *Los Angeles Times*, May 15, 1986.

95. Thomas B. Rosenstiel, "Gannett Chairman Expands Empire, Advancing into the 'Major Leagues,'" *Los Angeles Times*, July 6, 1986.

96. Thomas B. Rosenstiel, "We Take a Look at *USA Today*," *Los Angeles Times*, October 8, 1987.

97. "Author: Neuharth Invented a New-Style Newspaper," *USA Today*, April 19, 2013, https://www.usatoday.com/story/news/nation/2013/04/19/hartman-tribute-neuharth/2098369/.

98. Ronald Reagan, "Remarks at a Reception Marking the First Edition of *USA Today*," speech, Washington, DC, September 15, 1982, Ronald Reagan Presidential Library and Museum, https://www.reaganlibrary.gov/research/speeches/91582d.

CHAPTER TWO

1. Leonard Silk, "A Disappearing Way," *New York Times*, January 1, 1973.

2. Edward D. Berkowitz, *Something Happened: A Political and Cultural Overview of the Seventies* (New York: Columbia University Press, 2005); Peter N. Carroll, *It Seemed Like Nothing Happened: America in the 1970s* (New Brunswick, NJ: Rutgers University Press, 1990); Lizabeth Cohen, *A Consumers' Republic: The Politics of Mass Consumption in Postwar America* (New York: Vintage Books, 2004); Andreas Killen, *1973 Nervous Breakdown: Watergate, Warhol, and the Birth of Post-Sixties America* (New York: Bloomsbury USA, 2006); Bruce J. Schulman, *The Seventies: The Great Shift in American Culture, Society, and Politics* (Cambridge, MA: Da Capo Press, 2002); Bruce J. Schulman and Julian E. Zelizer, *Rightward Bound: Making America Conservative in the 1970s* (Cambridge, MA: Harvard University Press, 2008); Natasha D. Zaretzky, *No Direction Home: The American Family and the Fear of National Decline* (Chapel Hill: University of North Carolina Press, 2007).

3. Thomas J. J. Altizer and William Hamilton, *Radical Theology and the Death of God* (Indianapolis: Bobbs-Merrill, 1966); Gabriel Vahanian, *The Death of God* (New York: George Braziller, 1961).

4. Will Herberg, *Protestant, Catholic, Jew: An Essay in American Religious Sociology* (New York: Doubleday, 1960).

5. "Report Examines the State of Mainline Protestant Churches," Barna Group, December 7, 2009, https://web.archive.org/web/20111106134955/http://www.barna.org/barna-update/article/17-leadership/323-report-examines-the-state-of-mainline-protestant-churches.

6. Zaretzky, *No Direction Home*, 109.

7. Elizabeth Gumport, "The Forgotten Anger of 'Our Bodies, Ourselves,'" Sunday Review/Opinion, *New York Times*, April 28, 2018, https://www.nytimes.com/2018/04/28/opinion/sunday/the-forgotten-anger-of-our-bodies-ourselves.html.

8. Charles Champlin, "Philip Roth's Trendy Book, Trendy Movie," *Los Angeles Times*, April 6, 1969.

9. Robert B. Tapp, "The Once and Future Humanist Institute," *Humanist*, January 1, 1998, 46–47.

10. National Organization for Women (NOW), "Statement of Purpose," accessed August 19, 2022, https://feminist.org/resources/feminist-chronicles/part-iii-the-early-documents/national-organization-for-women-statement-of-purpose/.

11. NOW, "Statement of Purpose."

12. "The American Family: Future Uncertain," *Time*, December 28, 1970, 34, 35.

13. "Teen-Age Sex: Letting the Pendulum Swing," *Time*, August 21, 1972, 34.

14. "Teen-Age Sex," 35, 34.

15. The film opened in New York on February 1, 1973, but its distributor, United Artists, permitted a screening on October 14, 1972, the closing night of the New York Film Festival.

16. "Self Portrait of an Angel and a Monster," *Time*, January 22, 1973, http://content.time.com/time/magazine/article/0,9171,903717,00.html.

17. Letters, *Newsweek*, February 26, 1974, 4.

18. James Wall, "Tango Partners: Money and Media," *Christian Century*, February 28, 1973, 250.

19. "Abortions and the Right of Privacy," *Los Angeles Times*, January 23, 1973.

20. "Abortion and Privacy," *Wall Street Journal*, January 26, 1973.

21. "Indecision on Abortion," *Chicago Tribune*, January 23, 1973.

22. "Abortion on Demand," *Time*, January 29, 1973, 46–47.

23. J. Claude Evans, "The Abortion Decision: A Balancing of Rights," *Christian Century*, February 14, 1973, 195–97.

24. "Abortion Decision: A Death Blow?," *Christianity Today*, February 16, 1973, 48–49.

25. "Abortion and the Court," *Christianity Today*, February 16, 1973, 32–33.

26. "The Abortion Revolution," *Newsweek*, February 5, 1973, 27.

27. Stephanie Harrington, "An American Family Lives Its Life on TV," *New York Times*, January 7, 1973.

28. John J. O'Connor, "TV: 'An American Family' Is a Provocative Series," *New York Times*, January 23, 1973.

29. Zaretzky, *No Direction Home*, 11.

30. "Lyndon Johnson, 36th President, Is Dead; Was Architect of 'Great Society' Program," *New York Times*, January 23, 1973.

31. Carroll, *It Seemed Like Nothing Happened*, 95.

32. For example: "A Celebration of Men Redeemed," *Time*, February 19, 1973, 13–18.

33. "Nation Marks End of War Quietly," *Washington Post*, January 28, 1973.

34. "Letter from the People," *St. Louis Post-Dispatch*, October 31, 1967.

35. "At the End of the Tunnel," *Boston Globe*, January 25 1973.

36. "At Long Last," *Los Angeles Times*, January 24, 1973.

37. "The Nation's Editors React to Peace," *Wall Street Journal*, January 26, 1973.

38. "Celebration of Men Redeemed."

39. "Life with Father," *Time*, June 11, 1973, 23–24.

40. "Nixon's Other Crisis: The Shrinking Dollar," *Time*, June 18, 1973, 25–36.

41. Berkowitz, *Something Happened*, 63.

42. “The Energy Crisis: Time for Action,” *Time*, May 7, 1973, 41–49.

43. Edward Cowans, “President Offers Policy to Avert an Energy Crisis,” *New York Times*, April 19, 1973.

44. “At Last, the Energy Message,” *Time*, April 30, 1973, 57–58.

45. Paul L. Montgomery, “Some Sales Reported Off—Drive to Last a Week,” *New York Times*, April 2, 1973.

46. Carroll, *It Seemed Like Nothing Happened*, 130.

47. Cohen, *A Consumers' Republic*, 369.

48. Carl Bernstein and Bob Woodward, “FBI Finds Nixon Aides Sabotaged Democrats,” *Washington Post*, October 10, 1972.

49. David Crary, “Trump Impeachment Inquiry Heads to Live TV Coverage,” Associated Press, November 10, 2019, https://apnews.com/6f36c34ab6b845bf8b279db3ac559897.

50. Ted Johnson, “When Congressional Hearings Become ‘the Hottest Daytime Soap Opera,’” *Variety*, June 7, 2017, https://variety.com/2017/biz/news/john-dean-watergate-hearings-tv-moments-1202456418/.

51. William Greider, “Wonders of Watergate,” *Washington Post*, July 17, 1973; “Butterfield: Devices Were Installed for Historical Purposes,” *Washington Post*, July 17, 1973.

52. “Dirty Tricks,” *New York Times*, July 22, 1973; Nate Rawlings, “Top 10 Dirty Political Tricks,” *Time*, January 18, 2012, http://swampland.time.com/2012/01/19/top-10-dirty-political-tricks-2/slide/donald-segretti-and-the-nixon-gang/.

53. James Wooten, “Nixon's Men: All Work and No Frills,” *Washington Post*, March 21, 1973.

54. Mary McCarthy, *The Mask of State: Watergate Portraits* (New York: Harcourt and Brace, 1973), 3.

55. “How the Public Feels about Nixon and Watergate Now,” *Time*, November 19, 1973, 35.

56. “Seven Tumultuous Days,” *Time*, November 5, 1973, 15.

57. Lydia Saad, “Gallup Vault: More Said ‘Fire Nixon’ after Nixon Fired Cox,” Gallup.com, January 26, 2018, https://news.gallup.com/vault/226370/gallup-vault-fire-nixon-nixon-fired-cox.aspx.

58. “How the Public Feels,” 25–26.

59. “Operation Nickel Grass: Turning Point of the Yom Kippur War,” Richard Nixon Foundation, accessed August 25, 2022, https://www.nixonfoundation.org/2014/10/operation-nickel-grass-turning-point-yom-kippur-war/.

60. Martin Tolchin, “South Bronx: A Jungle Stalked by Fear, Seized by Rage,” *New York Times*, January 15, 1973.

61. Martin Tolchin, “Future Looks Bleak for the South Bronx,” *New York Times*, January 18, 1975.

62. Alvin M. Josephy Jr., “What the Indians Want,” *New York Times*, March 18, 1973.

63. A Harris Poll taken during the third week in March found that 51 percent of respondents agreed with the Native Americans and 28 percent with the gov-

ernment. Louis Harris, "Americans Sympathize with Indians at Wounded Knee," Louis Harris and Associates Poll, April 2, 1973, https://ropercenter.cornell.edu/ipoll/study/31107698.

64. Bryce Nelson, "Wounded Knee: The Months Only Deepen Division; Even Some Sympathizers Now Believe the Occupation Has Gone on Too Long," *Los Angeles Times*, May 5, 1973.

65. Paul Houston, "Property Tax Use for Schools Upheld," *Los Angeles Times*, March 22, 1973.

66. Keyes v. Denver School Dist. No. 1, 413 U.S. 189 (1973), accessed August 25, 2022, https://www.oyez.org/cases/1972/71-507.

67. For example, see Jon Nordheimer, "The 'New South' Is No Longer a Slogan; It's a Description," *New York Times*, December 30, 1973.

68. Mark A. Shibley, *Resurgent Evangelicalism in the United States: Mapping Cultural Change since 1970* (Columbia: University of South Carolina Press, 1996).

69. Lisa McGirr, *Suburban Warriors: The Origins of the New American Right* (Princeton, NJ: Princeton University Press, 2015), 8.

70. Daniel Robert McClure, *Winter in America: A Cultural History of Neoliberalism, from the Sixties to the Reagan Revolution* (Chapel Hill: University of North Carolina Press, 2021).

71. John Tracy Ellis, "American Catholicism in an Uncertain, Anxious Time," *Commonweal*, April 27, 1973, 178.

72. Ellis, 180.

73. Edward Fiske, "Conservative Church Growth Slower," *New York Times*, April 15, 1973.

74. "Milwaukee Jewish Council Statement on Key 73," May 1973, http://www.milwaukeejewish.org/wp-content/uploads/2016/02/1973-Key-73.pdf; Barrie Doyle, "Jewish Furor over Key 73," *Christianity Today*, December 22, 1972, https://www.christianitytoday.com/ct/1972/december-22/jewish-furor-over-key-73.html.

75. Martin E. Marty, "The Fire We Can Light: The Role of Religion in a Suddenly Different World," *Christian Century*, October 3, 1973, 986.

76. Robert A. Wright, "Los Angeles a Shadow of Its Usual Radiant Self," *New York Times*, December 27, 1973.

77. David Smothers, "One Family: Faith in the U.S. despite '73," *Washington Post*, December 30, 1973.

78. Martha M. Hamilton, "To Families in Brookland, Prospects for a Better 1974 Don't Look Good," *Washington Post*, January 1, 1974.

79. "Resolution for a New Era," *New York Times*, January 1, 1974.

80. Jack Anderson, "1973: U.S. Overtaken by Middle Age," *Washington Post*, January 1, 1974.

CHAPTER THREE

1. Katie Oxx, *The Nativist Movement in America: Religious Conflict in the Nineteenth Century* (New York: Routledge, 2013); Luke Ritter, *Inventing America's First Immigration Crisis: Political Nativism in the Antebellum West* (New York: Fordham University Press, 2020).

2. Thomas Frank, *The Conquest of Cool: Business Culture, Counterculture and the Rise of Hip Consumerism* (Chicago: University of Chicago Press, 1997).

3. Marshall Berman, *The Politics of Authenticity: Radical Individualism and the Emergence of Modern Society* (New York: Verso, 2009); Doug Rossinow, *The Politics of Authenticity: Liberalism, Christianity, and the New Left in America* (New York: Columbia University Press, 1998).

4. Bob Dylan, "The Times They Are A-Changin'," 1964, accessed August 20, 2022, http://bobdylan.com/songs/times-they-are-changin/.

5. The April 8, 1966, cover of *Time* magazine had asked, "Is God Dead?" *Time*, April 8, 1966, 21–24, https://content.time.com/time/subscriber/article/0,33009,835309,00.html.

6. For example: Hugh McLeod, *The Religious Crisis of the 1960s* (New York: Oxford University Press, 2008); Axel R. Schäfer, ed., *American Evangelicals and the 1960s* (Madison: University of Wisconsin Press, 2013); Paul Oliver, *Hinduism and the 1960s: The Rise of a Counter-Culture* (London: Bloomsbury Academic, 2014); Ann Gleig and Lola Williamson, eds., *Homegrown Gurus: From Hinduism in America to American Hinduism* (Albany: SUNY Press, 2014).

7. Jane Howard, "The Groovy Christians of Rye, N.Y." *Life*, May 14, 1971, 77–85. See, too, James T. Richardson and Rex David, "Experiential Fundamentalism: Revisions of Orthodoxy in the Jesus Movement," *Journal of the American Academy of Religion* 51, no. 3 (September 1983): 397–425.

8. Robert Bellah, Richard Madsen, William Sullivan, Ann Swidler, and Steven M. Tipton, *Habits of the Heart: Individualism and Commitment in American Life*, with a new preface (Berkeley: University of California Press, 2007).

9. Frank, *The Conquest of Cool.*

10. Larry Eskridge, "God's Forever Family: The Jesus People Movement in America, 1966–1977" (PhD diss., University of Stirling, 2005), abstract, http://hdl.handle.net/1893/1842.

11. Larry Eskridge, "'One Way': Billy Graham, the Jesus Generation, and the Idea of an Evangelical Youth Culture," *Church History* 67, no. 1 (March 1998): 83–106.

12. Earl C. Gottschalk Jr., "Hip Culture Discovers a New Trip: Fervent Foot-Stompin' Religion," *Wall Street Journal*, March 2, 1971.

13. Eskridge, "'One Way,'" 87.

14. Edward Fiske, "A 'Religious Woodstock' Draws 75,000," *New York Times*, June 16, 1972.

15. Edward Fiske, "Holler for Jesus," *New York Times*, June 18, 1972.

16. Fiske, "'Religious Woodstock' Draws 75,000."

17. "EXPLO '72: A Gospel of Affirmation from America's Youth," *Newsday*, June 20, 1972, n.p., Collection 360, BGEA—Scrapbooks, reel 34: March–October 1972, Archive and Research Center at the Billy Graham Library, Charlotte, North Carolina.

18. Eskridge, "God's Forever Family," 21.

19. Preston Shires, *Hippies of the Religious Right: From the Countercultures of Jerry Garcia to the Subculture of Jerry Falwell* (Waco, TX: Baylor University Press, 2007), 93–95.

20. Chuck Smith, *Calvary Chapel Distinctives* (Costa Mesa, CA: Word for Today, 2000), 54, https://archive.org/details/2000BookCalvaryChapelDistinctivesDigEd3.

21. Shires, *Hippies of the Religious Right*, 51.

22. Donald E. Miller, *Reinventing American Protestantism: Christianity in the New Millennium* (Berkeley: University of California Press), 1997.

23. Eskridge, "God's Forever Family," 366–69.

24. Lisa McGirr, *Suburban Warriors: The Origins of the New American Right*, updated ed. (Princeton, NJ: Princeton University Press, 2015); Shires, *Hippies of the Religious Right*.

25. Darren Dochuk, *From Bible Belt to Sunbelt: Plain-Folk Religion, Grassroots Politics, and the Rise of Evangelical Conservatism* (New York: W. W. Norton, 2011), 263.

26. Andrew E. Busch, "1966 Midterm Foreshadows Republican Era," the Ashbrook Center, July 1, 2006, https://ashbrook.org/viewpoint/oped-busch-06-1966/.

27. Heather Hendershot, *Open to Debate: How William F. Buckley Put Liberal America on the Firing Line* (New York: Broadside Books, 2016); Carl T. Bogus, *Buckley: William F. Buckley Jr. and the Rise of American Conservatism* (New York: Bloomsbury Press, 2013); Alan S. Felzenberg, *A Man and His Presidents: The Political Odyssey of William F. Buckley Jr.* (New Haven, CT: Yale University Press, 2018).

28. K. Healon Gaston, *Imagining Judeo-Christian America: Religion, Secularism and the Redefinition of Democracy* (Chicago: University of Chicago Press, 2019), 194–97.

29. Dochuk, *From Bible Belt to Sunbelt*, 199.

30. Bethany Moreton, *To Serve God and Wal-Mart: The Making of Christian Free Enterprise* (Cambridge, MA: Harvard University Press, 2010).

31. James Davison Hunter, *Culture Wars: The Struggle to Control the Family, Art, Education, Law, and Politics in America*, reprint ed. (New York: Basic Books, 1992).

32. See, for example, Robert Orsi, "Is the Study of Lived Religion Irrelevant to the World We Live In? Special Presidential Plenary Address, Society for the Scientific Study of Religion, Salt Lake City, November 2, 2002," *Journal for the Scientific Study of Religion* 42, no. 2 (June 2003): 169–74.

33. James Chappell, "A Servant Heart: How Neoliberalism Came to Be," *Boston Review*, November 30, 2015, http://bostonreview.net/books-ideas/james-chappel-servant-heart-religion-neoliberalism; Matthew Guest, *Neoliberal Religion: Faith and Power in the Twenty-First Century* (London: Bloomsbury, 2022); Jason Hackworth, *Faith Based: Religious Neoliberalism and the Politics of Welfare in the United States* (Athens: University of Georgia Press, 2012); Kathryn Lofton, *Consuming Religion* (Chicago: University of Chicago Press, 2017); James Dennis LoRusso, *Spirituality, Corporate Culture, and American Business: The Neoliberal Ethic and the Spirit of Global Capital* (London: Bloomsbury Academic, 2017); Moreton, *To Serve God and Wal-Mart*.

34. For example: Darren E. Grem, *The Blessings of Business: How Corporations Shaped Conservative Christianity* (New York: Oxford University Press, 2016); Amanda Porterfield, Darren Grem, and John Corrigan, eds., *The Business Turn in American Religious History* (New York: Oxford University Press, 2017); Timothy Gloege, *Guaranteed Pure: The Moody Bible Institute, Business, and the Making of Modern Evangelicalism* (Chapel Hill: University of North Carolina Press, 2015);

Kevin M. Kruse, *One Nation under God: How Corporate America Invented Christian America* (New York: Basic Books, 2016); LoRusso, *Spirituality, Corporate Culture, and American Business*; and Moreton, *To Serve God and Wal-Mart*.

35. Benedict Anderson, *Imagined Communities: Reflections on the Origin and Spread of Nationalism*, rev. ed. (London: Verso, 2016), 6–7.

36. David Paul Nord, *Faith in Reading: Religious Publishing and the Birth of Mass Media in America* (New York: Oxford University Press, 2004); John Lyden, ed., *The Routledge Companion to Religion and Film* (London: Routledge, 2009); Mark Ward, *The Lord's Radio: Gospel Music Broadcasting and the Making of Evangelical Culture, 1920–1960* (Jefferson, NC: McFarland, 2017); Michele Rosenthal, *American Protestants and TV in the 1950s: Responses to a New Medium* (Hampshire, UK: Palgrave MacMillan 2007); Lorne L. Dawson and Douglas Cowan, eds., *Religion Online: Finding Faith on the Internet* (London: Routledge, 2004), Tona J. Hangen, *Redeeming the Dial: Radio, Religion, and Popular Culture in America* (Chapel Hill: University of North Carolina Press, 2002).

37. Heather Hendershot, "God's Angriest Man: Carl McIntyre, Cold War Fundamentalism and Right-Wing Broadcasting," *American Quarterly* 59, no. 2 (June 2007): 373–96; Markku Ruotsila, *Fighting Fundamentalist: Carl McIntire and the Politicization of American Fundamentalism* (New York: Oxford University Press, 2016).

38. Robert Abelman, "The Selling of Salvation in the New Electronic Church," in *Religious Television: Controversies and Conclusions*, ed. Robert Abelman and Stewart Hoover (Westport, CT: Praeger, 1995), 173.

39. *Encyclopedia of Religion and Society*, s.v. "Televangelism," by Razelle Frankl, accessed August 30, 2022, http://hirr.hartsem.edu/ency/Televangelism.htm.

40. *Encyclopedia of Religion and Society*, s.v. "Televangelism."

41. William F. Fore, "Religion and Television: Report on the Research," *Christian Century*, July 18–24, 1984, reprinted on Religion Online, https://www.religion-online.org/article/religion-and-television-report-on-the-research/.

42. Fore, "Religion and Television."

43. Darren E. Grem, "*Christianity Today*, J. Howard Pew, and the Business of Conservative Evangelicalism," *Enterprise and Society* 15, no. 2 (2014): 353–54. See also Phyllis E. Alsdurf, "The Founding of *Christianity Today* Magazine and the Construction of an American Evangelical Identity," *Journal of Religious and Theological Information* 9, nos. 1–2 (2010): 20–43.

CHAPTER FOUR

1. Cathleen Decker, "1 Million 'Rejoice' at 94th Rose Tournament," *Los Angeles Times*, January 2, 1983.

2. Patrick Boyle, "Economy High on Deukmejian's List," *Los Angeles Times*, January 2, 1983.

3. "Economic Indicators," prepared for the Joint Economic Committee by the Council of Economic Advisers, January 1983, p. 1, https://fraser.stlouisfed.org/title/economic-indicators-1/january-1983-405.

4. John Greenwald, "Climbing Out of the Basement," *Time*, December 6, 1982, https://content.time.com/time/subscriber/article/0,33009,923103,00.html.

5. "Economic Indicators," 12.

6. Decker, "1 Million 'Rejoice.'"

7. Frank Newport, Jeffrey M. Jones, and Lydia Saad, "Ronald Reagan from the People's Perspective: A Gallup Poll Review," Gallup.com, June 7, 2004, http://www.gallup.com/poll/11887/ronald-reagan-from-peoples-perspective-gallup-poll-review.aspx.

8. David Domke and Kevin Cox, *The God Strategy: How Religion Became a Political Weapon in America*, updated ed. (New York: Oxford University Press, 2010); Christine Wicker, *The Simple Faith of Franklin Delano Roosevelt: Religion's Role in the FDR Presidency* (Washington, DC: Smithsonian Books, 2017); Randall Balmer, *God in the White House: A History; How Faith Shaped the Presidency from John F. Kennedy to George W. Bush* (San Francisco: HarperOne, 2008).

9. Patrick Henry, "'And I Don't Care What It Is': The Tradition-History of a Civil Religion Proof-Text," *Journal of the American Academy of Religion* 49, no. 1 (March 1981): 36.

10. Brian Kaylor, "A 'Transformative Moment' in SBC Political Activity," ethics.com, August 29, 2010, https://ethicsdaily.com/a-transformative-moment-in-sbc-political-activity-cms-16555/.

11. Dudley Clendinen, "Christian Right's New Rush to Power," *New York Times*, August 18, 1980.

12. Allan Lichtman, *White Protestant Nation: The Rise of the American Conservative Movement* (New York: Grove/Atlantic Press, 2008), 343.

13. Doug Wead, "Author of Op-Ed Is the Idiot, Not Trump," *Doug Wead: A Contrarian View of History and Events* (blog), September 11, 2008, https://dougwead.wordpress.com/2008/09/11/the-history-of-the-evangelical-vote-in-presidential-elections/.

14. Charlotte Saikowski, "Religious Right Throws Its Weight behind Reagan Reelection Effort," *Christian Science Monitor*, October 3, 1984, https://www.csmonitor.com/1984/1003/100335.html.

15. David John Marley, "Ronald Reagan and the Splintering of the Christian Right," *Journal of Church and State* 48, no. 4 (Autumn 2006): 851–68.

16. Howell Raines, "Reagan Backs Evangelicals in Their Political Activities," *New York Times*, August 23, 1980.

17. David E. Rosenbaum, "Conservatives Embrace Reagan on Social Issues," *New York Times*, April 21, 1980.

18. Paul Hendrickson, "Ronald Reagan: Rugged Runner in the Biggest Race; Reagan: The Cause, the Prize and the Rendezvous; At 68, Easing into the Campaign where Duty and Destiny Converge," *Washington Post*, November 13, 1979.

19. William L. Bird Jr., *Better Living: Advertising, Media and the New Vocabulary of Business Leadership, 1935–1955* (Evanston, IL: Northwestern University Press, 1999).

20. Paul Kengor, *God and Ronald Reagan: A Spiritual Life* (New York: Harper Perennial, 2011), 104.

21. Lou Cannon, *President Reagan: The Role of a Lifetime* (New York: Simon and Schuster, 1991), 288.

22. Darren Dochuk, *From Bible Belt to Sunbelt: Plain-Folk Religion, Grassroots Politics, and the Rise of Evangelical Conservatism* (New York: W. W. Norton, 2011), 263.

23. "The Reagan/Mondale Debates," *Debating Our Destiny*, PBS.org, accessed August 21, 2022, https://www.pbs.org/newshour/spc/debatingourdestiny/doc1984.html.

24. Kengor, *God and Ronald Reagan*.

25. Dochuk, *From Bible Belt to Sunbelt*, 370–71.

26. "The Reagan/Mondale Debates."

27. Bill Peterson, "For Reagan and the New Right, the Honeymoon Is Over," *Washington Post*, July 21, 1981.

28. James Conaway, "James Watt, in the Right with the Lord," *Washington Post*, April 27, 1983, https://www.washingtonpost.com/archive/lifestyle/1983/04/27/james-watt-in-the-right-with-the-lord/946026f4-3b79-4fcb-9a5f-082ca8150007/.

29. Benjamin Taylor, "Reagan Shoring Up Conservative Support," *Boston Globe*, May 16, 1983.

30. Adam Clymer, "Reagan in the Pulpit," *New York Times*, March 9, 1983.

31. For an in-depth perspective on Reagan, the freeze movement, and the "Evil Empire" speech, see Jon Richard Peterson, "'An Evil Empire': The Rhetorical Rearmament of Ronald Reagan" (PhD diss., Ohio University, 2010), https://etd.ohiolink.edu/!etd.send_file?accession=ohiou1273107940&disposition.

32. David Adams, *The American Peace Movements: History, Root Causes, and Future* (New Haven, CT: Advocate Press, 1986), 15, http://www.culture-of-peace.info/apm/title-page.html.

33. Jon Richard Peterson, "Peace through Strength or Strength through Peace? The Reagan Administration and the Nuclear Freeze Movement in 1982," *ERAS* 12, no. 2 (March 2011), https://www.monash.edu/__data/assets/pdf_file/0006/1668480/jpeterson-1.pdf.

34. Sean Wilentz, *The Age of Reagan: A History, 1974–2008* (New York: Harper, 2008), 163; Peterson, "Peace through Strength," 4.

35. Glenn H. Miller Jr., Karlyn Mitchell, and Dan Hoxworth, "The U.S. Economy and Monetary Policy in 1983," *Economic Review, Federal Reserve Bank of Kansas City* 68, no. 10 (December 1983): 3–21.

36. Newport, Jones, and Saad, "Reagan from the People's Perspective."

37. Marjorie Hyer, "Polls Show Evangelicals Support Nuclear Freeze," *Washington Post*, July 8, 1983.

38. Peterson, "Peace through Strength," 27.

39. John J. Pitney Jr., "The Man Who Called Out Evil," *National Review*, June 8, 2004, https://www.nationalreview.com/2004/06/man-who-called-out-evil-john-j-pitney-jr/.

40. G. Thomas Goodnight, "Ronald Reagan's Reformulation of the Rhetoric of War: Analysis of the 'Zero Option,' 'Evil Empire,' and 'Star Wars' Addresses," *Quarterly Journal of Speech* 72 (November 1986): 400; "Winning the Cold War, Part I: The Evil Empire Speech," the Other Half of History, January 23, 2011, http://historyhalf.com/winning-the-cold-war-the-evil-empire-speech/; Bill Peterson, "Reagan's Use of Moral Language to Explain Policy Draws Fire," *Washington Post*, March 23, 1983.

41. "Ronald Reagan, 'Evil Empire Speech,'" Voices of Democracy: The U.S. Oratory Project, March 8, 1983, http://voicesofdemocracy.umd.edu/reagan-evil-empire-speech-text/.

42. *Journal of John Wesley*, Christian Classics Ethereal Library, accessed August 22, 2022, http://www.ccel.org/ccel/wesley/journal.vi.ii.xvi.html.

43. "Ronald Reagan, 'Evil Empire Speech,'" March 8, 1983, transcript, Miller Center, University of Virginia, accessed August 22, 2022, https://millercenter.org/the-presidency/presidential-speeches/march-8-1983-evil-empire-speech.

44. "Ronald Reagan, 'Evil Empire Speech.'"

45. "Ronald Reagan, 'Evil Empire Speech.'"

46. Anthony Lewis, "Onward Christian Soldiers," *New York Times*, March 10, 1983; Tom Wicker, "Two Dangerous Doctrines," *New York Times*, March 15, 1983; Arthur Schlesinger Jr., "Pretension in the Presidential Pulpit," *Wall Street Journal*, March 17, 1983.

47. Peterson, "'An Evil Empire,'" 174–75.

48. Associated Press, "Reagan Appeals to Ministers on Freeze," *Los Angeles Times*, March 9, 1983.

49. Juan Williams, "Reagan Steps Up Defense Push," *Washington Post*, March 8, 1983.

50. Peterson, "'An Evil Empire,'" 149.

51. Cannon, *President Reagan*, 284.

52. "State of the Union Address: Ronald Reagan (January 25, 1983)," Infoplease, http://www.infoplease.com/t/hist/state-of-the-union/196.html.

53. "At U.N. Some Still Hope for a Reversal," *New York Times*, September 18, 1983.

54. Benjamin B. Fischer, "A Cold War Conundrum: The 1983 Soviet War Scare," Central Intelligence Agency, March 19, 2007, https://www.cia.gov/library/center-for-the-study-of-intelligence/csi-publications/books-and-monographs/a-cold-war-conundrum/source.htm.

55. Fischer, "A Cold War Conundrum."

56. Wilentz, *The Age of Reagan*, 164.

57. Fischer, "A Cold War Conundrum."

58. "The Andropov Speech," editorial, *Washington Post*, September 30, 1983.

59. Boris Egorov, "This American Girl Was a Celebrity in the USSR," *Russia Beyond*, accessed August 22, 2022, https://www.rbth.com/history/330761-one-little-american-girl-ussr; Anton Fedyashin, "Andropov's Gamble: Samantha Smith and Soviet Soft Power," *Journal of Russian American Studies* 4, no. 1 (May 2020): 1–23.

60. *The Day After*, Nuclear War/Deterrence Discussion Panel, *Viewpoint*, ABC News, November 20, 1983, YouTube video, 1:20:33, https://www.youtube.com/watch?v=PcCLZwU2t34.

61. Jon Niccum, "Nuclear Reaction: Cast, Crew of 'The Day After' Reunite for 25th Anniversary of Film Shot in Lawrence, KS," *Lawrence (KS) Journal-World*, November 16, 2008, http://www2.ljworld.com/news/2008/nov/16/nuclear_reaction/.

62. Dawn Stover, "Facing Nuclear Reality: 35 Years after *The Day After*," *Bulletin of the Atomic Scientists*, n.d., accessed August 22, 2022, https://thebulletin.org/2018/12/facing-nuclear-reality-35-years-after-the-day-after/.

63. "'The Day After': Nuclear-Attack TV Movie Horrifies America in 1983 | WABC-TV Vault," Eyewitness News ABC7NY, YouTube video, 8:06, accessed August 22, 2022, https://www.youtube.com/watch?v=aG-e52yAxfs.

64. Clymer, "Reagan in the Pulpit."

65. Peter Grier, "US Public Opinion Generally Favors 'Star Wars,'" *Christian Science Monitor*, November 21, 1985, http://www.csmonitor.com/1985/1121/asdi.html.

66. James Gerstenzang, "The Times Poll: Public Backs 'Star Wars,' Hopes for Arms Control," *Los Angeles Times*, November 19,1985, https://www.latimes.com/archives/la-xpm-1985-11-19-mn-7785-story.html.

67. Jason McGahan, "Before Stonewall, the Queer Revolution Started Right Here in Los Angeles," *Los Angeles Magazine*, May 29, 2019, https://www.lamag.com/citythinkblog/before-stonewall-gay-pride-history/.

68. Chad Painter, "How the New York Media Covered the Stonewall Riots," *Conversation*, June 19, 2019, https://theconversation.com/how-the-new-york-media-covered-the-stonewall-riots-117954.

69. Justin Taylor, "Fact-Checking Randall Balmer's Urban Legend on the Real Origin of the Religious Right," *Gospel Coalition*, August 8, 2022, https://www.thegospelcoalition.org/blogs/evangelical-history/fact-checking-randall-balmers-urban-legend-on-the-real-origin-of-the-religious-right/.

70. Thomas F. McDow, "A Century of HIV," *Origins: Current Events in Historical Perspective*, October 2018, https://origins.osu.edu/article/century-hiv-world-aids-day-africa-actup-unaids?language_content_entity=en.

71. Larry Gross, *Up from Invisibility: Lesbians, Gay Men, and the Media in America* (New York: Columbia University Press, 2001), 114.

72. Transcript of *Morning Edition*, January 28, 1983, program, National Public Radio.

73. *Morning Edition*, January 28, 1983.

74. *Morning Edition*, January 28, 1983.

75. Associated Press, "Immune Disease: A New Test," *New York Times*, March 8, 1983.

76. Claudia Wallis, "Medicine: Battling a Deadly New Epidemic," *Time*, March 28, 1983, 53–55.

77. Jean Seligman, "The AIDS Epidemic: The Search for a Cure," *Newsweek*, April 18, 1983, 74–79.

78. Glenn Collins, "Facing the Emotional Anguish of AIDS," *New York Times*, May 30, 1983.

79. Dudley Clendinen, "AIDS Spread Pain and Fear among Ill and Healthy Alike," *New York Times*, June 17, 1983.

80. Jerome Socolovsky, "Conservative Christian Approach to AIDS Evolves toward Compassion," Voice of America, July 26, 2012, https://www.voanews.com/usa/conservative-christian-approach-aids-evolves-toward-compassion.

81. S. Robert Lichter, Stanley Rothman, and Linda S. Lichter, *The Media Elite* (Bethesda, MD: Adler and Adler, 1986), 32.

82. Sue Cross, "Jerry Falwell Calls AIDS a 'Gay Plague,'" *Washington Post*, July 6, 1983.

83. Cross, "Jerry Falwell."

84. Eleanor Randolph, "Falwell Urges Government Officials to Launch Crack-down against AIDS," *Washington Post*, July 13, 1983.

85. Cross, "Jerry Falwell."

86. Dudley Clendinen and Adam Nagourney, *Out for Good: The Struggle to Build a Gay Rights Movement in America* (New York: Simon and Schuster, 1999), 482.

87. Transcript of July 13, 1983, program, National Public Radio.

88. Edwin Diamond, "Covering AIDS in the Nineties," *New York Magazine*, April 16, 1990, 12.

89. "Top of the Week," *Newsweek*, August 8, 1983, 3.

90. Tom Morganthau, Vincent Coppola, John Carey, Nancy Cooper, George Raine, John McCormick, and David Friendly, "Gay America in Transition," *Newsweek*, August 8, 1983, 30.

91. Morganthau et al., 30; italics in the original. Subsequent citations are made parenthetically in the text.

92. "Top of the Week," 3.

93. Morganthau et al., 30. Subsequent citations are made parenthetically in the text.

CHAPTER FIVE

1. Lou Cannon, "Reagan: Peace through Strength," *Washington Post*, August 19, 1980.

2. F. Richard Ciccone, "Reagan Vows Strong U.S.: VFW Speech Here Opens Campaign," *Chicago Tribune*, August 19, 1980.

3. Cannon, "Reagan."

4. Ciccone, "Reagan Vows Strong U.S."

5. Greg Schneider and Renae Merle, "Reagan's Defense Buildup Bridged Military Eras; Huge Budgets Brought Life Back to Industry," *Washington Post*, June 9, 2004.

6. Douglas Kellner, *Television and the Crisis of Democracy* (Oxfordshire: Routledge, 2019).

7. Janice Castro, "Keeping the Press from the Action," *Time*, November 7, 1983, 63–66.

8. Barry Sussman, "Grenada Move Earns President Broad Political Gains, Poll Shows," *Washington Post*, November 9, 1983.

9. Phuong Nguyen, "The 1983 Invasion of Grenada," *ESSAI* 7 (2009), article 36, 116, http://dc.cod.edu/essai/vol7/iss1/36.

10. For more, see Terry Nardin and Kathleen D. Pritchard, *Ethics and Intervention: The United States in Grenada, 1983* (New York: Carnegie Council on Ethics and International Affairs, 1990).

11. Nardin and Pritchard, 3.

12. Duncan Pindar, "The United States 1983 Invasion of Grenada: Reagan Foreign Policy and the Caribbean," unpublished paper presented at the Association of Third World Studies, Savannah, GA, October 2010.

13. Walter Isaacson, Laurence I. Barrett, and Strobe Talbott, "Weighing the Proper Role," *Time*, November 7, 1983, 42.

14. Walter Isaacson, "Hard Facts, Harsh Choices," *Time*, May 9, 1983, 22–30.

15. Russell Crandall, *Gunboat Diplomacy: U.S. Interventions in the Dominican Republic, Grenada and Panama* (Lanham, MD: Rowman and Littlefield, 2006), 127.

16. Eldon Kenworthy, "Grenada as Theater," *World Policy Journal* 1, no. 3 (Spring 1983): 645.

17. Nardin and Pritchard, *Ethics and Intervention*, 3.

18. Eric Pace, "Grenadian's Appeal to Young Was the Promise of Change," *New York Times*, October 21, 1983.

19. Nardin and Pritchard (*Ethics and Intervention*, 5) write that 354 were rescued from the two campuses. According to Ronald H. Cole, another 200 lived off campus. Ronald H. Cole, *Operation Urgent Fury: The Planning and Execution of Joint Operations in Grenada, 12 October–2 November 1983* (Washington, DC: Joint History Office, Office of the Chairman of the Joint Chiefs of Staff, 1997), 42, https://www.jcs.mil/Portals/36/Documents/History/Monographs/Urgent_Fury.pdf.

20. Nardin and Pritchard, *Ethics and Intervention*, 3.

21. The editors, "1983 Beirut Barracks Bombing," revised and updated by Amy Tikkanen, accessed September 8, 2022, *Encyclopaedia Britannica Online*, https://www.britannica.com/event/1983-Beirut-barracks-bombings.

22. "American Held Hostage," *New York Times*, October 24, 1983.

23. Ed Magnuson, Douglas Brew, Bernard Diederich, and William McWhirter, "D-Day in Grenada," *Time*, November 7, 1983, 28, 22

24. Patsy Lewis, "Revisiting the Grenada Invasion: The OECS' Role, and Its Impact on Regional and International Policy," *Social and Economic Studies* 48, no. 3 (September 1999): 85–120.

25. This is now named the Maurice Bishop International Airport.

26. Office of Public Communication, Bureau of Public Affairs, *Department of State Bulletin* 83, no. 2081 (December 1983): 89, https://heinonline.org/HOL/P?h=hein.journals/dsbul83&i=1151.

27. B. Drummond Ayres Jr., "Defense Dept. Says the Marines and Rangers Quickly Achieved Initial Goals," *New York Times*, October 26, 1983.

28. Bernard Gwertzman, "An Invasion Prompted by Previous Debacles," *New York Times*, October 26, 1983.

29. Steven V. Roberts, "Capitol Hill Is Sharply Split over the Wisdom of Invading Grenada," *New York Times*, October 26, 1983.

30. Alan J. Rosenblatt, "Aggressive Foreign Policy Marketing: Public Response to Reagan's 1983 Address on Lebanon and Grenada," *Political Behavior* 20, no. 3 (September 1998): 234–46.

31. Everett Carll Ladd, "On Mandates, Realignments and the 1984 Presidential Election," *Political Science Quarterly* 100, no. 1 (Spring 1985): 5.

32. William F. Lewis, "Telling America's Story: Narrative Form and the Reagan Presidency," *Quarterly Journal of Speech* 73, no. 3 (August 1987): 283, 291.

33. Craig von Buseck, "Why Reagan Was a Great Communicator," Christian Broadcasting Network, accessed August 26, 2022, https://www1.cbn.com/why-reagan-was-great-communicator.

34. Kellner, *Television and the Crisis of Democracy*, 248.

35. Stephen F. Ostertag, "Negotiating News: A Study of the Social Construction of News Realities" (PhD diss., University of Connecticut, 2008), UMI, 99.

36. Stephen Walt, "The Myth of American Exceptionalism," *Foreign Policy* 189 (November 1, 2011): 72.

37. "Transcript of Address by President on Lebanon and Grenada," *New York Times*, October 28, 1983.

38. "Transcript of Address."

39. "Transcript of Address."

40. Tom Noyes, "Semantics of Grenada Invasion/Rescue," transcript of November 4, 1983, program, National Public Radio.

41. "Transcript of Address."

42. Hedrick Smith, "Report to the Nation," *New York Times*, October 28, 1983.

43. "Transcript of Address."

44. Section 22 USC 2656f(d)(2), United States Department of State, *Country Reports on Terrorism 2018* (October 2019): 331, https://www.state.gov/wp-content/uploads/2019/11/Country-Reports-on-Terrorism-2018-FINAL.pdf.

45. Melani McAlister, *Epic Encounters: Culture, Media and U.S. Interests in the Middle East since 1945*, updated ed. (Berkeley: University of California Press, 2005), 206–10.

46. Ted Clark, "US Admits Bombing Grenada Mental Hospital," transcript of October 31, 1983, program, National Public Radio.

47. Mark Hertsgaard, *On Bended Knee: The Press and the Reagan Presidency* (New York: Farrar, Straus, and Giroux, 1988), 211.

48. Phil Gailey, "U.S. Bars Coverage of Grenada Action, News Groups Protest," *New York Times*, October 27, 1983.

49. William E. Farrell, "U.S. Allows 15 Reporters to Go to Grenada for Day," *New York Times*, October 28, 1983.

50. Jonathan Friendly, "Reporting the News in a Communique War," *New York Times*, October 26, 1983.

51. George Skelton and David Wood, "U.S. to Post Task Force Off Grenada," *Los Angeles Times*, October 22, 1983.

52. Noah Adams, "US Student Describes Grenada Situation," transcript of October 20, 1983, program, National Public Radio.

53. Ayres, "Defense Dept."

54. Francis X. Clines, "At Reagan Press Office, It's Avoid the Negative," *New York Times*, October 28, 1983.

55. Robert McFadden, "From Rescued Students, Gratitude and Praise," *New York Times*, October 23, 1983.

56. Steven V. Roberts, "Move in Congress," *New York Times*, October 28, 1983.

57. Smith, "Report to the Nation."

58. McFadden, "From Rescued Students."

59. Philip Taubman, "The Reason for Invading," *New York Times*, November 1, 1983.

60. Bill Buzenberg, "Communist Documents Found on Grenada," transcript of October 31, 1983, program, National Public Radio.

61. Stuart Taylor Jr., "In Wake of Invasion, Much Official Misinformation by the U.S.," *New York Times*, November 6, 1983.

62. Taylor, "In Wake of Invasion."

63. Alan Berlow, "Documents Show Grenada Was in Disarray," transcript of November 5, 1983, program, National Public Radio.

64. Cokie Roberts, “Congress Says Grenada Invasion Justified,” transcript of November 8, 1983, program, National Public Radio.

65. Roberts, “Grenada Invasion.”

66. Thomas Griffith, “Haunted by History,” *Time*, November 14, 1983, 76.

67. Griffith, 76.

68. Carroll J. Glynn, Susan Herbst, Garrett J. O’Keefe, Robert Y. Shapiro, and Mark Lindeman, *Public Opinion*, 2nd ed. (Boulder, CO: Westview Press, 2004), 18–32.

69. Rosenblatt, “Aggressive Foreign Policy Marketing,” 234–35.

70. Barry Sussman, ‘Reagan’s Talk Gains Support for Policies,” *Washington Post*, October 30, 1983.

71. Rosenblatt, “Aggressive Foreign Policy Marketing,” 239.

72. Hertsgaard, *On Bended Knee*, 209.

73. Farrell, “U.S. Allows 15 Reporters.”

74. Margaret A. Blanchard, “Press Criticism and National Reform Movements: The Progressive Era and the New Deal,” *Journalism History* 5, no. 2 (Summer 1978): 35.

75. Blanchard, 36.

76. Blanchard, 55–56.

77. Gerald F. Seib and Rich Jaroslovsky, “Reagan Charges Cuba Planned to Seize Grenada,” *Wall Street Journal*, October 28, 1983.

78. Associated Press, “3D Day of Combat,” *New York Times*, October 28, 1983.

79. Jack Nelson, “Cubans Sought Grenada Base for Terrorism, Reagan Charges,” *Los Angeles Times*, October 28, 1983.

80. Ostertag, “Negotiating News,” 34–45.

81. William Safire, “Us against Them,” *New York Times*, October 30, 1983.

82. Norman P. Lewis, “The Myth of Spiro Agnew’s ‘Nattering Nabobs of Negativism,’” *American Journalism* 27, no. 1 (Winter 2010): 89–115.

83. Paul Gronke and Timothy E. Cook, “Disdaining the Media: The American Public’s Changing Attitudes toward the News,” *Political Communication* 24, no. 3 (July 1, 2007): 259–60.

84. Gronke and Cook, 259–81.

85. Hertsgaard, *On Bended Knee*, 33.

86. Hertsgaard, 47.

87. Terry Teachout, “*The Media Elite*, by S. Robert Lichter, Stanley Rothman, and Linda S. Lichter (Book Review),” *Commentary* 83, no. 1 (1987): 78, https://www.commentarymagazine.com/articles/terry-teachout/the-media-elite-by-s-robert-lichter-stanley-rothman-and-linda-s-lichter/.

88. “Media Bias Basics,” Media Research Center, accessed August 23, 2022, http://archive.mrc.org/biasbasics/biasbasics3.asp.

89. Daniel C. Hallin, *The “Uncensored War”: The Media and Vietnam* (Berkeley: University of California Press, 1986), 116–17.

90. Walter Isaacson, Sam Allis, and Laurence Barrett, “A Rallying Round for Reagan,” *Time*, November 14, 1983, 51–54.

91. Jonathan Friendly, “Press Voices Criticism of ‘Off-the-Record’ War,” *New York Times*, November 4, 1983.

92. Art Harris, "The New Patriotism: Flags and Fatigues on the March Again," *Washington Post*, December 18, 1983.

93. George J. Church, "Sunny Mood at Midsummer: Americans Take a Brighter View of Reagan," *Time*, July 18, 1983, 12–15.

94. "A Perky New Look," *Time*, August 29, 1983, 43.

95. Winston Williams, "A Classic Recovery, After All," *New York Times*, November 20, 1983.

96. David Shribman, "The Return to Normal Is a Slow Journey for Grenada," *New York Times*, November 20, 1983.

97. Sussman, "Grenada Move."

98. Isaacson, Allis, and Barrett, "Rallying Round for Reagan," 51–54.

99. Adam Clymer, "The Nation's Mood," *New York Times*, December 11, 1983.

100. Associated Press, "Patriotism Is Making a Comeback, Flag Dealer Says," *Baltimore Sun*, July 5, 1981; Melvin Maddocks, "The New Patriotism—Some Tunes Can't Be Played on a Bugle," *Christian Science Monitor*, January 4, 1984; Steve Farnsworth, "A Surge in Popularity for ROTV," *Los Angeles Times*, March 4, 1984.

101. R. W. Apple, "New Stirrings of Patriotism," *New York Times*, December 11, 1983; Hodding Carter III, "Reagan's 'New Patriotism' Is Old Chauvinism," *Wall Street Journal*, August 2, 1984.

102. Stephen Farber, "Promotion during Olympics Helps 'Call to Glory,'" *New York Times*, August 22, 1984.

103. John Corry, "A Serial about the Military Gambles on Patriotism," *New York Times*, August 12, 1984.

104. Kurt Anderson, "America's Upbeat Mood," *Time*, September 24, 1984, 16.

105. Jay Sharbutt, "Air Force, ABC Flying 'Gloriously,'" *Los Angeles Times*, September 4, 1984.

106. Mark Dolan, "Born in the U.S.A.: When the President Met the Boss," *Salon*, May 28, 2012, http://www.salon.com/2012/05/28/born_in_the_u_s_a_when_the_president_met_the_boss/.

107. Ronald Reagan, "Remarks at a Reagan-Bush Rally in Hammonton, New Jersey," speech, September 19, 1984, Ronald Reagan Presidential Library and Museum, https://www.reaganlibrary.gov/research/speeches/91984c.

108. Dudley Clendinen, "Ads Try to Tie Reagan with the Best of Times," *New York Times*, June 17, 1984. The costs for these seven commercials were $400,000 for making the ads and $1.6 million for the local and national media buys. The projected cost for the entire advertising campaign was projected to run $20 million to $25 million.

109. Clendinen, "Ads Try to Tie Reagan."

110. Ronald Reagan TV ad, "It's Morning in America Again," YouTube video, 0:59, accessed August 26, 2022, https://www.youtube.com/watch?v=EU-IBF8nwSYm.

111. Ronald Reagan, "Remarks at an Ecumenical Prayer Breakfast in Dallas, Texas," speech, August 23, 1984, Ronald Reagan Presidential Library and Museum, https://www.reaganlibrary.gov/research/speeches/82384a.

112. Ronald Reagan, "Remarks at a Spirit of America Rally, Atlanta, Georgia," speech, January 26, 1984, Ronald Reagan Presidential Library and Museum, https://www.reaganlibrary.gov/research/speeches/12684g.

113. Ronald Reagan, "Remarks at the St. Ann's Festival in Hoboken, New Jersey," speech, July 26, 1984, Ronald Reagan Presidential Library and Museum, https://www.reaganlibrary.gov/research/speeches/72684c.

114. Ronald Reagan, "Address to the Nation on the Eve of the Presidential Election," broadcast speech, Oval Office, Washington, DC, November 5, 1984, Ronald Reagan Presidential Library and Museum, https://www.reaganlibrary.gov/research/speeches/110584e.

115. Evan Thomas and Douglas Brew, "Yankee Doodle Candidate," *Time*, June 25, 1984, 14.

116. Thomas and Brew, 18–20.

117. Lou Cannon, "'Gipper' Rallies U.S. Invoking 'New Patriotism,' Reagan Urges Athletes to 'Go for It,'" *Washington Post*, July 29, 1984.

118. Scott Harris, "A Partisan Crowd Whoops It Up for Reagan in S.D.," *Los Angeles Times*, November 6, 1984.

119. Lewis H. Lapham, "Notebook: The New Patriotism," *Harper's*, June 1984, 7.

120. Robert M. Entman, *Projections of Power: Framing News, Public Opinion and Foreign Policy* (Chicago: University of Chicago Press, 2004), 23–24.

CHAPTER SIX

1. "What Meese Said to Reporters," *New York Times*, December 15, 1983.

2. Storer Rowley, "Critics Growl over Meese's Hunger Remarks," *Chicago Tribune*, December 10, 1983; Marlene Cimons, "Meese Remarks on Hunger Stir Angry Protests," *Los Angeles Times*, December 10, 1983; Robert D. McFadden, "Comments by Meese on Hunger Produce a Storm of Controversy," *New York Times*, December 10, 1983; David Hoffman, "Discussing Hunger in U.S., Meese Sparks a Firestorm," *Washington Post*, December 10, 1983.

3. Rowley, "Meese's Hunger Remarks."

4. Cimons, "Meese Remarks on Hunger."

5. McFadden, "Comments by Meese."

6. Hoffman, "Discussing Hunger in U.S."

7. Ronald Reagan, "Radio Address to the Nation," December 3, 1983, Ronald Reagan Presidential Library and Museum, https://www.reaganlibrary.gov/research/speeches/120383a.

8. Daniel Robert McClure, *Winter in America: A Cultural History of Neoliberalism, from the Sixties to the Reagan Revolution* (Chapel Hill: University of North Carolina Press, 2021), 203.

9. Brian Steensland, *The Failed Welfare Revolution: America's Struggle over Guaranteed Income Policy* (Princeton, NJ: Princeton University Press, 2008), 7.

10. Steensland, 12.

11. John Winthrop, *A Modell of Christian Charity* (1630), Collections of the Massachusetts Historical Society (Boston, 1838), 3rd ser., 7:31–48, accessed August 28, 2022, https://history.hanover.edu/texts/winthmod.html.

12. Marisa Chappell, *The War on Welfare: Family, Poverty, and Politics in Modern America* (Philadelphia: University of Pennsylvania Press, 2010); John O'Connor, "US Social Welfare Policy: The Reagan Record and Legacy." *Journal of Social Policy*

27, no. 1 (January 1, 1998): 37–61; David Stoesz and Howard Jacob Karger, "Deconstructing Welfare: The Reagan Legacy and the Welfare State," *Social Work* 38, no. 5 (September 1, 1993): 619–28.

13. Frances Fox Piven and Richard A. Cloward, "The Weight of the Poor: A Strategy to End Poverty," *Nation*, May 2, 1966, 510–17, https://www.thenation.com/article/archive/weight-poor-strategy-end-poverty/.

14. Steensland, *The Failed Welfare Revolution*, 1.

15. McClure, *Winter in America*, 137–40.

16. "'Welfare Queen' Becomes an Issue in Reagan Campaign," *New York Times*, February 15, 1976.

17. Josh Levin, "The Welfare Queen," *Slate*, December 19, 2013, http://www.slate.com/articles/news_and_politics/history/2013/12/linda_taylor_welfare_queen_ronald_reagan_made_her_a_notorious_american_villain.html.

18. "'Welfare Queen' Becomes an Issue"; Levin, "The Welfare Queen."

19. Franklin D. Gilliam, "The 'Welfare Queen' Experiment," *Nieman Reports* 53, no. 2 (Summer 1999): 49–52, https://niemanreports.org/articles/the-welfare-queen-experiment/.

20. Jill Quadagno, *The Color of Welfare: How Racism Undermined the War on Poverty* (New York: Oxford University Press, 1994).

21. Dorothy E. Roberts, "Welfare and the Problem of Black Citizenship," *Yale Law Review* 195, no. 6 (April 1996): 1571, 1572.

22. Sheldon Danziger, "Welfare Reform Policy from Nixon to Clinton: What Role for Social Science?," paper presented at "The Social Sciences and Policy Making," Institute for Social Research, University of Michigan, Ann Arbor, March 13–14, 1998, revised 1999, 6. https://www.researchgate.net/publication/237409671_Welfare_Reform_Policy_From_Nixon_to_Clinton_What_Role_for_Social_Science, accessed August 23, 2022.

23. Danziger, 8.

24. "Federal 1979 Government Spending," accessed August 23, 2022, https://www.usgovernmentspending.com/fed_spending_1979USon.

25. Alan S. Blinder and Jeremy B. Rudd, "The Supply-Shock Explanation of the Great Stagflation Revisited" (NBER Working Paper no. 14563, National Bureau of Economic Research, Inc., 2008), https://EconPapers.repec.org/RePEc:nbr:nberwo:14563.

26. John O'Connor, "US Social Welfare Policy: The Reagan Record and Legacy," *Journal of Social Policy* 27, no. 1 (January 1, 1998): 38.

27. O'Connor, 46.

28. Chappell, *The War on Welfare*, 201.

29. Michael J. New, "Morning in California," *National Review*, June 10, 2004, http://www.nationalreview.com/article/211036/morning-california-michael-j-new.

30. The program's success was limited. See Richard C. Paddock, "Gov. Reagan's Workfare: No 'Gang Busters' in a Short Life," *Los Angeles Times*, February 10, 1986.

31. Margaret H. Kunde, "Ronald Reagan and the Resurgence of the Puritan Covenantal Tradition: The 'City on a Hill' and Reorientation of the People of the

United States into an 'Economy of Grace'" (PhD diss., University of Minnesota, 2012), http://hdl.handle.net/11299/133839.

32. Monica Prasad, "The Popular Origins of Neoliberalism in the Reagan Tax Cut of 1981," *Journal of Policy History* 24, no. 3 (July 2012): 363.

33. David Vogel, "The Inadequacy of Contemporary Opposition to Business," *Daedalus* 109, no. 3 (July 1, 1980): 52.

34. John Berry, "Reagan's World v. the Real One: He Left Out a Few Facts in His Defense of Reaganomics," *Washington Post*, February 13, 1983.

35. Ronald Reagan, first inaugural address (speech, presidential inauguration, Washington, DC, January 20, 1981), Ronald Reagan Presidential Library and Museum, https://www.reaganlibrary.gov/research/speeches/inaugural-address-january-20-1981.

36. Stoesz and Karger, "Deconstructing Welfare," 620.

37. O'Connor, "US Social Welfare Policy," 40.

38. Robert Pear, "Most of Those Taken Off Welfare Are Said Not to Leave Their Jobs," *New York Times*, April 29, 1983.

39. Floyd Norris, "From 1983, Hope for Jobs in 2011," *New York Times*, February 4, 2011.

40. New York Times News Service, "Reagan Support Waning, Polls Show," *Chicago Tribune*, January 25, 1983.

41. Robert Pear, "Reagan Asks Wide Cuts in Programs to Aid Poor," *New York Times*, January 29, 1983.

42. Francis X. Clines, "Reagan, Saying Recovery Is Near, Vows to Fight Tax-Cut 'Sabotage,'" *New York Times*, February 2, 1983.

43. Ronald Reagan, "Radio Address to the Nation on the Economic Recovery Program," February 5, 1983, the American Presidency Project, https://www.presidency.ucsb.edu/documents/radio-address-the-nation-the-economic-recovery-program.

44. John M. Berry, "Reagan's World v. the Real One," *Washington Post*, February 13, 1983, https://www.washingtonpost.com/archive/opinions/1983/02/13/reagans-world-v-the-real-one/be8085cc-3d1b-459c-8e9f-6ce1f00fc856/m.

45. Walter Isaacson, Neil MacNeil, and Laurence Barrett, "Searching for the Recovery," *Time*, February 21, 1983, 16, 17.

46. "Gauging the Recovery as Birthday Nears," Outlook, *Wall Street Journal*, September 29, 1983.

47. William Eaton, "Reagan Suffers Setback in House Budget Vote," *Los Angeles Times*, March 24, 1983.

48. Eaton, "Reagan Suffers Setback."

49. Michael Isikoff, "Welfare Caseload Is Growing Again, Confounding Economizers," *Washington Post*, April 1, 1983.

50. Dennis Farney, "Reagan Said to Cut $110 Billion Social Aid over 4 Years; Poorer Families Bear Brunt," *Wall Street Journal*, August 26, 1983.

51. Associated Press, "Reagan Cuts Blamed for Tax Increases," *Baltimore Sun*, August 27, 1984.

52. Robert D. Hershey Jr., "Despite Reagan Tax Cuts, Many Are Taxed More," *New York Times*, April 15, 1983.

53. [Michael Kinsley,] "Mondale's Task," *New Republic*, July 2, 1984, 7.

54. Don E. Wallin, "Dr. Reagan Didn't Deliver," *Los Angeles Times*, September 29, 1983.

55. William Serrin, "Recovery Irrelevant to Workers Left Behind," *New York Times*, September 4, 1983.

56. David Hoffman, "War on Spending to Take Back Seat to Reagan's Political Aims," *Washington Post*, September 26, 1983.

57. Winston Williams, "Tales of the Economic Recovery," *New York Times*, September 4, 1983; "An Economic Recovery Stirs, and a Campaign Curtain Rises," *New York Times*, December 29, 1983.

58. "Text of President's Address to World Financial Community," *New York Times*, September 28, 1983.

59. Leonard Silk, "Economic Scene," *New York Times*, October 28, 1983.

60. Helen Dewar, "Representatives Find That Deficits Dominate Talk back Home," *Washington Post*, October 16, 1983.

61. "Firms' Earnings Soared 20% in Third Quarter; Best Rise in 4 1/2 Years," Roundup, *Wall Street Journal*, November 3, 1983.

62. David Treadwell, "The Times Poll: Reaganomics Works, Most in U.S. Believe," *Los Angeles Times*, December 21, 1983.

63. "An Economic Recovery Stirs."

64. ProQuest search, April 29, 2015, on "fairness issue" January 20, 1981, to December 31, 1983.

65. Francis X. Clines, "Can Reagan Defuse the 'Fairness' Issue," *New York Times*, December 25, 1983.

66. Lou Cannon, "Fairness-to-Poor Offensive Launched," *Washington Post*, March 25, 1982.

67. Lynn Rossellini, "First Lady Tells Critics: 'I Am Just Being Myself,'" *New York Times*, October 13, 1981.

68. "Reagan and the Rich," editorial, *Boston Globe*, June 30, 1983.

69. Steve V. Roberts, "Democrats Base Campaign Plans on Reagan's Economic Record," *New York Times*, September 4, 1982.

70. Dan Balz and Margot Hornblower, "Democrats Gain 26 Seats in House," *Washington Post*, November 4, 1982.

71. Ronald Reagan, "Radio Address to the Nation on the American Family" (speech, Camp David, MD, December 3, 1983), Ronald Reagan Presidential Library and Museum, https://www.reaganlibrary.gov/research/speeches/120383a.

72. Ronald Reagan, "Radio Address to the Nation on Economic and Fair Housing Issues" (speech, Camp David, MD, July 9, 1983), Ronald Reagan Presidential Library and Museum, https://www.reaganlibrary.gov/research/speeches/70983a.

73. Associated Press, "Reagan Defends Policy, Raps 'Misery Merchants,'" *Chicago Tribune*, July 10, 1983.

74. Reagan, "On Economic and Fair Housing Issues."

75. Juan Williams, "New Poverty Rationale May Be Emerging," *Washington Post*, August 13, 1983.

76. Kenneth H. Bacon, "The Outlook: Fatherless Families; Key Poverty Problem," *Wall Street Journal*, August 8, 1983.

77. Williams, “New Poverty Rationale.”

78. Steven R. Weisman, “Reagan Says Blacks Were Hurt by Works of the Great Society,” *New York Times*, September 16, 1982.

79. Williams, “New Poverty Rationale.”

80. Milton Coleman, ”More Reliant on Aid Than Whites, Blacks Hit Harder by Cuts,” *Washington Post*, December 4, 1983.

81. Morton Kondracke, “The Fairness of It,” *Baltimore Sun*, December 23, 1983.

82. Paul Taylor, “Voters Wary of Fairness Theme,” *Washington Post*, November 22, 1985.

83. Louis Harris, “The Reagan Mandate,” Louis Harris and Associates Poll, November 12, 1984, https://ropercenter.cornell.edu/ipoll/study/31104081.

84. Seymour Martin Lipset, “The Elections, the Economy and Public Opinion: 1984,” *PS: Political Science and Politics* 18, no. 1 (Winter 1985): 32.

85. Lipset, 32.

86. Heather E. Bullock, Karen Fraser Wyche, and Wendy R. Williams, “Media Images of the Poor,” *Journal of Social Science Issues* 57 (Summer 2001): 229.

87. Michael Brüeggmann, “Between Frame Setting and Frame Sending: How Journalists Contribute to News Frames,” *Communication Theory* 24, no. 1 (February 2014): 61–82.

88. Bullock, Wyche, and Williams, “Media Images of the Poor,” 236, 235.

89. Bullock, Wyche, and Williams, 236.

90. Max Rose and Frank R. Baumgartner, “Framing the Poor: Media Coverage and U.S. Poverty Policy, 1960–2008,” *Policy Studies Journal* 41, no. 1 (February 2013): 25.

91. Rose and Baumgartner, “Framing the Poor,” 26; Franklin D. Gilliam Jr., “The ‘Welfare Queen’ Experiment: How Viewers React to Images of African-American Mothers on Welfare,” UCLA Center for Communications and Community, July 1, 1999, accessed August 24, 2022, https://escholarship.org/uc/item/17m7r1rq; Ange-Marie Hancock, *The Politics of Disgust: The Public Identity of the Welfare Queen* (New York: New York University Press, 2004); Joya Misra, Stephanie Moller, and Marina Karides, “Envisioning Dependency: Changing Media Depictions of Welfare in the Twentieth Century,” *Social Problems* 50 (November 2003): 482–504.

92. John C. White and Joseph A. Reaves, “Family Break-Up Hurts Black Progress,” *Chicago Tribune*, October 20, 1983.

93. Judith Cummings, “For Black Families, the Odds Are Formidable,” *New York Times*, November 27, 1983.

94. Milton Coleman, “More Reliant on Aid Than Whites, Blacks Hit Harder by Cuts,” *Washington Post*, December 4, 1983.

95. Bullock, Wyche, and Williams, “Media Images of the Poor,” 237.

96. Thomas Ford, “Effects of Stereotypical Television Portrayals of African-Americans on Person Perception,” *Social Psychology Quarterly* 60, no. 3 (September 1, 1997): 273–75.

97. Robert Staples and Terry Jones, “Culture, Ideology and Black Television Images,” *Black Scholar* 16, no. 3 (May 1, 1985): 14.

98. Jess Brooks, “Black Best Friend: A Manifesto,” *Black Camera* 11, no. 2 (Spring 2020): 244–45.

99. "'The Toy' Is Family Fun," *Washington Post*, December 10, 1982.

100. Robert Pear, "U.S. Panel Says Hunger Cannot Be Documented," *New York Times*, January 9, 1984.

101. Christopher Drew, "Proud Working Class Becomes 'New Poor,'" *Chicago Tribune*, December 10, 1984.

102. Margaret Shapiro, "House Votes to Increase Food Stamp Payments," *Washington Post*, August 2, 1984.

103. William Raspberry, "The Almighty Pocketbook," *Washington Post*, September 30, 1984.

104. Raspberry, "The Almighty Pocketbook."

105. Milton Coleman and David S. Broder, "'Fairness' Issue Loses Potency," *Washington Post*, October 7, 1984.

106. Coleman and Broder, "'Fairness' Issue Loses Potency."

107. Ellen Goodman, "Real Election Losers: Society's Have-Nots," *Chicago Tribune*, November 15, 1984.

EPILOGUE

1. Brad Schiller, "Op-Ed: Why Did Trump Win? The Economy, Stupid," *Los Angeles Times*, November 9, 2016, https://www.latimes.com/opinion/op-ed/la-oe-schiller-trump-victory-economy-20161109-story.html.

2. Ronald Reagan, "Acceptance Speech at 1980 Republican Convention," July 17, 1980, https://teachingamericanhistory.org/library/document/acceptance-speech-at-1980-republican-convention/.

3. Zach Montague, "Holding It Aloft, He Incited a Backlash. What Does the Bible Mean to Trump?," *New York Times*, June 2, 2020, https://www.nytimes.com/2020/06/02/us/politics/trump-bible-st-johns.html.

4. John Homans, "Ivan the Terrible," *New York*, March 30, 2012, https://nymag.com/news/features/scandals/ivan-boesky-2012-4/.

5. "Donald J. Trump: The Long Road to the White House, 1980–2017," YouTube video, 43:15, accessed August 24, 2022, https://www.youtube.com/watch?v=305-erOr3jk.

6. "1980s: How Donald Trump Created Donald Trump," NBC News, July 6, 2016, https://www.youtube.com/watch?v=_FL014GMYos.

7. Russ Buettner and Charles V. Bagli, "Donald Trump's Business Decisions in '80s Nearly Led Him to Ruin," *New York Times*, October 3, 2016, https://www.nytimes.com/2016/10/04/nyregion/donald-trump-taxes-debt.html.

8. Dan Alexander, "Donald Trump Has at Least $1 Billion in Debt, More Than Twice the Amount He Suggested," *Forbes*, October 16, 2020, https://www.forbes.com/sites/danalexander/2020/10/16/donald-trump-has-at-least-1-billion-in-debt-more-than-twice-the-amount-he-suggested/?sh=734613464330.

9. Andrea Micocci and Flavia Di Mario, *The Fascist Nature of Neoliberalism* (Oxfordshire: Routledge, 2017).

10. Jessica Gantt Shafer, "Donald Trump's 'Political Incorrectness': Neoliberalism as Frontstage Racism on Social Media," *SM+S Social Media + Society*, July–September 2017, 1–10.

11. Curt Devine and Maegan Vazquez, "Trump-Branded Properties Charged Federal Government at Least $1.2 Million, Records Show," CNN, March 16, 2020, https://www.cnn.com/2020/03/12/politics/trump-branded-properties-charge-taxpayers-a-million-invs/index.html.

12. Nicholas Confessore and Karen Yourish, "$2 Billion Worth of Free Media for Donald Trump," *New York Times*, March 15, 2016, https://www.nytimes.com/2016/03/16/upshot/measuring-donald-trumps-mammoth-advantage-in-free-media.html.

13. Jay Rosen, "The View from Nowhere," *Pressthink*, September 18, 2003, http://archive.pressthink.org/2003/09/18/jennings.html.

14. Ronald Reagan, "Debate between the President and Former Vice President Walter F. Mondale in Kansas City, Missouri," October 21, 1984, Ronald Reagan Presidential Foundation and Institute, https://www.reaganfoundation.org/ronald-reagan/reagan-quotes-speeches/debate-between-the-president-and-former-vice-president-walter-f-mondale-in-kansas-city-missouri/.

15. Lee Dembart, "Carter's Comments on Sex Cause Concern," *New York Times*, September 23, 1976.

16. During Pope John Paul II's 1987 trip to the United States, I watched several high-profile reporters discuss the day's events and decide on the news angle to use for their stories. This shielded them from editors second-guessing their work, because their peer publications had the same angle. Moreover, since their work went on wire services to local and regional news outlets, those papers and broadcasts followed suit.

17. Benedict Anderson, *Imagined Communities: Reflections on the Origin and Spread of Nationalism*, rev. ed. (New York: Verso, 2016).

18. Anne Murphy, introduction to *Time, History and the Religious Imaginary in South Asia*, ed. Anne Murphy (New York: Routledge, 2011), 4.

19. Murphy, 115.

20. Daniel T. Rodgers, *As a City on a Hill: The Story of America's Most Famous Lay Sermon* (Princeton, NJ: Princeton University Press, 2018); Abram C. Van Engen, *City on a Hill: A History of American Exceptionalism* (New Haven, CT: Yale University Press, 2020).

21. Rodgers, *As a City on a Hill*, 204–36.

22. H. Howell Williams, "'Personal Responsibility' and the End of Welfare as We Know It," *PS: Political Science and Politics* 50, no. 2 (October 2017): 379–83.

23. Kevin D. Reyes, "'We Must Help Them Build Free Institutions': Neoliberal Modernization and American Nation-Building in Iraq," *Global Societies Journal* 4 (2016): 42–55.

24. Caren Bohan, "Obama Tells Blacks They Must Take Responsibility," Reuters, July 14, 2008, https://www.reuters.com/article/us-usa-politics-obama/obama-tells-blacks-they-must-take-responsibility-idUSN1447659320080715.

25. William Greider, "Reagan's Reelection: How the Media Became All the President's Men," *Rolling Stone*, December 20, 1984, https://www.rollingstone.com/politics/politics-news/reagans-reelection-how-the-media-became-all-the-presidents-men-73809/; Mark Hertsgaard, *On Bended Knee: The Press and the Reagan Presidency* (New York: Farrar, Straus, and Giroux, 1988); Craig R. Smith, "Ronald Reagan's Rhetorical Re-invention of Conservatism," *Quarterly Journal of Speech*

103, nos. 1–2 (2017): 33–65; Steven R. Weisman, "The President and the Press," *New York Times*, October 14, 1985.

26. Internet Live Stats, accessed August 24, 2022, https://www.internetlivestats.com/total-number-of-websites/.

27. Seth Fiegerman, "Facebook Is Closing In on 2 Billion Users," CNN Business, February 1, 2017, https://money.cnn.com/2017/02/01/technology/facebook-earnings/index.html; Daniel Sparks, "How Many Users Does Instagram Have?," Motley Fool, May 16, 2017, https://www.fool.com/investing/2017/05/16/how-many-users-does-instagram-have.aspx; GMI Blogger, "Twitter Users Statistics 2016," Global Media Insight, December 12, 2016, https://www.globalmediainsight.com/blog/twitter-users-statistics/.

28. Jon Allsop and Peter Vernon, "How the Press Covered the Last Four Years of Trump," *Columbia Journalism Review*, October 23, 2020, https://www.cjr.org/special_report/coverage-trump-presidency-2020-election.phpm; Jim Rutenberg, "Trump Is Testing the Norms of Objectivity in Journalism," *New York Times*, August 7, 2016, https://www.nytimes.com/2016/08/08/business/balance-fairness-and-a-proudly-provocative-presidential-candidate.html; Pablo J. Boczkowski and Zizi Papacharissi, eds., *Trump and the Media* (Cambridge, MA: MIT Press, 2018).

29. Paul Farhi, "Lies? The News Media Is Starting to Describe Trump's 'Falsehoods' That Way," *Washington Post*, June 5, 2019, https://www.washingtonpost.com/lifestyle/style/lies-the-news-media-is-starting-to-describe-trumps-falsehoods-that-way/2019/06/05/413cc2a0-8626-11e9-a491-25df61c78dc4_story.html.

30. Trump Twitter Archive, accessed August 24, 2022, https://www.thetrumparchive.com.

31. Joseph D. Lyons, "Guess How Many Times Trump Generally Tweets Per Day," Bustle.com, May 21, 2018, https://www.bustle.com/p/how-many-times-does-trump-tweet-a-day-the-president-basically-lives-on-twitter-8909583.

32. Connor Perrett, "Trump Broke His All-Time Tweeting Record amid Nationwide Protests, Sending More Tweets in a Single Day Than He Did during His Impeachment Trial," *Insider*, June 6, 2020, https://www.insider.com/trump-breaks-record-most-tweets-in-a-single-day-2020-6.

Index

Page numbers in italics refer to illustrations.